The
Biblical Doctrine
of Heaven

The
Biblical Doctrine
of Heaven

By
WILBUR M. SMITH

MOODY PRESS

CHICAGO

ACKNOWLEDGMENTS. The author expresses appreciation to the following publishers for permission to quote from copyrighted sources: Association Press, New York, publishers of *He Ascended into Heaven* by John G. Davies; Augsburg Publishing House, Minneapolis, publishers of *Exposition of Genesis* by H. C. Leupold; Concordia Publishing House, St. Louis, publishers of *The Minor Prophets* by Theodore Laetsch; T. & T. Clark, Edinburgh, Scotland, publishers of *Church Dogmatics*, III, by Karl Barth; Wm. B. Eerdmans Publishing Company, Grand Rapids, publishers of *The Doctrine of God* by Herman Bavinck, *The Epistle to the Hebrews* by F. F. Bruce, and *The Epistle to the Romans*, I, by John Murray; Holt, Rinehart and Winston, New York, publishers of *Basic Christian Doctrines*, edited by Carl F. H. Henry; Moody Press, Chicago, publishers of *The Revelation of Jesus Christ* by John F. Walvoord; J. Nisbet and Company, Welwyn, England, publishers of *Theological Examination* by G. F. Woods; Westminster Press, Philadelphia, publishers of *The Creed in Christian Teaching* by James Smart and *The Psalms* by Artur Weiser.

The Bible text quoted in this book, unless otherwise indicated, is from the *American Standard Version of the Bible,* copyrighted 1901 by Thomas Nelson & Sons.

ISBN: 0-8024-0705-6

Moody Paper Edition, 1980
First Printing

LIBRARY OF CONGRESS CATALOG CARD NUMBER: 68-18883

Contents

APPENDIXES

Preface

In regard to literature pertaining to the Biblical doctrine of Heaven, it is strange that the latter part of the nineteenth century saw a flood of books on various aspects of this subject while the twentieth century has witnessed comparatively few. Yet in spite of this so-called library on Heaven, we do not have in the English language, as far as I am aware, any volume attempting to embrace all the basic passages about Heaven and the heavens in the Scriptures. Only two really significant volumes on Heaven have been published in the last quarter century. Dr. Ulrich Simon has published two books on Heaven, only one of which discusses the Biblical data: *Heaven in the Christian Tradition* (1958). In 1966 Dr. Calvin R. Schoonhoven published his doctoral thesis, *The Wrath of Heaven*, which discusses only one major aspect, the antagonistic powers of a Heavenly Rule, and Heaven as the originating source of the outpouring of the wrath of God.

In this volume I have not felt it necessary to assign a chapter to the well-worn subject of Immortality, assuming this as a basic truth when considering the subject of life in heaven. Most books on Heaven contain chapters on the recognition of loved ones in heaven, but this I have not attempted to discuss, having thought for years that it is almost ridiculous to

7

even question whether we will know our loved ones in heaven
—of course we will! It has not seemed important to attempt
to trace New Testament teachings about Heaven to the complicated Jewish literature created in the period between the
Old and New Testaments, for such does not offer anything
regarding Heaven that is not more authoritatively expressed
in the Old and New Testaments. Even though the Qumran
literature may contain some expressions parallel to those
found in the Scriptures, it does not contribute to the thought
of Jesus or the theology of St. Paul. It would have been interesting to attempt discussions of Heaven in some of the
great classics of European literature, such as Dante's *Paradise,* and Milton's *Paradise Lost.* But, however important
these works are, they do not give us anything new about
Heaven deriving from divine inspiration. Neither anthro-
pology nor philosophy nor comparative religion can make
any vital contribution to the understanding of Heaven.

While I hope this volume will be found helpful by all students of the Scriptures and all Christian believers, I have not
been able to divorce myself from continually having in mind
particularly those men whose lives are devoted to the interpretation of the Bible—ministers and Bible teachers—and
therefore I have thought it not out of order to indicate with
some detail, sources for the further investigation of subjects
herein discussed. The most important literature is referred
to in the footnotes, and the most extensive bibliography on
the subject of Heaven that has yet appeared in any volume in
our language is assigned to an appendix. I trust that an occasional quotation of extended length will not prove irritat-
ing, for I realize that some of the literature referred to is not
easily come upon, and some works are so lengthy that few
would even think of reading them through, for instance, that
great classic of Richard Baxter, *The Saints' Everlasting Rest,*
which extends to some 460,000 words.

There are five subjects which originally I had hoped to consider in separate chapters or appendixes in this volume; but to have done so would have postponed its publication for at least another year. If a second edition should be required, they would then be added. These five subjects are as follows: (1) the experiences of some saints who in the hour of death have been given a glimpse of heaven as, for example, the experiences of D. L. Moody; (2) the testimonies of famous modern astronomers of their own conviction that the heavens declare the glory of God; (3) the treatment of Heaven in such classic works as Dante's *Paradise,* long sections in Milton and others; (4) Heaven in the creeds of the church. (5) Then there certainly should be a chapter on the Beatific Vision, which plays such an important part in Catholic Eschatology, but concerning which most Protestant works treat with regretful brevity or entirely fail to consider. I am not the mystic that I ought to be, and I would find this chapter rather difficult to write, but we all need to more frequently think of the meaning of that great experience when we shall behold the Lord.

I have one great regret (among minor ones) in sending out this volume, and that is my realization that for a book on Heaven, an author ought to have what might be called a heavenly style, such as we find so often in the exhilarating pages of Thomas Dick or Isaac Watts, so that readers might feel lifted into a rarefied atmosphere of celestial glory. But this style I do not have. There are problems here regarding which the church has had differences of opinion, and this volume does not pretend to give a final solution to all of them. Regarding some themes we know so very little, as for example, the life and occupations of the redeemed between death and resurrection.

San Marino, California   WILBUR M. SMITH

The first man came out of the earth, a material creature. The second man came from Heaven and was the Lord himself.

For the life of this world men are made like the material man; but for the life that is to come they are made like the one from Heaven.

So that just as we have been made like the material pattern, so we shall be made like the Heavenly pattern.

I CORINTHIANS 15:47-49 (PHILLIPS)

1 Introduction

Any careful student of Christian doctrine who wishes to obtain a well-balanced knowledge of the great basic truths set forth in the Scriptures will soon discover how little has been written on the subject of Heaven as set forth in the Bible in spite of its hundreds of statements pertaining thereto. The Reformers are in part to blame for this. Calvin himself avoided coming to grips with the great eschatological problems of the Scriptures. As a recent authoritative work has accurately said,

> Real and universal eschatology continually declines, both among the Lutheran and the Reformed. . . . The Reformed doctrine of the last things (that of Calvin more than that of Luther) did not do full justice to essential Biblical concerns. . . . Up to now the Reformed Churches suffer from the consequences of that corruption of the Biblical expectation of the future.[1]

A spiritual descendant of John Calvin, the late Professor Charles Hodge of Princeton, the outstanding theologian of the nineteenth century, after acknowledging that Eschatology is "a very comprehensive and very difficult subject," added an amazing confession at the end of his great *Systematic Theology*:

The subject cannot be adequately discussed without taking a survey of all the prophetic teachings of the Scriptures both of the Old Testament and of the New. This task cannot be satisfactorily accomplished by any one who has not made the study of the prophecies a specialty. The author, knowing that he has no such qualifications for the work, purposes to confine himself in a great measure to a historical survey of the different schemes of interpreting the Scriptural prophecies relating to this subject.[2]

Almost all Systematic Theologies devote infinitely more space to Hell than Heaven as, for instance, Shedd, who assigns two pages in his *Dogmatic Theology* to Heaven, and eighty-seven pages to Eternal Punishment! Theological dictionaries often pass by the subject entirely, as in the valuable work by Blunt. The standard work by the late Professor Salmond, *The Christian Doctrine of Immortality*, has an index extending to eight hundred subjects, but Heaven is not there! In Reinhold Seeberg's *Text Book of the History of Doctrines*, though there are eighty columns of index, Heaven does not appear! In Dr. Reinhold Niebuhr's exhaustive work, *The Nature and Destiny of Man*, there is no treatment of Heaven whatever, and the only reference appears in a single sentence, which in itself many will think a regrettable statement: "It is unwise for Christians to claim any knowledge of either the furniture of heaven or the temperature of hell."[3]

A quarter of a century ago, Professor John Baillie was even then regretting the infrequency of Heaven as a subject in the preaching of his age:

I will not ask how often during the last twenty-five years you and I have listened to an old-style warning against the flames of hell. I will not even ask how many sermons have been preached in our hearing about a future day of reckoning when men shall reap according as they have sown. It will be enough to ask how many preachers, during these years, have dwelt on the joys of the heavenly rest with anything like the old ardent love and impatient longing, or have spoken of the world that now is as a place of sojourn and pilgrimage.[4]

A Roman Catholic theologian of that same era echoed a similar regret in reminding his readers thus:

> It is surprising how seldom nowadays we see or hear any theological discussion of the goal to which all Christians are presumably striving; how seldom do we hear a sermon on the beatific vision, the essential characteristic of heaven? And the lack of emphasis on heaven and the joys awaiting man in the next life is noticed in non-Catholic churches also.[5]

Suddenly the space age broke upon us. The attention of all mankind is directed more forcibly, with profounder inquiries, toward the celestial heavens above than ever before in the history of the human race. It is thus inevitable that with our rapidly expanding knowledge of the universe, questions are bound to arise regarding this subject of the heavens above us, which the Christian church has been teaching and preaching these many centuries.

The United States government has recently published a manual for teaching children with the significant title *What's Up There?* The subtitle of this book is exceedingly significant: "A Source Book in Space-Oriented Mathematics for Grades Five Through Eight. Prepared from Materials Furnished by the National Aeronautics and Space Administration in Cooperation with the United States Office of Education by a Committee on Space Science Oriented Mathematics." The preface states, "The space program has given young boys and girls throughout the land new heroes and a dramatic new frontier with which to identify." This bro-

chure terminates with a "Glossary of Terms Used in Exploration of Space," extending to fifty-five columns.[6]

The above words seem to me tremendously important.
Who are those that are going to be taught "What's Up
There?" They are our young boys and girls from ages ten to
fourteen! How many of these are going to hear from some
other source what the Bible says about what exists far beyond
the space which our instruments are now traversing? I do
not know what he has in mind, but in a recent volume of
essays on *Outer Space in World Politics,* one of the authors
says, "The idea of space travel has profound spiritual significance for a number of believers to whom the space age marks
a new era of mankind climaxing all previous human history."[7]

In attempting to write on this subject, I am aware of the
vastness of the themes involved and the difficulties therein
embraced, and I am also aware of the many different opinions
that are held by different Biblical scholars on some of the
matters that we will be considering. I would take as my own
confession the words of Dr. Alexander Whyte in a sermon on
Isaiah 57:15 which he entitled "The Geometry of Prayer":

> Much and long as I have thought on this subject, and
> with great care and labor as I have composed this dis-
> course, I am keenly sensible of how immature and un-
> finished my treatment of this great topic has been. The
> subject demands and deserves all my might and all your
> might too—both as preachers and hearers; for it is our
> very life.[8]

Before actually entering upon a study of our subject, many
readers will be spiritually refreshed in this materialistic age
with words written long ago by Richard Baxter in the greatest
treatment on Heaven ever to appear:

> If it had not been to make comfortable our present life,
> and fill us with the delights of our foreknown blessed-

ness, he might have kept his purpose to himself, and never have let us know till we come to enjoy it, nor have revealed it to us till death had discovered it, what he meant to do with us in the world to come; yea, when we had got possession of our rest, he might still have concealed its eternity from us, and then the fears of losing it again, would have bereaved us of much of the sweetness of our joys. But it hath pleased our Father to open his counsel, and to let us know the very intent of his heart, and to acquaint us with the eternal extent of his love; and all this that our joy may be full, and we might live as the heirs of such a kingdom. And shall we now overlook all, as if he had revealed no such matter? Shall we live in earthly cares and sorrows, as if we knew of no such thing? And rejoice no more in these discoveries, than if the Lord had never written it? If thy prince had sealed thee but a patent of some lordship, how oft wouldst thou be casting thine eye upon it, and make it thy daily delight to study it, till thou shouldst come to possess the dignity itself. And hath God sealed thee a patent of heaven, and dost thou let it lie by thee, as if thou hadst forgot it! O that our hearts were as high as our hopes, and our hopes as high as these infallible promises![9]

NOTES

1. Heinrich Quistorp, *Calvin's Doctrine of the Last Things* (London: 1955), p. 194. Similarly, James P. Martin stated, "Both Luther and Calvin neglected the special content of Eschatology" (*The Last Judgment* [Grand Rapids: 1963], p. 4).
2. Charles Hodge, *Systematic Theology*, III (New York: 1873), 990. For a similar acknowledgment of Luther's inadequate eschatology, see Julius Kostlin, *The Theology of Luther* (Philadelphia: 1897), II, 573.
3. Reinhold Niebuhr, *The Nature and Destiny of Man* (New York: 1942). Vol. II.
4. John Baillie, *And the Life Everlasting* (London: 1934), p. 15.
5. D. J. Lehy, *St. Augustine on Eternal Life* (London: 1939), pp. xi-xii. For a similar statement, J. P. McCarthy, *Heaven* (New York: 1958), p. 8.
6. *What's Up There? A Source Book in Space-Oriented Mathematics for Grades Five Through Eight.* Prepared from materials furnished by the

National Aeronautics and Space Administration in cooperation with the United States Office of Education by a Committee on Space Science Oriented Mathematics. Washington, D.C.: U.S. Government Printing Office, 1964.

7. Paul Kecskemeti, *Outer Space in World Politics*, J. M. Goldsen (ed.) (New York: 1963). Some additional statements emphasizing the significance of this space age may not be out of place here. "Space is the theater of strategy of tomorrow-space and the human mind" (James M. Gavin, *War and Peace in the Space Age* [New York: 1958], p. 220). And this well-needed warning from Dr. Abraham J. Heschel, Professor of Jewish Ethics and Mysticism at the Jewish Theological Seminary, New York: "I question the enthusiasm with which many people rejoice in our scientific and technological achievements in space. Some religious leaders have praised them as a great triumph of the spirit of man. A more realistic appraisal is that the triumph belongs to science and technology, which threatens the enslavement of the spirit of man by inhibiting freedom of choice" (A. J. Heschel, *Space: Its Impact on Man and Society*, Lillian Levy (ed.) [New York: 1965], p. 177).

8. Alexander Whyte, *Lord, Teach Us to Pray* (New York: 1928), p. 26.

9. Richard Baxter, *Practical Works*, XXIII (London: 1830), 253.

2 The Repudiation of the Idea of Heaven in Modern Thought

There has always been strong opposition to the great truths of the Christian faith, indeed from the time of the apostles. But almost all agree that it was with the coming of the French Revolution that the stream of opposition to Biblical truth developed into a torrent and swept before it a great mass of the people of Europe. As a recent scholar has said, "The French Revolution witnessed the first concerted attack on the Christian Church since the days of Diocletian." Soon there appeared on the horizon the most blasphemous opponent of the Christian faith, exercising extended influence, of any of his generation, namely, Nietzsche. Some of his shuddering statements are these: "We have killed God . . . there has never been a more grandiose act and those who are born after us will belong, because of this act, to a higher history . . . we are God's assassins."[1]

Just at this time there was also spawned in Europe the beginning of Communism, and the writings of Karl Marx began to grip the empty hearts of millions of Europeans. These are the familiar words of Marx regarding religion in general, which include his attack upon the Christian concept of Heaven:

Man makes religion; religion does not make man. Religion, indeed, is the self-consciousness and the self-feeling of the man who either has not yet found himself, or else (having found himself) has lost himself once more. But man is not an abstract being, squatting down somewhere outside the world. Man is the world of men, the State, society. This State, this society, produce religion, produce a perverted world consciousness, because they are a perverted world. Religion is the generalized theory of this world, its encyclopaedic compend, its logic in a popular form. . . . The fight against religion is, therefore, a direct campaign against the world whose spiritual aroma is religion. . . .

Religion is the sigh of the oppressed creature, the feelings of a heartless world, just as it is the spirit of unspiritual conditions. It is the opium of the people.

The people cannot be really happy until it has been deprived of illusory happiness by the abolition of religion. The demand that the people should shake itself free of illusion as to its own condition is the demand that it should abandon a condition which needs illusion.

Thus, it is the mission of history, after the other-worldly truth has disappeared, to establish the truth of this world. In the next place, it is the mission of philosophy, having entered into the service of history after the true nature of the reputed sainthood of human self-estrangement has been disclosed, to disclose all the unsaintliness of this self-estrangement. Thus the criticism of heaven is transformed into a criticism of earth, the criticism of religion into a criticism of law, the criticism of theology into a criticism of politics.[2]

Lenin, in his writings, echoed the verdict of Marx:

Religion teaches those who toil in poverty all their lives to be resigned and patient in this world, and consoles them with the hope of reward in heaven. As for those who live upon the labour of others, religion teaches them to be charitable in earthly life, thus providing a cheap justification for their whole exploiting existence and selling them at a reasonable price tickets to heavenly bliss. "Religion is the opium of the people." Religion is a kind of spiritual intoxicant, in which the slaves of capital drown their humanity and blunt their desires for some sort of decent human existence.[3]

Communism has continued to pound away at this idea of life in heaven. Soviet cosmonaut Gherman Titov said that during his orbit seventeen times around the world, he looked into space and did not see God.[4] I feel that we as Christians have not yet allowed ourselves to fully realize the fearful religious consequences of the whole of the vast nation of China adopting atheistic Communism. Professor James H. Nichols of Harvard has well said, "The Communist revolution in China meant that a full third of the world's population, some eight hundred million men and women, were under the control of this passionate and ruthless atheist religion. In one generation Communism has expanded as no other religion in world history."[5]

THE IMPACT OF SCIENCE UPON CHRISTIAN FAITH

At the beginning of our century, the German philosopher Friedrich Paulsen did not exaggerate the situation when he wrote:

It cannot be denied that, since the beginning of modern times, advancing scientific knowledge has more and more deprived the objects of faith of the forms in which they were formerly conceived, yes, of the very possibility of their representation at all. Since the great revolution that has taken place in our views of the cosmos, we can no longer, with Aristotle and Aquinas, think of God, the eternal and holy will, whom we worship as the great First Cause, as "the prime mover," enthroned beyond and above the finite world. Since the world has constantly become larger and man smaller the human understanding has shown itself less and less adapted to serve as a model for the Creator.[6]

Even the great Harvard philosopher, William James, clearly foresaw some of the consequences of total absorption in the pursuit of natural sciences:

The scope of the practical control of nature newly put into our hand by scientific ways of thinking vastly exceeds the scope of the old control grounded on common sense. Its rate of increase accelerates so that no one can trace the limit; one may even fear that the *being* of man may be crushed by his own powers, that his fixed nature as an organism may not prove adequate to stand the strain of the ever-increasingly tremendous functions, almost divine creative functions which his intellect will more and more enable him to yield.[7]

The discoveries in the area of astronomy have led both Christian and non-Christian writers to speak as though the reality of any such a locality as heaven must be abandoned. From the standpoint of non-Christian philosopher Alfred North Whitehead, the verdict is: "The clash between religion and science which has relegated the earth to the position of a second-rate planet attached to a second-rate sun has been greatly to the benefit of the spirituality of religion by dispersing these medieval fancies of Hell and Heaven in the sky."[8]

The famous astronomer of Harvard University, Professor Harlow Shapley, boldly states it as his conviction that "logical proofs of the existence of a beneficent personal God are to most scientists meaningless because they cannot accept the assumptions upon which the logic operates. The historical bases of divine revelation are devoid of the evidential qualities essential for conclusions." Linked with his rejection of the reality of God is rejection of the idea of man being a special creature of God's creative work. "If there is some grandeur in our position in space and time, I fail to find it. Our glory must lie elsewhere. Also should we not openly question the rather vain and tedious dogma that man somehow is something very special, very superior?"[9]

Few would question the verdict of Professor H. J. Paton, Professor of Moral Philosophy in the University of Oxford, who in his Gifford Lectures boldly stated that "the gradual spread of the scientific outlook—and we are all affected by it—has tended not so much to refute religious belief, but rather to make it fade and wither."[10]

THE VERDICT OF PHILOSOPHY

Philosophy itself never did have a place for Heaven; consequently, we need not be amazed at coming upon statements in many philosophical works simply brushing aside the whole idea of life in heaven. Even so, one is surprised at the sarcasm and irreverence of no less a person than the late Dr. Alfred Whitehead, who once wrote, "As for the Christian theology, can you imagine anything more appallingly idiotic than the Christian idea of heaven?" The strong atheistic position of Professor W. T. Stace, Professor of Philosophy in Princeton University for thirty years, is well known:

> No such vast mind running the universe or a part of the universe, however enormous, magnificent, powerful, intelligent, good it might be, could be God. For it would be merely another natural being, a part of the natural order or perhaps the whole of it. God so thought of is a superstition, a gigantic and perhaps benevolent ghost, an immense and disembodied super-earthly clergyman.[11]

The late Professor Willard L. Sperry, for many years Dean of the Divinity School at Harvard University, in expressing the same opposition to this very doctrine of Heaven, asks this question: "Is it possible to save what was intended by the doctrine of Heaven at the same time that we dispense with the antithetical idea of Hell? The two terms have usually traveled together." Then after stating in regard to Hell that "most of us are through with that doctrine," he goes on to say, "Perhaps the fact that we are through with it has in some measure contributed to our skepticism as to Heaven. If we cannot have Heaven, save at the price of Hell, then we will forego the hope of Heaven."[12] Perhaps one more statement will suffice for our purpose. In 1965, Dr. A. J. Ayer, Professor of Logic at Oxford University, speaking to the entire British nation over BBC, frankly said, "We only think that if someone examines the question rationally and dispassionately, he will probably come to the conclusion there is no evidence for the existence of God."[13] Of course, if there is no existence of God, then it is utterly foolish to talk about such a thing as Heaven.

THE ABANDONMENT OF HEAVEN AMONG LIBERAL THEOLOGIANS

Not only Communism, contemporary philosophy and modern science on the whole (though there are some exceptions) but also liberal theology have not hesitated to refer to Heaven as a superstition, a myth, an outworn concept. Dean Inge, forty years ago, then listened to so intently and followed by many who had loose ideas about the Christian faith, though he was dean of St. Paul's Cathedral, did not hesitate to say,

> The discovery that the earth, instead of being the centre of a finite universe, like a dish with a dish-cover above it, is a planet revolving round the sun, which itself is only one of millions of stars, tore into shreds the Christian map of the universe. Until that time the ordinary man, whether educated or uneducated, had pictured the sum of things as a three-storeyed building, consisting of heaven, the abode of God, the angels, and beatified spir-

its; our earth; and the infernal regions, where the devil,
his angels, and lost souls are imprisoned and tormented.
. . . The Copernican astronomy, and all the knowledge
about the heavens which has been built upon this foundation, leave no room for a geographical heaven. Space
seems to be infinite, or as some prefer to say, boundless—
a distinction not very intelligible except to the mathe-
maticians; and among all the stars, planets, satellites, and
nebulae which are sparsely scattered over its vast empty
distances we can hardly imagine that one has been
chosen as the abode of the Creator and the site of the
heavenly Jerusalem.[14]

We must not forget what the ultimate end of Dean Inge's
abandonment of so many Christian truths ultimately meant
for him. During his last days, he said to those near him that
he had no certain knowledge whatever concerning what was
ahead for him after his death.

Even a New Testament student such as Canon B. H.
Streeter, who would consider himself somewhat orthodox,
flippantly wrote in a famous essay of his, "The heaven of
Sunday School teaching or popular hymnology is a place
which the plain man does not believe to exist, and which he
would not want to go to when he died."[15]

Of course we cannot speak of the oppositions to the Christian faith without referring to the verdict of the new school
of demythologizing. Bultmann himself often speaks of the
so-called necessary repudiation of Heaven, for instance, in
his famous *Kerygma and Myth*:

The concept of a Christ Who pre-existed as a heavenly
being, and the corresponding concept of man's own
translation to a heavenly world of light, in which the self
is destined to receive a celestial vesture, a spiritual body,
are to him not merely inapprehensible by any rational
process, they are totally meaningless. For he cannot
understand how it could be that salvation could take the

form of the attainment of such a condition, or that in it
he could reach the fulfilment of human life, and of his
own authentic character as a personal being.[16]

If the concept of Heaven as held in general by the Christian church of every age is in this twentieth century to be
given up, there is admittedly nothing to take its place. Of
course, I am referring here to those who claim to be Christians. There is no need of defending the doctrine of Heaven
to an unbelieving world, which first of all needs faith in Jesus
Christ. The character of life in the future fades into a fic-
tional meaninglessness, every man left to create his own idea
of what the future holds, if the belief of the church concerning Heaven is abandoned. Wherever such a forfeiting of the
idea of Heaven is urged, then some new and danger-fraught
principles of hermeneutics will have to be created by which
what the Bible says regarding Heaven will be reinterpreted
as referring to something else or to nothing. If the idea of
Heaven is put aside, then many words of the Lord Jesus will
seem unjustified, indeed mythological, such as "Our Father
who art in heaven." Furthermore, if such takes place, then a
large section of all our standard hymnals will have to be lifted
out or left unsung. Confronted by this modern attack on
Heaven from so many different directions, what is the believing Christian to do? He can do only one thing—turn again
to the Word of God with the prayer "I believe, help thou my
unbelief."

The Scriptures are our only resource in these days of doubt
if it is the truth we sincerely want. An outstanding theologian
of our generation, Professor E. C. Rust, has well said,

  If man is to know the truth about God, the divine
  meaning of history, and his own historical destiny, he
  needs a revelation of the eternal order which shall, at
  the same time, redeem him from his sinful bondage. The
  living God must enter into a saving and personal en-

counter with the human spirit, and He must do this within the continuum of historical existence, the divinely ordained sphere of personal encounter.[17]

Granting the justification for all sound methods of New Testament exegesis and the best of modern scholarship, after all, we must each decide for ourselves if the Bible is the Word of God and, if it is, that we are going to believe it. For this reason in the following chapters, I have set out with only one purpose, to examine what the *Bible* tells us about Heaven and our heavenly life.

NOTES

1. Friedrich Nietzsche, *The Joyful Wisdom*, Section 125, in *Thus Spake Zarathustra* (New York: 1937). Of course, when a personal God is denied, it is ridiculous to speak of the possibility of another life, and Heaven at once becomes an outworn myth. When Nietzsche published his *Thus Spake Zarathustra* (1883-91) he was, in general, considered a sort of antichrist, as he was, and the Western world for the most part shuddered with horror; now some of our larger denominations are publishing books by professors of religion actually advocating atheism. For a survey of the background of this movement, see Gabriel Vahanian, *The Death of God* (New York: 1961); Karl Löwith, *From Hegel to Nietzsche* (New York: 1964). For a summary of the recent theological discussion, John Warwick Montgomery, *The "Is God Dead?" Controversy* (Grand Rapids: 1966). Vahanian's work begins with this unchallenged statement: "Ours is the first attempt in recorded history to build a culture upon the premise that God is dead."

2. Quoted in Otto Rühle, *Karl Marx: His Life and Work* (New York: 1928), pp. 57-58. See also Karl Marx, *Selected Writings on Sociology and Social Philosophy*, T. Bottomore and M. Riebel (eds.) (London: 1956), p. 27.

3. Quoted in Franklin Le Van Baumer (ed.), *Main Currents of Western Thought* (New York: 1952), p. 625.

4. There is an excellent testimony to faith in God by our astronaut John Glenn, in *Queen's Work* (1962), p. 17.

5. James H. Nichols, *History of Christianity, 1650-1950* (New York: 1956), p. 453.

6. Friedrich Paulsen, *The German Universities* (New York: 1906), pp. 385-86.

7. William James, *Pragmatism* (New York: 1907), p. 187.

8. Alfred North Whitehead, *Science and the Modern World* (New York: 1927), p. 272.

9. Harlow Shapley, *The Scientific Life*, Theodore Berland (ed.) (New York: 1962), p. 19.

10. H. J. Paton, *The Modern Predicament* (London: 1955), p. 104.

11. W. T. Stace, *Religion and the Modern Mind* (New York: 1952), p. 218.

12. Willard L. Sperry, *Man's Destiny in Eternity* (Boston: 1949), p. 215.

13. A. J. Ayer, quoted in *The Listener* (October 21, 1965), p. 622. See also Ayer's earlier work, *Language, Truth, and Logic* (London: 1946).

14. William R. Inge, *The Church in the World* (London: 1927), pp. 156-57.

15. B. H. Streeter, "The Life of the World to Come," *Immortality* (New York: 1917), p. 135.

16. Giovanni Miegge, *Gospel Myth in the Thought of Rudolf Bultmann* (Richmond: 1960), pp. 10, 94. This repudiation of the concept of Heaven is developed at great length by Miegge, pp. 5-10, where one will find full references to Bultmann's writings. See also L. Malerez, *The Christian Message and Myth* (London: 1957), p. 159.

17. E. C. Rust, *The Christian Understanding of History* (London: 1947), p. 48.

*   *   *

For further statements relating to the decline of belief in Christian teaching regarding the future life, see L. E. Elliott-Binns, *English Thought, 1860-1900, The Theological Aspect* (London: 1956), p. 252; John Herman Randall and J. H. Randall, Jr., *Religion and the Modern World* (New York: 1929), pp. 66-67, 206; Harry Elmer Barnes, *The Twilight of Christianity* (New York: 1929), pp. 281-82. A good summary of what we are saying here is by Professor Ralph E. Knudsen: "The rapid changes in Western civilization have subjectivized and secularized heaven. In the nineteenth century, the concept grew increasingly vague, with wide scope in meaning. Eschatology which gathered up the 'apparatus of celestial being' gave much assurance and comfort, but lacked reality. The twentieth century has been ever more devastating to the idea of heaven. The word 'heaven' has been appropriated for many purposes, and used in connection with dreams, loves, lyrics, and fiction, until now it has been deprived of meaning for much of society. The protest and misunderstanding reached its height in the slogan 'pie in the sky.' Theological thought today finds itself involved in a world of science which is bent on demythologizing religion. There is no unanimous opinion that heaven exists, and there are some who ignore the concept altogether. . . . Human existence demands heaven, Christian faith and experience apprehend heaven, and Christian revelation announces heaven" (*Theology in the New Testament* [Philadelphia: 1964], p. 408).

Ulrich Simon, in the most important book on Heaven of our generation, sums up what we have been attempting to say in this chapter in the following words: "Many schools of thought try to come to grips with the basic difficulty that the modern world-view no longer supports belief in the ancient Christian Heaven. . . . Since all values are threatened and the world itself in peril, Heaven figures again as the macrocosm which the earth mirrors as microcosm" (*Heaven in the Christian Tradition* [New York: 1958], pp. 34, 36).

3 The Meaning of "Heaven" and "Heavens" in the Bible

Of the hundreds of occurrences of the word *heaven* in an English Bible, almost all of them are translations of the Hebrew word *shamayim* and the Greek word *ouranos*. The Hebrew word means literally "the heights," while the Greek word has a related but slightly different meaning, "that which is raised up." Considering all the various shades of meaning which may be said to attach to the original words, and to the English word, it is undeniable that the primary meaning of the actual word *heaven* is "*that which is above.*" By this is meant, of course, that which is above man or the earth. Basically, heaven has reference to those phenomena whose loci are perpendicular from us, phenomena that are a part of the vast space which surrounds the earth, phenomena which embrace the stellar bodies. Thus, whenever man turns his eyes *from* that which is immediately *before* him, or that which is *under* his feet, he focuses his sight on the things that are *above* him. Whatever various meanings heaven might connote in the Scriptures, the very idea of that which is *above* carries with it generally the ethical concept of something high, as against that which is low, something noble rather than common, something of a celestial nature rather than terrestrial or earthy.[1]

We might say, in anticipation, that almost without exception in the hundreds of occurrences of the word *heaven* in the Old and New Testaments, there is a direct relationship to the earth, and to men dwelling on the earth—a fact clearly announced in the very first sentence of the Bible: "In the beginning God created the heaven and the earth" (Gen. 1:1).

The word *heaven* in the Bible may refer to one of three major realms: (1) the atmospheric heavens which are immediately above us, in which we live and move; (2) the stellar heavens, which ultimately must include the entire universe; and (3) the heaven of heavens, the abode of God. In Catholic and medieval theology, these three realms are referred to as Coelum Aqueum, Coelum Sidereum, and Coelum Empyreum. These are exactly the three basic meanings of the word *heaven* in classical Greek literature. From the time of Homer, the words first of all referred to the sky, to the heavens immediately above us, then to the entire universe, particularly in the writings of Plato and Aristotle. Finally, also from the days of Homer, it referred to the seat of the gods, generally Mount Olympus. There is an interesting summary of these three concepts in the famous work of Aristotle *On the Heavens,* which reads in part as follows:

> Let us first establish what we mean by *ouranos,* and in how many senses the word is used, in order that we may more clearly understand the object of our questions. (1) In one sense we apply the word *ouranos* to the substance of the outermost circumference of the world, or to the natural body which is at the outermost circumference of the world; for it is customary to give the name of *ouranos* especially to the outermost and uppermost region, in which also we believe all divinity to have its seat. (2) Secondly we apply it to that body which

occupies the next place to the outermost circumference of the world, in which are the moon and the sun and certain of the stars; for these, we say, are in the *ouranos*. (3) We apply the word in yet another sense to the body which is enclosed by the outermost circumference; for it is customary to give the name of *ouranos* to the world as a whole.

Trusting, then, to the foregoing arguments, we may take it that the world as a whole was not generated and cannot be destroyed, as some allege, but is unique and eternal, having no beginning or end of its whole life, containing infinite time and embracing it in itself. . . . Our forefathers assigned heaven, the upper region, to the gods, in the belief that it alone was imperishable; and our present discussion confirms that it is indestructible and ungenerated.[2]

Aristotle's conclusion that the universe is uncreated is an indication of how even men of greatest genius need divine revelation.

The Atmospheric Heavens

The first of the three heavens depicted for us in the Holy Scriptures is, as we have said, the atmospheric heaven, specifically the atmosphere which surrounds our globe. The blanket of air that surrounds the earth, that which we breathe, is contained within the space known as the troposphere, which does not extend more than twenty miles above the earth. All normal clouds are within a distance of seven miles above the earth. From twenty to thirty miles beyond, the space is known as the stratosphere, while the space from thirty to fifty miles high is known as the mesosphere. "The ionosphere ranges from fifty, up to three hundred miles. The exosphere, beginning at two hundred or three hundred miles, can be argued as extending anywhere from eight hundred to twenty thousand miles."[3]

At seven miles up the temperature is normally about fifty-five degrees below zero, centigrade. Above this, the temperature does not decrease until beyond the stratosphere, when, strangely enough, the temperature begins to rise. The exosphere gradually merges into interplanetary space. It is generally recognized that what we call air ends at about one thousand miles above sea level.

While we are on this technical matter, it might be of interest to note that Sputnik I ascended 156 miles into space, while Explorer I in 1958 ascended 1,575 miles, and Explorer III the same year ascended 2,100 miles. In the fall of 1958 Pioneer I ascended 70,000 miles. In 1959 the Soviet Lunik I, orbiting the sun, sent back observations from a distance of 373,000 miles above the earth, while in the same year the United States Pioneer IV sent back observations from 407,000 miles above the earth. During the last ten years one of the greatest discoveries concerning spacial phenomena was what are now called the Van Allen radiation belts, the inner one extending from 1,000 to 3,000 miles above the earth, and the outer band from 8,000 to 12,000 miles. The density of the air at 150 miles above the earth is one ten-millionth of that at sea level, and at 225 miles above the earth the density is one-trillionth of the air which we breathe. It is most significant, as all scientists are agreed, that "the earth's oxygen filled atmosphere (which is unique in the solar system) is a modern development that has been in existence for only ten percent of the earth's lifetime."

Atmospheric Phenomena in Scripture. All the phenomena referred to in the Scriptures as occurring within the atmospheric heavens are confined to within an area not more than ten miles above sea level, and it is surprising how many different phenomena are mentioned in the Scriptures as being displayed in these atmospheric heavens. Probably the most frequent of all is that basically necessary element for biological existence, water, which comes to the earth regularly as rain! The promise to the Israelites was that the land which they were about to possess "is a land of hills and valleys and drinketh water of the rain of heaven" (Deut. 11:11); or, in a later address of Moses, "Jehovah will open unto thee his good treasure the heavens, to give the rain of thy land in its season" (Deut. 28:12).

Along with the rain, of course, is the rarer phenomenon (in Palestine) of snow, as in the profound passage which begins, "For as the heavens are higher than the earth, so are my ways higher than your ways, and my thoughts than your thoughts. For as the rain cometh down and the snow from heaven, and returneth not thither, but watereth the earth, and maketh it bring forth and bud, and giveth seed to the sower and bread to the eater; so shall my word be that goeth forth out of my mouth: it shall not return unto me void, but it shall accomplish that which I please, and it shall prosper in the thing whereto I sent it" (Isa. 55:9-11). One of the most solemn aspects of divine judgment upon Israel in her disobedience to God would be "the shutting up of the heavens that they should not drop down rain" (Deut. 11:17; II Chron. 7:13). This idea of rain coming from the heavens is picturesquely set forth in a passage in Job: "Who can number the clouds by wisdom? Or who can pour out the bottles of heaven?" (38:37). This, of course, can only be a figure of speech.

Frost also is said to be sent from heaven as in Job 38:29. And we frequently find in the Bible the idea of dew from heaven as in the great song of Moses: "Blessed of Jehovah be his land for the precious things of heaven, for the dew . . ." (Deut. 33:13; cf. Gen. 27:39; Hag. 1:10).

In the solemn warnings of judgment that would follow disobedience on the part of Israel, there are a number of passages which speak of God as changing the normal order of

weather: "I will make your heaven as iron" (Lev. 26:19).
In one of the final messages of Moses, he warned the Israelites that if they disobeyed the Lord "Jehovah will make the rain of thy land powder and dust: from heaven shall it come down upon thee, until thou be destroyed" (Deut. 28:24).

Probably in the description of the battle of Gibeon, when we read that "Jehovah cast down great stones from heaven," the reference is to huge hailstones (Joshua 10:11). Frequently we read of thunder from heaven (Ps. 18:13; I Sam. 2:10; II Sam. 22:14).

With equal frequency the Scriptures refer to the clouds of heaven: "Who covereth the heavens with clouds, who prepareth rain for the earth, who maketh grass to grow upon the mountains" (Ps. 147:8; cf. Dan. 7:13). To clouds also is attached an eschatological importance, for our Lord repeatedly said that when He returned, it would be with clouds and great glory (Matt. 24:30; 26:74; Mark 13:25; 14:62),[4] of which we will have more to say in a later chapter.

Closely identified, of course, with the clouds are the phenomena of the winds, sometimes referred to as "the four winds of heaven" (Zech. 2:6; 6:5; Dan. 7:2; 11:4; Jer. 49:36; Ps. 78:26; Rev. 7:1).

It is hardly necessary to refer to the frequent statements in Scripture that the manna which was divinely provided for the daily food of Israel is said to have come "from heaven," which probably has a dual reference, that is, it was a gift from the God of heaven, and it probably dropped from the atmosphere (Exodus 16:4; Neh. 9:15; Ps. 78:23-24; 105:40).

Turning from inanimate phenomena to biological, over and over again in the Scriptures we read of the *birds* of heaven, sometimes specifically. A reference is made to the eagles that fly in the heavens (Prov. 23:5). In fact, these birds of the heavens are announced in the very initial account of creation (Gen. 1:26, 30; 2:19-20). It is interesting that while the Scriptures never indicate that man is given the control of weather, rain or snow, he is given dominion over the birds that fly in the air, as well as over the beasts that walk upon the earth (see II Sam. 21:10; Job 12:7; 35:11; Ps. 104:12; Ezek. 38:20; Hosea 2:18; 4:3; 7:12).

While these phenomena are generally beneficial in their relationship to men upon earth, sometimes God chooses to rain down from the atmospheric heavens fire and brimstone, as at Sodom and Gomorrah (Gen. 19:24 ff.; Ezek. 39:22; Luke 17:29) or, for the destruction of the property of a certain individual, as Job (1:16).[5] On rare occasions God sends down fire from this heaven testifying of His acceptance of certain sacrifices offered to Him (II Kings 1:10, 14; II Chron. 7:1; I Chron. 21:26).

Likewise, occasionally the birds of heaven are tokens of God's anger with men for their disobedience, and they become scavengers in a time of judgment (e.g., Deut. 28:26; Ezek. 29:5). Both in the Old and New Testaments, birds lodging in the branches of a tree are indicative of something evil (Dan. 4:12, 21; Ezek. 31:6, 13; Matt. 13:32). One more matter ought to be mentioned bearing upon the consideration that men give to these atmospheric phenomena. That is that man is forbidden to make any likeness of any of the birds flying in the heavens above him (Deut. 4:17; 5:8).

In such a day as ours, when our attention is being continually directed toward what is called man's conquest of space and the vast significance of air in military matters, we could hardly ignore the few occurrences in the Bible of the Greek word *aer* from which, of course, is directly derived our English word *air*. As we have already seen, our Lord referred to "the fowls of the air" or "the birds of the air" (Matt. 6:26; 8:20; Mark 4:4, 32; cf. Acts 10:12; 11:6). This is the word which our Lord used when He talked about the sky being red (Matt. 16:3). Twice it is used in a most incidental way, as in the act of throwing dust into the air (Acts 22:23), or in the rebuke concerning speaking into the air (I Cor. 14:9). Strange to say, this word is found only twice in the entire Greek text of the Old Testament. In fact, only on one occasion, when David sang his great psalm of praise "in the day that Jehovah delivered him out of the hand of all of his enemies and out of the hand of Saul." This exquisite psalm occurs in II Samuel 22 and in Psalm 18. Specifically the text reads, "He made darkness pavilions round about him, gathering of waters, thick clouds of the skies" (v. 12).

There are, however, four occurrences of this word *aer* which have profound eschatological significance. In Ephesians 2:2, Satan is referred to as the prince of the power of the air. In the first letter to the Thessalonians, we are told in that famous passage on the Lord's return that we will be caught up "to meet the Lord in the air" (4:17). Twice in the book of Revelation the air comes under what might be called an act of judgment. At the sounding of the fifth trumpet, when the pit of the abyss was opened, we are told that "there went up a smoke out of the pit, as the smoke of a great furnace; and the sun and the air were darkened by reason of the smoke of the pit. And out of the smoke came forth locusts upon the earth" (Rev. 9:2-3). The last vial of judgment was poured out "upon the air; and there came forth a great voice out of the temple from the throne saying it was done." This was followed by lightnings, voices, thunders, and a great earthquake (Rev. 16:17).[6]

The Celestial Heavens

The celestial heavens are, of course, the sphere in which the sun and the moon and the stars appear. In scores of occurrences when these heavenly bodies are mentioned in the Scriptures, it is repeatedly stated that these are *in the heavens*. Even at the very beginning of the creation account, we have the phrase "lights in the firmament of heaven" (Gen. 1:14). The stars are said to be of heaven (Gen. 15:5; Deut. 4:19). Over and over again we read, as the writer to the Hebrews reminds us, "The heavens are the works of thy hands" (e.g., Heb. 1:10; Ps. 33:6). Among the planets, Venus and Saturn are expressly named (Isa. 14:12; Amos 5:26). And among the so-called fixed stars, several constellations are named in the book of Job, as the Pleiades and Orion (Job 9:9; 38:31; and Amos 5:8). As the phenomena of the atmospheric heavens are sometimes involved in God's warnings to men, so in relation to the celestial heavens, two kinds of warnings are frequently uttered, especially in the Old Testament. On the one hand the children of Israel were forbidden to worship any of the stellar bodies or any likeness in the heavens, even as announced in the Decalogue (Exodus 20:4; Ezek. 8:16); and especially were they condemned for offering sacrifices and gifts to the Queen of Heaven (Jer. 7:18; 44:17-25). Furthermore, the Israelites were forbidden to attempt to discover from the movements of the heavenly bodies any events to take place in the future, and astrologers were mocked (Isa. 47:13; Jer. 10:2). This great truth of God as the Creator of the heavens interpenetrates many aspects of Old Testament theology and sometimes even New Testament experiences. When Israel was in trouble she turned to God the Creator of heaven and earth (II Kings 19:15; Isa. 37:16), even as the early church did as persecution began (Acts 4:24). The infinite greatness and power of God are emphasized by Isaiah as in the famous statement "Lift up your eyes on high, and see who hath created these, that bringeth out their host by number; he calleth them all by name; by the greatness of his might, and for that he is strong in power, not one is lacking" (40:26).

While the word *heaven* (*shamayim*) occurs with the greatest frequency, sometimes the Hebrews use the word *shackaq*, which in the Authorized Version is generally translated "clouds" but in the later revised versions normally is translated "sky." Here we have some of the same phenomena which we have just been discussing, as for instance, the reference to "the thick clouds of the sky" (II Sam. 22:12; Ps. 18:1); "the skies drop down the dew" (Prov. 3:20); or "water" (Job 36:28). The book of Job, so crowded with beautiful passages on various phenomena of nature, speaks of the time when "men see not the light which is bright in the skies" (37:21; cf. Prov. 8:28; Ps. 36:5; 78:23). It is because God is so omnipotent that He not only knows the future (Isa. 45:12), but He will be able to fulfill His promises to His people (Isa. 42:5). It is from God the Creator of heaven and earth that His children may expect help in time of need (Ps. 121:2; 124:8). Over and over again, the prophets call attention to the fact that the pagan gods of nations surrounding Israel are incapable of creating anything, not to mention the heavens and the earth. "Thus shall ye say unto them, The gods that have not made the heavens and the earth, these shall perish from the earth, and from under the heavens. He hath made the earth by his power, he hath established the world by his wisdom, and by his understanding hath he stretched out the heavens" (Jer. 10:11-12; see also Isa. 44:24; Ps. 96:5; Acts 14:15).

We should not forget that the Bible itself bears testimony to a fact always emphasized in works on astronomy that the stars are so numerous that "they cannot be numbered" (Jer. 33:22; Deut. 1:10; 28:62; Exodus 32:13; Neh. 9:23; Gen. 22:17; 26:4; Heb. 11:12; Rev. 12:4). When we read in the song of Deborah and Barak, after the defeat of Sisera, that "they fought from heaven; the stars in their courses fought against Sisera" (AV), we must, of course, take this as a poetic way of expressing the fact that even the elements of nature participated in the defeat of this pagan king (Judges 5:20).[7]

Occasionally statements are made in relation to the concept of Heaven which we may designate as hyperbole, for instance, in the report that the tree in Nebuchadnezzar's dream "reached to heaven" (Dan. 4:11, 20, 22), or the report of the spies that they saw cities that were "fortified up to heaven" (Deut. 1:28; see Jer. 51:32).

Whenever a statement is made in which the phrase *"under the whole heaven"* or something similar is used, this simply stands for the totality of mankind, as "the kingdoms under the whole heaven" (Dan. 9:27; Acts 2:5); "all that is done under heaven" (Eccles. 1:13; 2:3); "all flesh from under heaven" (Gen. 6:17); and, particularly, in our Lord's Olivet Discourse regarding the gathering of all "from one end of heaven to the other" (Matt. 24:31; Mark 13:27; see also Deut. 2:25; 7:24; 9:14; 25:19; Exodus 17:14; Gen. 7:19). This, of course, is the meaning of Paul's statement to the Colossians that the "gospel was preached in all creation under heaven" (1:23), and Peter's affirmation that there is none other name under heaven by which men may be saved but the name of the Lord Jesus (Acts 4:12).

When the phrase "heaven and earth" is found in a given text, it is normally to be interpreted as embracing the entire universe, no area and no individual to be found outside of the jurisdiction of God and His truth. Thus, even in that heavenly book of Deuteronomy, the phrase appears in the question that demands a negative: "What God is there in heaven or in earth that can do according to thy works and according to thy mighty acts?" (3:24; cf. 4:32). This same truth is stated affirmatively in a nearby passage: "Know therefore this day, and lay it to thy heart, that Jehovah he is God in heaven above and upon the earth beneath; there is none else" (Deut. 4:39). Toward the close of Deuteronomy this concept of universality is introduced in one of the most solemn utterances of the Old Testament: "I call heaven and

earth to witness against you this day, that I have set before
thee life and death, the blessing and the curse: therefore
choose life, that thou mayest live, thou and thy seed" (Deut.
30:19; 31:28). With an altogether different connotation the
psalmist reminds us that "the heavens are the heavens of
Jehovah; but the earth hath he given to the children of men"
(Ps. 115:16; 89:11). It is for another purpose that Jehovah
through Jeremiah reminds the sinful nation of Israel: "Can
any hide himself in secret places so that I shall not see him?
saith Jehovah. Do not I fill heaven and earth? saith Jehovah"
(Jer. 23:24). It is, of course, with this idea of absolute universality that our Lord begins His great commission with the
words: "All authority hath been given me in heaven and on
earth" (Matt. 28:10). The Apostle Paul in speaking of the final absolute victory of Christ in the age to come in that so profound a passage opening his epistle to the Ephesians, speaks
of the fullness of the times when God will "sum up all things
in Christ, the things in the heavens and the things upon the
earth" (Eph. 1:10). In a somewhat similar Christological
chapter beginning his epistle to the Colossians, Paul speaks
of God through Christ purposing "to reconcile all things unto
himself, having made peace through the blood of his cross;
through him, I say, whether things upon the earth, or things
in the heavens" (Col. 1:20). This is not the place to discuss
with any detail the profounder meanings of these words, but
simply to emphasize the universality that is implied in the
phrase "the heavens and the earth."

It is inevitable that in any treatment of the theme of
Heaven and the heavens in the Scriptures, there must be included a discussion of what the Bible says about the creation
of the heavens, concerning which there are over seventy different passages. Here we shall treat the subject in general.
It would be generally agreed, in any generation, that as the
distinguished astronomer A. C. B. Lovell has recently said,

"The problem of the origin of the universe is the greatest challenge to the intellect which faces man, and I cannot pretend that I have any new solution to offer you."[8]

THE CREATION OF THE HEAVENS

In that ever glorious and ever reassuring statement with which the Bible begins, the heavens are declared, along with the earth, to be the result of the creative activity of God and of God only.[9] "In the beginning God created the heavens and the earth." It is, by the way, interesting to note that these two great objects, the heavens, or heaven, and the earth, are brought together in over forty different statements in the New Testament. Even before examining the statement in detail, we ought to be reminded, in the words of a famous theologian of a former generation, W. Lindsay Alexander:

> In this short sentence, the Bible places itself in antagonism to a whole phalanx of opinions taught in ancient schools of philosophy or incorporated with ancient systems of religion. This sentence is a denial of the Greek doctrine of the eternity of matter; of the Epicurean doctrine of a fortuitous concourse of atoms, as that out of which the Kosmos arose; of the stoic doctrine of an all-compelling fate; of the Pantheistic doctrine of the identity of God with the universe; of the Polytheistic doctrine of a plurality of gods; and of the dualistic doctrine of a good and a bad principle dividing the formation and the rule of the world between them.[10]

At the threshold of our study, we should remind ourselves that the Hebrew word here translated "heaven" is a plural form technically known as a plural of intensity; and the very fact that the first occurrence of the word is in the plural certainly implies that there are more than one heavenly sphere, one rising above the other. When the writer uses the phrase "the heavens and the earth," he is reminding us that "in reality the word is bipartite; it is not a unit as far as we are concerned. The two parts constitute the world or the universe."[11]

While the studies in this volume are all related to the subject of Heaven itself, in its various manifestations, one can hardly leave this opening statement of the Word of God without a word concerning the fact of creation itself. As to the meaning of the very word so translated, I have not seen anything more helpful than the comment of the distinguished Old Testament scholar H. C. Leupold in what is certainly the most important commentary on the book of Genesis to appear in the last two score years:

> The verb describing God's initial work is "created" (*bara'*). This verb is correctly defined as expressing the origination of something great, new and "epoch-making," as only God can do it, whether it be in the realm of the physical or of the spiritual. The verb *bara'* does not of itself and absolutely preclude the use of existing material; cf. Isaiah 65:18b: "Behold I create Jerusalem a rejoicing, and her people a joy." Also note v. 27 of this chapter. However, when no existing material is mentioned as to be worked over, no such material is implied. Consequently, this passage teaches *creatio ex nihilo*, "creation out of nothing," a doctrine otherwise also clearly taught by the Scriptures; Romans 4:17; Hebrews 11:3; cf. also Psalm 33:6, 9; Amos 4:13. The verb is never used of other than DIVINE activity.[12]

While it is true that the creation narrative which this declaration introduces is in itself limited to this stellar galaxy in which our sun, stars and this earth are a part, still there is nothing here or elsewhere in the Scriptures to forbid our believing that the "heavens" here embrace the entire universe. Later references to God's initial creative activity support such a view. In the well-known prologue of John's gospel when we are told that "without him was not anything made that hath been made" (John 1:3), there is no possibility that other galaxies are not included. The same idea embracing the entire universe was expressed by Paul when, in addressing the Athenian philosophers, he said, "The God that made the world and all things therein, he, being Lord of heaven and earth. . . ." (Acts 17:24).

How strange that as modern man has become increasingly aware of the vastness of the universe, of the very heavens spoken of at the beginning of the Bible, he has felt that the idea of an eternal home located somewhere in these heavens must be abandoned (as we have noted previously). I have felt that in a work of this kind we ought to frankly and gladly acknowledge the latest conclusions of contemporary astronomers regarding the size of our universe. We will begin with a word concerning the earth, then the sun, then the galaxy in which our sun moves in its orbit, and then the vast universe itself of innumerable galaxies.

The Size of the Universe

Our *earth* is one of nine planets revolving around the sun, and has a diameter of 8,000 miles. Its mass is estimated to be 6,600,000,000,000,000,000,000,000 tons. The distance from the earth to the moon is 250,000 miles; while the distance to the sun is 93,000,000 miles.

The *sun* has a diameter of 866,500 miles, and a mass 330,000 times that of the earth. The sun—and here the mind begins to stagger at such enormous distances and innumerable masses—is only one star in a galaxy of some one hundred billion other stars (100,000,000,000!), a galaxy that has a mass of about seventy billion times that of the sun.

Distances now become so great that we will find it so cumbersome to use the measure of a *mile* that it is necessary to construct a more practical unit which is called a *light year*. Light travels at the speed of 186,000 miles per second (generally referred to as m.p.s.), or 11,160,000 miles in one minute. (The sun is eight light minutes away.) A *light year,* then, means the distance light will travel in one year, or 5,880,000,000,000 miles. Our solar system has a diameter of 660 light minutes; but the galaxy of which it is a very small part has a diameter of 100,000 light years!

Enormous as is the galaxy in which our solar system moves, it is only one of innumerable other galaxies—possibly one thousand million of them, the nearest of which is the Andromeda galaxy, 1,500,000 light years distant!

If in *each* of these thousand million galaxies there are, as astronomers believe, 100,000 million stars, then in the entire universe there are some 150 million million million (150,000,-000,000,000,000,000) stars.

On a clear night as many as 2,000 stars can be seen with the naked eye by a person standing at one spot. The total number of stars visible in the entire sky is estimated at about 6,000. By the one-inch telescope, some 225,000 stars can be observed. With the one-hundred-inch telescope about 1,500,000,000 stars. However, with the two-hundred-inch telescope nearly one billion *galaxies* are brought within observation, which includes objects as far away as two billion light years.

Very recently the frontiers of space have been pushed even farther back by Dr. Maarten Schmidt, Professor of Astronomy at California Institute of Technology. He has found five *quasars,* that is, quasi-stellar radio noise sources that are farther from the earth than any other known object. The most distant of these five quasars is labeled 3C-9. "The light we see from 3C-9," says Professor Schmidt, "left there many billions of years ago, long before the sun and the earth were born, when the expanding universe was only a third as big as it is now."[13]

AGE OF THE UNIVERSE

While the subject of the age of our universe is not as relevant to the problem of the space which is embraced by these heavenly bodies, it should have brief notice, even if only in summarized form. The concept of the age of our earth, as well as the age of the universe, has in our century undergone as great changes as conceptions of the size of this universe. Hardly more than forty years ago, the age of our earth was estimated to be about one hundred million years. Thirty years ago this figure was extended from 210 to 340 million years. It is now generally acknowledged that this earth is from 4.5 to 5 billion years in age. Within this very decade it was generally thought that life originated on the earth at least two billion years ago. In 1965 an international research team at the University of California, in Berkeley, found life-produced molecules in rocks from the Soudan formation of Minnesota that are estimated to be 4 billion years old.

The age of the universe has been variously estimated. In 1958 Sandage calculated it to be somewhere between thirteen to twenty billion years.

There is nothing in the initial accounts of creation in the Bible, nor in the later numerous references to this great theme, that can be interpreted as in direct contradiction to such estimates of enormous time periods. In fact, poetic language as it is, even the Hebrews themselves would seem to have considered the earth to have a great age, when they spoke of "the everlasting hills" (Gen. 49:26; Hab. 3:6). Note also the phrase "the ancient mountains" in the Blessing of Moses (Deut. 33:15).

There is no need in a work such as this to enter into the complicated subject of how this universe of ours came into existence. The theories held by different competent authorities testify to the inability of contemporary scientists to agree on any one theory attempting to explain the origin of this vast universe. Dr. W. M. Smart, the Regius Professor of Astronomy in the University of Glasgow, in his authoritative work, *The Origin of the Earth*, enumerates the following different theories, held with equal convictions by astronomers and physicists today. Without defining them, Professor Smart mentions The Tidal Theory, The Collision Theory, The Binary Star Hypothesis, The Fission Theory, The Nebular-Cloud Theory, The Electromagnetic Theory, and The Nova Theory. And then he is forced to conclude that "all the theories proposed up to date as to the mechanism by which the Solar System has come into being failed to carry conviction." But in the same paragraph, he makes this interesting confession: "We feel some assurance in asserting that the Solar System is derived from a single activity on a great scale in the distant past."[14]

Probably the most frequently quoted volume on cosmology is the one by Dr. E. A. Milne, the late Rouse Ball Professor of Mathematics in the University of Oxford, who concludes his work with the simple statement "I do most fervently believe that this universe was created by Almighty God."[15]

The second chapter of Genesis opens with a statement regarding this initial creative activity that contains a word not found in the earlier pronouncement: "And the heavens and the earth were finished and all the *host* of them." The Hebrew word here translated "host" derives from a root meaning to go forth as a soldier, and is often applied to angels (Luke 2:13; I Kings 22:19, etc.) as well as to the celestial bodies (Matt. 24:29; Isa. 34:4)—subjects concerning which we will have more to say later on. Leupold is probably right in remarking that "since the creation account has up to this point said nothing about angels, it will hardly be safe to advance the claim that the angels are meant to be included in this term. We simply know nothing definite as to the time of their creation."

We should add one new theory, however, to this list, and that is what is known as the Continuous Creation Theory, which has been vigorously set forth by one of the most distinguished astronomers of our day, Dr. Fred Hoyle, the Professor of Physics in Cambridge University. These are Hoyle's own words: "From time to time people ask where the created material comes from. Well, it does not come from anywhere. Matter simply appears—it is created. At one time the various atoms composing the material do not exist and at a later time they do."[16] Does not this statement sound mysteriously like the concept we have mentioned above, the view held by most orthodox theologians, namely, that God created the world out of nothing, a doctrine referred to as *Creatio ex Nihilo*. This subject needs careful consideration now before we proceed any further and we can do no better than to have before us the restrained but specific statement of Dr. G. F. Woods stated in a lecture which he recently delivered in Cambridge University:

> In so far as our use of some kind of analogy from an act of human construction leads us to think that God made use in the creation of some kind of material, which He had not Himself created, we do not attain to a final explanation but remain at a loss before an unexplained fact.
>
> God is the absolute creator of the world. He did not use any kind of given material. He did not act in accordance with some given body of laws or principles which were not His own.
>
> The final theory of creation *ex nihilo* leaves many points obscure but it represents a faith in God as the ultimate explanation of the world. It is an expression of faith in the ultimate explicability of the world by reference to God rather than an account of what took place when the world came into being.[17]

That there was a definite time when this universe came into existence, by which is meant that it is not eternal, is the general verdict of both scientists and philosophers at this present time. No discoveries have altered the accuracy of the words of the famous astronomer, Sir J. H. Jeans, when he said, nearly forty years ago:

> Everything points with overwhelming force to a defi-nite event, or series of events, of creation at some time or times, not infinitely remote. The universe cannot have originated by chance out of its present ingredients, and neither can it have been always the same as now. For in either of these events no atoms would be left save such as are incapable of dissolving into radiation; there would be neither sunlight nor starlight but only a cool glow of radiation uniformly diffused through space. This is, indeed, so far as present-day science can see, the final end towards which all creation moves, and at which it must at long last arrive.[18]

Though the Bible often refers to the phenomena of the atmospheric and celestial heavens, the most important mean-ing of Heaven in the Bible, and for Christians, is of course, the abode of God and the ultimate destiny of believers. Our next chapter then will be entirely devoted to the Biblical data that reveals heaven as the habitation of God.

At the close of these two chapters considering the Biblical data referring to the atmospheric and celestial heavens and to heaven as the abode of God, before we begin a more ex-haustive consideration of the relationships of Jesus Christ to heaven, the inhabitants of heaven, and heaven as the Holy City, we might do well just at this point to remind ourselves that this simple word *heaven*, probably more than any other single word in the English language, consistently connotes what is wholly beautiful, satisfying and perfect. Even the word *God* can be debased as happens in the Bible when the immoral and mythological deities of the heathen are called gods even though they are condemned. In the latest edition of Roget's thesaurus the word *heaven* is placed in a group of words referring to such exquisite concepts as delightful, beautiful, divine, angelic, boundlessness, bliss, the afterlife, the promised land, celestial, spaciousness, and blessedness. As an adverb or adjective, it may mean radiant, spiritual, pure in heart, unearthly, angelic. Some of these ideas are found in the definition for the word *heavenly* in the great *Oxford English Dictionary*: "Having the excellence, beauty, or delight that belongs to heaven; of more than earthly or human excellence; divine." To be heavenly minded, says this same authority, and here the language is almost identical with the New Testament, is "having the thoughts and affections set on things above; holy, devout." Consequently, anything that is said to be from heaven partakes in part of the very character of God and may be expected to bring blessing, cleansing, hope and deliverance, to whom a messenger from heaven, or a revelation from heaven, is sent. This is the basic theme in the famous words of James that "every good gift and every perfect gift is from above, coming down from the Father of lights, with whom can be no variation, neither shadow that is cast by turning" (James 1:17).

NOTES

1. Some of the definitions of "high" in the *Oxford English Dictionary* have a direct bearing upon our theme: "Of exalted rank, station, dignity, position, or estimation. (Of persons or their attributes; also, with emphatic force, in *high* God.) . . . Of lofty, elevated, or superior kind." There is a profound discussion of the influence of contemplating the heavenly regions in M. Eliade, *Patterns in Comparative Religion* (London: 1958), pp. 38-39. He remarks that "the sky symbolizes transcending power and changelessness simply by being there."
2. Aristotle, *On the Heavens*, I. ix, in *Loeb Classical Library* (Cambridge, Mass.: 1953), p. 89.
3. On the atmosphere there are two excellent chapters, "The Ocean of Air" and "The Sea of the Ionosphere," pp. 73-94, 134-53, in Alexander Marshall, *The World in Space* (New York: 1958). For an earlier discussion from a Christian standpoint, see F. T. Farmer, "The Atmosphere: Its Design and Significance in Creation," *Transactions of the Victoria Institute* (1939), LXXI, 38-48.
4. In Psalm 68:4, the Hebrew word *arabah* means a mixed cloud; in 77:18, *galgal*, a rolling cloud; in 89:6, 37, *shackaq*, a thin cloud; and in Isaiah 5:30, *ariphim*, dropping clouds.

5. The judgment of God upon Sodom deserves a further note. The word translated "brimstone" is *gophrith*, which is always used in the Old Testament in reference to some form of judgment, as Deuteronomy 29.23; Psalm 11:6. In the LXX it is translated as *theion*, a very mysterious word, which is believed by many to be derived from *theios*, meaning *of/from the gods,* and thus *divine.* Jude uses this very word in his reference to this event (v. 7); and it occurs five times in the book of Revelation (9:17-18; 14:10; 19:20; 21:8), in reference to hell. See Wilbur M. Smith, *This Atomic Age and the Word of God* (Boston: 1948), pp. 282-94.

6. Of course the significance of the atmospheric heavens, i.e., air, takes on profounder meanings in our space age. Who will control the air, for radio communications, for biological warfare, for intercontinental warfare? These are increasingly acute problems. Bishop Charles J. Ellicott, a recognized authority on the Greek text of the New Testament, has said: "Paul's use of the word *aer* in Ephesians 2:2 to designate the atmosphere around the earth, leads us to the conclusion that he uses it in the same way in I Thessalonians 4:17. Our Lord will descend into the very atmosphere inhabited by demons when He comes to take the Church out of the midst of this enemy territory, with Him to Heaven. The Greeks made a distinction between the lower atmosphere *aner* and the purer, rarefied atmosphere of the mountain tops *aither*. Therefore, Our Lord will descend below the mountain tops to the lower atmosphere where both the saints and the demons are." He then defines the air of Ephesians 2:2 as "all that supra-terrestrial but super-celestial region which seems to be if not the abode yet the haunt of evil spirits" (*A Critical and Grammatical Commentary on St. Paul's Epistle to the Ephesians* [rev. ed.; London: 1864], pp. 44-45). Dr. Robert S. Candlish in his profound lectures on the first epistle of John, gives a spiritual interpretation of this passage—and both interpretations may well be true: "He is 'the prince of the power of the air.' He rules, as a powerful prince, the world's atmosphere; its moral and spiritual atmosphere; impregnating it with his own venom; the poisonous vapours of his own dark and godless hell. The air which the world breathes is under his control; he is the prince of the power of it; its powerful prince. It is, as it were, compounded, concocted and manufactured by him. Very wisely does he use his power; very cunningly does he compose the air which he would have his victims and subjects to breathe. He mingles in it many good ingredients. Even for the worst he does so, making it palatable and seductive. For the lowest company, he must needs prepare an atmosphere with something good in it; good fellowship at the least, and a large measure of good humour and good feeling. Then, as he rises to higher circles, how does he contrive, in the exercise of his princely power, to make the air that is to intoxicate his votaries, or lull them to unsuspecting sleep, all redolent, as it might seem, of good; good sense, good taste, good temper; good breeding and behaviour; good habits and good-heartedness! Many noisome vapours also that might offend he carefully excludes; so that the inhaling breath perceives nothing but what is pure and simple in what it imbibes and absorbs. But it is the wicked one's air or atmosphere after all. He is the prince of the power of it. He contrives to have it all pervaded with the latent influence of his own ungodliness. His godless spirit is in it all through. Have you not felt something of what it is to breathe the air of which the wicked one is thus the powerful prince—to breathe it at the time almost unconsciously, and afterwards to find the fruit of your

having breathed it all but inexplicable?" (*The First Epistle of John Expounded in a Series of Lectures* [Edinburgh: 1866], pp. 496-500).
7. Among volumes on astronomical matters that include "Heavens" in their titles may be mentioned the epochal work of Copernicus (in Latin) *De revolutionibus orbium Coelesticum* (1543); two titles by the famous professor of astronomy at Princeton University: Charles A. Young, *God's Glory in the Heavens* and *Uranography* (Boston: 1936); George Ellery Hale, *The New Heavens* (1922); and Edwin B. Frost, *The Heavens Are Telling.*
8. A. C. B. Lovell, *The Individual and the Universe* (New York: 1959), p. 74.
9. There is a fairly complete list of these passages relating to creation in Paul A. Zimmerman (ed.), *Darwin, Evolution, and Creation* (St. Louis: 1959), p. 39. And, for a helpful classification of the data, Henry W. Frost, *Outline Bible Studies* (Philadelphia: 1924), pp. 28-29.
10. W. Lindsay Alexander, *Biblical Theology* (Edinburgh: 1888), p. 130.
11. H. C. Leupold, *Exposition of Genesis* (Columbus, Ohio: 1942), p. 41.
12. Leupold, *ibid.*, pp. 40-41.
13. See *Time*, May 21, 1965.
14. W. M. Smart, *The Origin of the Earth* (Cambridge: 1951), p. 220. For recent discussions of these scientific conclusions, see Alexander Marshack, *The World in Space* (New York: 1958); Herman Bondi, *The Universe at Large* (New York: 1960); James A. Coleman, *Modern Theories of the Universe* (New York: 1963); H. C. King, *The Exploration of the Universe* (New York: 1964). *Creatio ex nihilo* is emphasized throughout Langdon Gilkey, *Maker of Heaven and Earth* (New York: 1959), p. 53.
15. E. A. Milne, *Modern Cosmology and the Christian Idea of God* (Oxford: 1962), p. 160. For a number of earlier testimonies to God as Creator, see Wilbur M. Smith, *Therefore Stand* (Boston: 1945), pp. 298-308.
16. Fred Hoyle, *The Nature of the Universe* (Oxford: 1950), p. 125.
17. G. F. Woods, *Theological Examination* (Welwyn, England: 1958), pp. 166, 172.
18. J. H. Jeans, *Eos, or the Wider Aspects of Cosmogony* (London: 1928), p. 55.

*   *   *

On the subject of creation from the standpoint of the Bible, the following will be found helpful: L. F. Gruber, *Whence Came the Universe?* (Boston: 1921), F. Alton Everest (ed.), *Modern Science and the Christian Faith* (2d ed.; Wheaton, Ill.: 1950); Bernard Ramm, *The Christian View of Science and Scripture* (Grand Rapids: 1954); Charles Hauret, *Beginnings: Genesis and Modern Science* (Dubuque: 1955); R. L. Mixter (ed.), *Evolution and Christian Thought Today* (Grand Rapids: 1957); N. H. Ridderbos, *Is There a Conflict Between Genesis 1 and Natural Science?* (Grand Rapids: 1957); Langdon Gilkey, *Maker of Heaven and Earth* (New York: 1959); Paul A. Zimmerman (ed.), *Darwin, Evolution, and Creation* (St. Louis: 1959).

4 Heaven—The Abode of God

Even though we are told in the Scriptures that the "heaven of heavens cannot contain God" (I Kings 8:27; II Chron. 2:6), and that God is everywhere present, on the earth as well as in heaven (Deut. 4:39; Joshua 2:11), nevertheless, the same Scriptures clearly teach that God does dwell particularly in heaven, a place often designated as *His habitation.* While such statements were made in the later period of Israel's history, we might well begin our study of this subject by having before us what may be called the two most comprehensive statements regarding God dwelling in heaven that are to be found anywhere in the Bible, both of them toward the end of the book of Isaiah: "For thus saith the high and lofty One that inhabiteth eternity, whose name is Holy: I *dwell* in the *high* and *holy place,* with him also that is of a contrite and humble spirit, to revive the spirit of the humble, and to revive the heart of the contrite" (57:15).[1] "Look down from heaven, and behold from *the habitation of thy holiness and of thy glory*: where are thy zeal and thy mighty acts? The yearning of thy heart and thy compassions are restrained toward me" (63:15; see also 66:1).

Some of the very titles of God imply His heavenliness, embracing the factor that He is lifted high above all mankind, and above the earth on which the destinies of men are determined. He is often referred to as "the God Most High" even as far back as the account of the interview of Abraham with Melchizedek, "priest of the Most High God." In speaking to Abraham, he twice uses this very title: "Blessed be Abram of God Most High, possessor of heaven and earth: and blessed be God Most High who hath delivered thine enemies into thy hand" (Gen. 14:18-20; cf. Heb. 7:1). In the Hebrew text, this title is *El Elyon,* which, as applied to God, reveals that "because He is the highest He has power to rule and turn them as He will should they be disobedient or seek to exalt themselves against Him." In this Melchizedek passage two factors appear which we will find as constant in the later occurrences of this title, namely, that God as Most High is the God of all mankind, not merely the God who enters into a covenant with Israel; and that, because He is Most High, He possesses abundant power to overcome His enemies. The psalmists use this title when they wish to give praise to God for delivering them in an hour of trouble, or when they cry unto Him for such deliverance (7:17; 18:13; 57:2; 78:35). It is significant that this title appears most frequently in the book of Daniel in passages where pagan rulers are prominent. When Nebuchadnezzar saw that the three men thrown into the fiery furnace had been divinely protected from the flame, he called out, "Ye servants of the Most High God, come forth, and come hither" (3:26). Similarly, he himself on the day when he was unaware of the tragedy that was to overtake him declared, "It hath seemed good unto me to show the signs and wonders that the Most High God hath wrought toward me" (4:2), an unjustified assumption on his part, for he himself otherwise always boasted that it was he who had accomplished all these things. Daniel then warned him of this coming period of semi-insanity, which would teach him that "the Most High ruleth in the kingdom

of men, and giveth it to whomsoever He will," a lesson which
he was to hearken to (4:25, 34). When Daniel rebuked Bel-
shazzar, he reminded him that it was the Most High God who
had given his father the kingdom (5:18, 21). In the great
prophecy of the four kingdoms recorded in chapter 7, an
angel interpreter three times speaks of "the saints of the Most
High who shall receive the kingdom, and possess the kingdom for ever" (vv. 18, 25, 27).[2] We should repeat here what
was said above that this title of God as the Most High implies
what all these passages speak of, the sovereignty of God over
the kingdoms of this earth.

Closely related to this title is the more often used one,
"Jehovah the God of heaven," frequently in passages which
are concerned with the relationship of Israel to the nations
around about. Even Cyrus himself, king of Persia, used this
title when he was about to allow the captive Israelites to return to Israel: "Thus saith Cyrus king of Persia, All the kingdoms of the earth hath Jehovah, the God of heaven, given
me; and he hath charged me to build him a house in Jerusalem, which is in Judah. Whosoever there is among you of
all his people, Jehovah his God be with him, and let him go
up" (II Chron. 36:23; cf. Ezra 1:2). It was at the time of
the return that Nehemiah in praying to God directed his
prayer to "the God of heaven" (Neh. 1:4-5; 2:4, 20; cf. Jonah
1:9; Ps. 136:26). Daniel also presented his petitions to "the
God of heaven" (2:18-19) and, in a later statement to Nebuchadnezzar, emphasized again the relationship of this title
of God to his dealings with the nations of the earth: "Thou,
O King, art king of kings, unto whom the *God of heaven* hath
given the kingdom, the power, and the strength, and the
glory. . . . And in the days of those kings shall *the God of
heaven* set up a kingdom which shall never be destroyed, nor
shall the sovereignty thereof be left to another people; but

it shall break in pieces and consume all these kingdoms, and it shall stand for ever" (Dan. 2:37, 44; 5:23).[3]

In the New Testament, as we might expect, the idea of God Most High appears in the Gospels and, almost exclusively in the gospel of St. Luke, a gospel for the whole world, as his supplementary work, the book of Acts, so clearly indicates. The angel Gabriel when announcing to Mary that she should bring forth a son declared, "He shall be great, and shall be called the Son of the Most High: and the Lord God shall give unto him the throne of His father David; . . . and of his kingdom there shall be no end" (Luke 1:32-33). Here again we note that this title of God naturally refers to the ultimate dominion of His sovereign reign. In the same hallowed message the angel told Mary, "The power of the Most High shall overshadow you" (1:35). Zacharias used the same title when in the Benedictus he said of his son, "Thou, child, shalt be called the prophet of the Most High" (1:76). The angelic host echoed this idea in their song, "Glory to God in the highest and on earth peace among men in whom he is well pleased" (2:14). As J. M. Creed has said, "The former proclaims God's glory in heaven, the second His gift of peace to His chosen upon earth."[4]

Once our Lord used this title, in a passage found exclusively in Luke (though the idea is elsewhere): "But love your enemies, and do *them* good, and lend, never despairing; and your reward shall be great, and ye shall be sons of the Most High: for he is kind toward the unthankful and evil" (Luke 6:35). Strange to say, the demon-possessed boy at Gerasa used this very title when he cried out, "What have I to do with thee, Jesus, thou Son of the Most High God?" (Luke 8:28; Mark 5:7). (See also the utterance of the demon-possessed woman at Philippi in Acts 16:17.)[5] The final occurrence of any reference to the God Most High in the Gospels significantly is not found in Luke's narrative. It is in the cry of the multitude at the time of the triumphal entry, "Hosanna to the Son of David: blessed is he who cometh in the name of the Lord; hosanna in the highest" (Matt. 21:9; Mark 11:10), a passage which Swete rightly says "must be taken to mean 'let the prayer for our deliverance be ratified in high heaven.'"

Only once in the subsequent books of the New Testament do we find this concept of God's exaltation. St. Stephen, quoting the opening statement of Isaiah 66, reminded his belligerent audience that "the Most High dwelleth not in houses made with hands; as saith the prophet, The heaven is my throne, and the earth the footstool of my feet" (Acts 7:48-49).[6] Here again in the word *throne* we have the idea of the sovereignty of God.

There are a great number of statements, both in the Old and New Testaments, which find their real meaning in this concept of heaven being the abode of God. Jehovah said to the children of Israel at the time of their sojourn at Sinai, "I have talked with you from heaven" (Exodus 20:22). Later Moses reminded the Israelites, "Out of heaven he made thee to hear his voice" (Deut. 4:36; see also Neh. 9:13).

This recalls the statement concerning the transfiguration that there was a voice heard *from heaven* saying, "This is my beloved son, hear ye him" (see also Jer. 25:30). This conviction that God is in heaven is the basis for the frequent pleas of the children of God. Solomon in his great dedicatory prayer so often pled, "Hear thou in heaven thy dwelling-place" (I Kings 8:30, 32, 34, 36, 39, 43, 45, 49). Nehemiah expressed his profound gratitude to God, recognizing that at times when Israel was flagrantly disobedient to God and was being punished for this, when they cried unto God, He had heard "from heaven" (Neh. 9:27-28; II Chron. 7:14; Deut. 26:15).

Often in the Scriptures we are admonished to lift up our

eyes unto heaven (Deut. 4:19, 34; Isa. 51:6). Jeremiah remarked in an unexpected moment, "Let us lift up our heart with our hands unto God in the heavens" (Lam. 3:41). It is especially, however, in the Psalms that David and others in Israel are said to cry unto God Most High (57:2), to sing praises to the Most High (9:2; 7:17). Once we read, "I will remember the years of the right hand of the Most High" (77:10); and once the children of Israel are called sons of the Most High (82:6). So like the psalmist, the children of God, down through the ages, can unite in saying, "Unto the Lord do I lift up my soul" (Ps. 86:4).

HEAVEN AS A HABITATION

We are now ready to consider in detail the nomenclature of heaven as the *abode* of God.

There are, it would seem, seven words used in the Old and New Testaments in reference to heaven, all of which have in them the idea of *dwelling* and *habitation*. Perhaps we might do well, first of all, to take two words from the great description of our heavenly abode in St. John's account of the Holy City to which we will be giving more minute study in a later chapter. John tells us that he heard a great voice out of the throne saying, "Behold the *tabernacle* of God is with men, and he shall *dwell* with them, and they shall be his people, and God himself shall be with them, and be their God" (Rev. 21:3). In this statement we have the final consummation of the entire revelation in the Old and New Testaments concerning God's dwelling among men, that is, among His redeemed, and their being with Him forever.

Tabernacle

Let us begin with the word *tabernacle*. All students of the Bible recognize this as the name of that first structure ordained by God to be built, in which He would reveal Himself to His people Israel. The central passage on this deserves to be quoted here: ". . . at the door of the tent of meeting before Jehovah, where I will meet with you, to speak there unto thee. And there I will meet with the children of Israel; and *the Tent* shall be sanctified by my glory. And I will sanctify the tent of meeting, and the altar: Aaron also and his sons will I sanctify, to minister to me in the priest's office. And I will *dwell* among the children of Israel, and will be their God" (Exodus 29:42-45). In the Greek text of the Old Testament and in the Greek New Testament, the word is *skene*. This same word is often used in reference to the temple, as "In Salem also is his tabernacle, and his dwelling-place in Zion" (Ps. 76:2). This is the word used in the apostolic literature, as for instance, in Paul's statement regarding our "earthly house of this tabernacle" (II Cor. 5:1, 4; see also II Peter 1:13-14). It is used twice by the writer to the Hebrews in a definite reference to Heaven itself. Christ is spoken of as "a minister of the *sanctuary*, and of the true *tabernacle*, which the Lord pitched, not man." "Christ having come a high priest of the good things to come, through the greater and more perfect tabernacle, not made with hands, that is to say, not of this creation" (Heb. 8:2; 9:11; see also Ps. 61:4; Rev. 15:5).

In the very verse with which we began this section, we have the verbal form of the noun tabernacle, translated *dwell*. This is exactly the word that is to be found in the early revelation concerning the tabernacle which was quoted above. It is this idea of God *dwelling* in the midst of His people which is so frequently referred to in the great dedicatory prayer of Solomon. "Then spake Solomon, Jehovah hath said that he would dwell in the thick darkness. I have surely built thee a house of habitation, a place for thee to *dwell* in for ever" (I Kings 8:12-13; see also vv. 30, 39, 43; II Chron. 6:2). (In anticipation of the building of the temple as the dwelling place of God, see Deuteronomy 23:16.) It is this verb which we find in that remarkable statement of the Apostle John that "the Word became flesh, and *dwelt* among us (and we beheld his glory, glory as of the only begotten from the Father), full of grace and truth" (John 1:14). It may be of interest to my readers that this verb is found elsewhere in the New Testament only in Revelation 7:15; 12:12; 13:6; and as we have said, in 21:3.

Sanctuary

Closely related to the idea of a *tabernacle*, a word often used in descriptions of the tabernacle is the word *sanctuary*, which in the Greek text of the Old and New Testaments is *hagion*, found also in the early description of the original tabernacle: "Let them make me a *sanctuary*, that I may dwell among them" (Exodus 25:8). This is the word sometimes used when the temple of Solomon is in mind (I Chron. 22:19; Ps. 68:24). In the epistle to the Hebrews the word is sometimes used when the author is referring to the earthly tabernacle (9:1-3, 24-25; 13:11), but it is used with equal frequency by the same author in referring to heaven, which is in some verses translated "the holy place" (8:2; 9:8, 12; 10:19). This idea of the holy place is also referred to by Solomon in his dedicatory prayer (I Kings 8:6, 8, 10).

Habitation

Another word frequently used in reference to the dwelling place of God, whether in the tabernacle, in the temple or in heaven, is *habitation*. In the song of Moses and Miriam, after the destruction of the Egyptian hosts, we come upon a most interesting exclamation: "Thou in thy lovingkindness hast led the people that thou hast redeemed: Thou hast guided them in thy strength to thy holy *habitation*" (Exodus 15:13). This word *habitation* is occasionally used in reference to the tabernacle: "Jehovah, I love the *habitation* of thy house, and the place where thy glory dwelleth" (Ps. 26:8), but most often in reference to the temple, as in Solomon's statement at the time of the finishing of the temple where we have four of these concepts brought together in a single statement: "I have built thee a house of habitation, and a place for thee to dwell in for ever" (II Chron. 6:2). This word is certainly made to refer to God's abode in heaven in such passages as "From the place of his *habitation* he looketh forth upon all the inhabitants of the earth" (Ps. 33:14), and in the exclamation of the psalmist, "Whom have I in heaven but thee? And there is none on earth that I desire besides thee" (Ps. 73:25). The word is used, most interestingly, in the statement of our Lord regarding our being received "into the eternal *tabernacles*" (Luke 16:9). The church itself is once referred to as "the *habitation* of God" (Eph. 2:22). Near the end of his great series of prophecies, Isaiah prays, "Look down from heaven and behold from the *habitation* of thy holiness and of thy glory" (Isa. 63:15). This is the truth implied in the statement regarding one aspect of the great revival under Hezekiah when we are told that when the priests and the Levites blessed the people, their prayer "came up to his holy habitation, even unto heaven" (II Chron. 30:27; see also Jer. 25:30; Zech. 2:13).

House

A word that appears with far greater frequency in reference to Heaven, as well as to earthly sacred structures, is the word *house*, the Greek word being *oikos*. Indeed this is the word used in the first occasion in the Scriptures when a child of God speaks of the heavenly abode. It occurs, as all will recall, in Jacob's exclamation as he awoke after the vision at Bethel and cried out, "How dreadful is this place! This is none other than the house of God, and this is the gate of heaven" (Gen. 28:17). It is the word used fifteen times in Solomon's dedicatory prayer (and its immediate context). In this prayer at the dedication of the temple in which the presence of God in this earthly sanctuary is constantly recognized, we have the tremendous statement "But will God in very deed dwell on the earth? Behold, heaven and the heaven of heavens cannot contain thee; how much less this house that I have builded!" (I Kings 8:27). While we are speaking of this rich chapter, it may be of interest to note the great frequency of the word *heaven,* both in I Kings 8 and in II Chronicles 6, where Solomon, in predicting the judgments of God yet to fall upon Israel in days to come because of her disobedience, urges the nation to seek God in prayer, and pleads with God that in that hour He would hear from Heaven and forgive the sin of His people Israel. This idea of the dwelling place of God on earth as a house is, of course, to be found in our Lord's well-known words "Make not my Father's house a house of merchandise" (John 2:16). It is not difficult to understand that when St. Peter speaks of believers as "living stones built upon a spiritual house" he has in mind the invisible church of all true believers (I Peter 2:5; also probably 4:17). But one wonders to what St. Paul might be referring when he exhorts believers that they should be careful how they "behave themselves in the *house of God,* which is the church of the living God" (I Tim. 3:15). Of course, this is the word also used by the apostle in reference to our earthly bodies, which he calls our "earthly house" (II Cor. 5:1). At the same time St. Paul uses another form of this Greek word (*oikterion*) when he speaks of "our habitation [house] which is from heaven" (II Cor. 5:2). This is the word used by our Lord in His famous statement regarding His return to prepare mansions for His own in His Father's house (John 14:2). An interesting verse for further study is the prophetic statement by Isaiah "Even them will I bring

to my holy mountain, and make them joyful in my house of
prayer: their burnt-offerings and their sacrifices shall be accepted upon mine altar; for my house shall be called a house
of prayer for all peoples" (56:7). (For other references to
heaven as the house of God, see Ps. 27:4; 61:4; 65:4.)

Temple

There is another term referring to Heaven that may be
included in this particular classification, and that is the word
temple, the Greek word *naos.* It is interesting to note that
this word *temple* is found even in reference to the first tabernacle (I Sam. 1:9; 3:3), and with great frequency, of course,
in reference to the temple of Solomon, and to the second
temple built by the returning exiles. One wonders why the
actual word *temple* is never used by Solomon in the great
dedicatory prayer, though it appears in other passages of the
same period (I Kings 6:3 ff.; 7:50 ff.; see also Zech. 6:12-15).
Probably in David's great psalm of praise after the victory
over the Philistines, the word is used in reference to God's
abode in heaven: "In my distress I called upon Jehovah; yea,
I called unto my God: and he heard my voice out of his temple, and my cry *came* into his ears" (II Sam. 22:7). Certainly
it is to the heaven of heavens that the experience of Isaiah
is related (6:1); and in the description of the Holy City, God
and the Lamb are the temple of that eternal abode. As with
the words *tabernacle* and *house,* so also with the word *temple,* sometimes the reference is to our own bodies, especially
in this case, as temple of the Holy Spirit (I Cor. 3:16-17;
6:19; II Cor. 6:16; Eph. 2:21).

Sanctuary

The words *sanctuary* (see p. 57) and *temple* are closely
related, sanctuary referring to the inner or holiest part of the
temple (Matt. 23:35). Since both words are used with ref-

erence to Heaven as the abode of God this identification may have been in the mind of the psalmist when he says, "He hath looked down from the height of his sanctuary; from heaven did Jehovah behold the earth" (Ps. 102:19; 20:2). The word sanctuary appears in the New Testament in the rich treatment of the place into which Christ has entered (Heb. 8:2) and is a common expression with the Apostle John (Rev. 3:12; 7:15; 16:17). It is used in reference to the tabernacle (Exodus 25:8; Lev. 4:6), to the temple of Solomon (Ps. 68:24; I Chron. 22:19), and even to the temple of Herod (Luke 23:45).

Throne of God

Sometimes Heaven is actually designated as the *throne of God* (Isa. 61:1; Matt. 5:34) which is closely related to the theme that the throne of God is in heaven (Ps. 103:19), sometimes called "the throne of thy glory" (Jer. 14:21). Closely related to this is the phrase of Daniel that God is "the King of heaven" (4:37).

All the basic words used in the Old Testament in reference to the tabernacle and the temple—that is, habitation, house, temple, sanctuary—are also found in the passages which describe for us the ministry of the Lord in heaven as our high priest, especially in the epistle to the Hebrews. We will have much more to say about our Lord's ministry in heaven in a later chapter.

The church itself is called a spiritual *house* (I Peter 2:5), and Christ is said to minister in the house of God (Heb. 3:6; 10:21). Christians, especially their bodies, are called the temple of God or the temple of the Holy Ghost (I Cor. 3:16-17; 6:19; Eph. 2:21; Rev. 21:22). In the use of the word *habitation*, which is the one found in the phrase "everlasting habitations" (Luke 16:9), it is said that our Lord "having come a high priest of the good things to come, through the greater and more perfect tabernacle, not made with hands, that is to say, *not* of this creation . . . entered in once for all into the holy place, having obtained eternal redemption" (Heb. 9:11-12). In the great description of the Holy City concluding the New Testament, the concept of habitation is found both as a noun and in verbal form, when we read: "And I heard a great voice out of the throne saying, Behold, the tabernacle of God is with men, and he shall dwell with them, and they shall be his peoples, and God himself shall be with them, *and be* their God" (Rev. 21:3). Using another word, but still keeping to the idea, we are called a habitation of God (Eph. 2:22). Finally, Christ is said now to be ministering in a heavenly sanctuary: "We have such a high priest, who sat down on the right hand of the throne of the Majesty in the heavens, a minister of the sanctuary, and of the true tabernacle, which the Lord pitched, not man" (Heb. 8:1-2). It is into this very holy place, this sanctuary, that we have the privilege of entering. "Having therefore, brethren, boldness to enter the holy place by the blood of Jesus, by the way which he dedicated for us, a new and living way, through the veil, that is to say, his flesh" (Heb. 10:19-20).

All these terms—temple, tabernacle, habitation, sanctuary and dwelling place—have one common denominator, or one basic characteristic often specifically expressed, and that is *holiness.* Thus the holy tabernacle and its holy place and the holy of holies, and later the holy temple, find their fundamental character, *holiness,* eternally perfected in what will be called at the end of the Scriptures the *Holy City,* in which only those will dwell who have been made holy by the grace of God. It is this God, none other, who high and lifted up, has absolute sovereignty over the nations of the earth. It is to such a God, holy and omnipotent, that we in fullest confidence direct our prayers, knowing that He is able to answer us above all we can think or ask. Finally, by the marvelous grace of God in His glorious plan of redemption, it is with us that God will dwell, so that forever we will be united in this family relationship bearing the image of God's Son. "It doth not yet appear what we shall be: but we know that, when he shall appear, we shall be like him; for we shall see him as he is" (I John 3:2, AV).

All the words we have found to be synonyms for heaven set forth four concepts permeating the whole revelation concerning our future life. To speak of a habitation, a dwelling place, a house, first of all connotes intimate relationship of individuals, not a collection of inanimate objects. This great group of individuals enjoys the most intimate and precious fellowship with God and with one another. In contrast to the temporalness of our pilgrimage here on earth, this fellowship will abide forever, never interrupted by sickness, change of character, alienation or death.

There is one word which perhaps should be discussed at this point, and that is the word *glory*. When the tabernacle was finished, we are told that "then the cloud covered the tent of meeting, and the glory of Jehovah filled the tabernacle. And Moses was not able to enter into the tent of meeting, because the cloud abode thereon, and the glory of Jehovah filled the tabernacle" (Exodus 40:34-35). Occasionally this concept of glory reappears in the older Biblical literature, and we read of God upon "the throne of glory" (I Sam. 2:8; see also Jer. 14:21; Matt. 25:31). Appropriately St. Stephen begins his famous address by referring to God thus: "The God of glory appeared unto our father Abraham" (Acts 7:2). And when he was being stoned, we are told that looking steadfastly into heaven he saw "the glory of God, and Jesus standing on the right hand of God" (Acts 7:55). The voice that spoke to our Lord on the mount of transfiguration is referred to by one who was present as a voice from glory (II Peter 1:17). St. Paul tells us that our Lord at the time of His ascension was "received up into glory" (I Tim. 3:16). On one occasion St. Paul speaks of God as "the Father of glory" (Eph. 1:17). Frequently in the New Testament, glory is a synonym for the heavenly destiny of the believer as in Paul's phrase "the hope of glory" (Col. 1:27). St. Peter in a similar way speaks of the Lord who has "called us unto his eternal glory" (II Peter 1:3, free trans.); and the author of the epistle to the Hebrews says, "It became him, for whom are all things, and through whom are all things, in bringing many sons unto glory, to make the author of their salvation perfect through sufferings" (Heb. 2:10). Somewhat related to this is, of course, those inexhaustible words of our Lord uttered toward the end of His high priestly prayer, when He said, "Father, I desire that they also whom thou hast given me be with me where I am, that they may behold my glory, which thou hast given me: for thou lovedst me before the foundation of the world" (John 17:24).[7]

HEAVEN AS A SYNONYM FOR GOD

Heaven is so vitally and constantly referred to as the abode of God that actually it is used both in the Old and New Testaments as a synonym for God in a metonymical way. Generally the phrase "looking up to heaven" implies that the person here referred to looks in that direction because there is where God abides to whom he will be praying, as in the prayer our Lord taught us to pray (Matt. 14:19; Luke 9:16), or in the experience of St. Stephen (Acts 7:55; see also Luke 18:13; Dan. 4:34; Deut. 32:40; II Chron. 32:20). It is quite certain that when Jehovah said unto Moses, "Stretch forth thy hand toward heaven that there may be hail in all the land of Egypt" (Exodus 9:22-23; 10:21-22; Dan. 12:7) the implication is not that he simply lifted up his hand as a token of authority, but that it was as it were an appeal to God. This idea of heaven as a synonym for God is, of course, fully understood in the confession of the prodigal son: "I have sinned against heaven" (Luke 15:18, 21).

When our Lord asked His critics whether the baptism of John was of Heaven or of man, He meant whether the baptism was of God or of man (Matt. 21:25; Mark 11:30-31; Luke 20:4-5). Often heaven is used in place of God in relation to the bountifulness of the Lord: "A man can receive nothing, except it have been given him from heaven" (John 3:27; cf. John 1:32). When the disciples looked toward heaven at the time of our Lord's ascension (Acts 1:10-11), while the initial meaning could be that they looked in the direction of heavenly objects, ultimately this must refer to the place where our Lord went, which would be the heaven of heavens. When the Apostle Paul asks the question, "Who shall ascend into heaven?" (Rom. 10:6, quoting Deut. 30:12), of course he means who shall ascend unto God. When we are told we are not to swear either by the earth or by heaven, this, of course, means we are not to swear using the name of God (Matt. 23:22; James 5:12). The "blessings of heaven above" (Gen. 49:25) are the blessings bestowed by God. Quite often in passages where these words relating to habitation are found, we have two, sometimes three, and sometimes four, terms gathered together. This is observed particularly in the Psalms: "In Salem also is his tabernacle, and his dwelling-place in Zion" (76:2); "Jehovah bless thee out of Zion: and see thou the good of Jerusalem all the days of thy life" (128:5); "Great is Jehovah, and greatly to be praised, in the city of our God, in his holy mountain" (48:1). The most remarkable illustration of multiplied references is in the following passage: "There is a river, the streams whereof make glad the city of God, the holy place of the tabernacles of the Most High" (46:4). The most frequently used term in calling attention to the temple is the one generally translated "house," which occurs in the Revised Version some sixteen times with particular emphasis upon the need for holiness on the part of those who approach the house of God (see 52:8; 55:14; 135:2, etc.). A classic illustration is in a psalm attributed to David: "Blessed is the man whom thou choosest, and causest to approach *unto thee,* that he may dwell in thy courts: we shall be satisfied with the goodness of thy house, thy holy temple" (65:4).

The Nomenclature of the Psalms

If our examination of these passages is complete, then only once do we have a word in the Psalter sometimes referring to God's earthly habitation and once to His heavenly habitation. This is the word *throne.* In such a passage as "His throne is in the heavens" (103:19), the reference certainly is to the heaven of heavens, but elsewhere the reference must be to the throne of Jerusalem, even though the word *throne* in the Scriptures is never directly related to the tabernacle.

Before discussing the very few passages where these terms may have a more spiritual implication than when employed in reference to the earthly tabernacle, attention should be called to the continuous emphasis upon the concept of holiness as a basic characteristic of God's dwelling place on earth. We read of "the holy hill of Zion" (2:6); "his holy hill" (3:4; 15:1); "his holy mountain" (48:1); "the holy temple" (5:7); "his holy habitation" (68:5); "his holy place" (24:3); "his holy throne" (47:8); and "the holy oracle" (28:2). This gives support to the constantly recurring concept that God is holy (22:3); "the holy one of Israel" (71:22, etc.).

There is no question but that in some passages in the

Psalter, where are references to the sanctuary, the temple and the house of God, the psalmist has in mind something more than an Israelite's actual approach to the literal temple, as at the conclusion of Psalm 23: "I shall dwell in the house of Jehovah for ever." Most would agree with Leupold:

> The broader thought is not physical presence in the temple or sanctuary but rather actual communion with God. Therefore, the claim that these words require a temple built in Jerusalem and therefore point beyond the days of David misses their deeper import. True, deep, and real fellowship with God, that is the climax of all the blessings enjoyed when a man is under the protecting care of this true Shepherd.[8]

So it is in the expression of gratitude and joy introducing Psalm 84: "How amiable are thy tabernacles, O Jehovah of hosts! My soul longeth, yea, even fainteth for the courts of Jehovah; my heart and my flesh cry out unto the living God" (vv. 1-2; see also 15:1; 24:3, etc.). This higher spiritual experience is certainly the one which the psalmist refers to in his words "But as for me, in the abundance of thy lovingkindness will I come into thy house: in thy fear will I worship toward thy holy temple" (5:7). To quote Leupold again:

"The higher privilege is under consideration, that of venturing into the personal presence of God in true fellowship." The idea of worshiping *toward* the holy temple implies that "all worship would very naturally be directed in thought toward the place where God had promised to manifest His presence, so that even a physical turning toward this place came to be customary in the course of time (Dan. 6:10)."[9]

A recent scholarly commentator on the Psalms, the German exegete Artur Weiser, in commenting on Psalm 84, writes as follows:

> It is hardly possible to imagine what the divine service

which as a layman he could attend only in the forecourt of the Temple, may have meant to this man who can say of himself that he was consumed with such yearning for the forecourts of Yahweh that he was pining away! To long for God is for him a vital expression of his own being so deeply and naturally rooted that the whole man, "heart and flesh", breaks into a sudden shout of joy as soon as he becomes fully and almost physically aware that God is near him in the Temple. The poet feels man, in his uttermost depths, to be a unity, integrated and unaffected; so here he blends the material and spatial with the spiritual and emotional.[10]

See also Psalm 65:4 and 27:4-5 for further Biblical examples of the use of the word *temple* in the sense of house.

There is one passage in the Psalter where possibly the word *temple* refers not to some holy structure in Jerusalem but to heaven itself: "In my distress I called upon Jehovah, and cried unto my God: he heard my voice out of his temple, and my cry before him came into his ears" (18:6). Many will certainly agree with Leupold and others that this "may well describe the heavenly dwelling place of the Most High." Weiser has added to this single concept an additional thought in which he says:

Embracing the widest possible dimensions, the prayer reflects the hard struggle in which the worshipper is involved whilst he prays, his thoughts dwelling first on the uttermost depths of hell, into which the hopeless despair of his affliction had thrown him, and then gradually rising to the heavenly sanctuary of God. And the great miracle comes to pass: God himself appears in his adversity to rescue him.[11]

SKIES

In the later versions of our English Bible, we frequently come upon references to God in relation to Heaven where, instead of the word *heaven* appearing, we have the word *sky,* especially in the book of Psalms. The earliest reference, I believe, is toward the close of the inexhaustible song of the blessing of Moses where both words are brought together: "There is none like unto God, O Jeshurun, who rideth upon the heavens for thy help, and in his excellency on the skies" (Deut. 33:26). The same two words are found also in an interesting exclamation of Isaiah (45:8; see also Jer. 51:9). In the Psalter the Hebrew word *shachaq* was generally translated "clouds" or "heaven," but in the later versions invariably "skies," and only rarely referred to the atmospheric heavens surrounding the earth as in Psalm 78:23, where again both words *skies* and *heaven* are found. There might be some difference of opinion as to the exact meaning of David's words when he exhorted his nation: "Ascribe ye strength unto God: his excellency is over Israel, and his strength is in the skies" (Ps. 68:34). One could hardly doubt but that Heaven as the abode of God is what is in the mind of the psalmist: "For thy lovingkindness is great unto the heavens, and thy truth unto the skies" (Ps. 57:10; 108:4). So likewise in such a question as "Who in the skies can be compared unto Jehovah?" (Ps. 89:6). There have been a number of interpretations of a later phrase in the same psalm: "the faithful witness in the sky" (v. 37).

The Omnipresence of God

There is one problem which we cannot avoid in discussing the subject of heaven as the abode of God, and that is, how can we reconcile this with the fundamental truth of the omnipresence of God? This is a subject which is so rarely heard today from our pulpits or in our classrooms that perhaps we would do well to have before us a few lines from the most extensive treatment of this attribute of God that we have in the English language by Stephen Charnock.

Charnock begins by reminding us of the frequently uttered statement that God fills the heaven and the earth which, he says, must be a reference not to God's knowledge or mere power but to the very essence of God.

That "I" notes the essence of God, as distinguished according to our capacity, from the perfections pertaining to his essence, and is in reason better referred to the substance of God, than to those things we conceive as attributes in him. Besides, were it meant only of his authority or power, the argument would not run well. I see all things, because my authority and power fills heaven and earth. Power doth not always rightly infer knowledge, no, not in a rational agent. Many things in a kingdom are done by the authority of the king, that never arrive to the knowledge of the king. Many things in us are done by the power of our souls, which yet we have not a distinct knowledge of in our understandings. There are many motions in sleep, by the virtue of the soul informing the body, that we have not so much as a simple knowledge of in our minds. Knowledge is not rightly inferred from power, or power from knowledge. By filling heaven and earth is meant, therefore, a filling it with his essence. No place can be imagined that is deprived of the presence of God; and therefore when the Scripture anywhere speaks of the presence of God, it joins heaven and earth together: He so fills them, that there is no place without him. . . .

There is an influential omnipresence of God. 1. Universal with all creatures. He is present with all things by his authority, because all things are subject to him: by his power, because all things are sustained by him: by his knowledge, because all things are naked before him. He is present in the world, as a king is in all parts of his kingdom regally present: providentially present with all, since his care extends to the meanest of his creatures. His power reacheth all, and his knowledge

pierceth all. As everything in the world was created by
God, so everything in the world is preserved by God;
and since preservation is not wholly distinct from creation, it is necessary God should be present with everything while he preserves it, as well as present with it
when he created it. "Thou preservest man and beast"
(Psalm 36:6). "He upholds all things by the word of
his power" (Hebrews 1:3). There is a virtue sustaining
every creature, that it may not fall back into that nothing
from whence it was elevated by the power of God. . . .
This virtual presence of God is evident to our sense, a
presence we feel; his essential presence is evident in our
reason. This influential presence may be compared to
that of the sun, which though at so great a distance from
the earth, is present in the air and earth by its light,
and within the earth by its influence in concocting those
metals which are in the bowels of it, without being substantially either of them. God is thus so intimate with
every creature, that there is not the least particle of any
creature, but the marks of his power and goodness are
seen in it, and his goodness doth attend them, and is
more swift in its effluxes than the breakings out of light
from the sun, which yet are more swift than can be
declared; but to say he is in the world only by his virtue,
is to acknowledge only the effects of his power and wisdom in the world. . . .

The essential presence is without any division of himself. "I fill heaven and earth," not part in heaven, and
part in earth; I fill one as well as the other: one part
of his essence is not in one place, and another part of his
essence in another place, he would then be changeable;
for that part of his essence which were now in this place,
he might alter it to another, and place that part of his
essence which were in another place to this; but he is
undivided everywhere. As his eternity is one indivisible
point, though in our conception we divide it into past,
present, and to come, so the whole world is as a point

to him, in regard of place, as before was said; it is as a small dust, and grain of dust: it is impossible that one part of his essence can be separated from another, for he is not a body, to have one part separable from another. The light of the sun cannot be cut into parts, it cannot be shut into any place and kept there, it is entire in every place. . . .

There is no space, not the least, wherein God is not wholly, according to his essence, and wherein his whole substance doth not exist; not a part of heaven can be designed wherein the Creator is not wholly; as he is in one part of heaven, he is in every part of heaven. Some kind of resemblance we may have from the water of the sea, which fills the great space of the world, and is diffused through all; yet the essence of water is in every drop of water in the sea, as much as the whole; and the same quality of water, though it comes short in quantity; and why shall we not allow God a nobler way of presence without diffusion, as is in that? or take this resemblance; since God likens himself to light in the Scripture, "he covereth himself with light." . . .

To dwell in heaven, and in one part of the earth at the same time, is all one as to dwell in all parts of heaven, and all parts of earth. If he were in heaven, and in the ark and temple, it was the same essence in both, though not the same kind of manifestation of himself. If by his dwelling in heaven he meant his whole essence, why is it not also to be meant by his dwelling in the ark? It was not, sure, part of his essence that was in heaven, and part of his essence that was on earth; his essence would then be divided; and can it be imagined that he could be in heaven and the ark at the same time, and not in the spaces between? Could his essence be split into fragments, and a gap made in it, that two distant spaces should be filled by him, and all between be empty of him, so that God's being said to dwell in heaven, and in the temple, is so far from impairing the truth of this doctrine, that it more confirms and evidences it.[12]

That we also might have on this subject the verdict of a modern scholar, let me quote from the learned Dr. Herman Bavinck:

> He is not present in the same degree and manner everywhere. Scripture everywhere teaches that heaven, though also created, has been God's dwelling and throne ever since it was called into being. . . .
>
> Both time and space are internal modes of existence pertaining to all finite being. This leads to the conclusion that space, as well as time, cannot be predicated of God, the Infinite. He transcends all space. Philo and Plotinus already held this view, and Christian theology also maintained that God "contains all things and is himself alone uncontained." In his manichaean period Augustine thought that like a fine ether God penetrated the whole mass of the universe and the immeasurable and boundless spaces. Later on, however, he learned to see things differently. God transcends all space and whereness. He is not "somewhere"; yet he fills heaven and earth; he does not permeate space as does the light or the air, but he is present at every place with his whole being. He is "wholly everywhere, yet nowhere in space." There is no place or measure of space which contains him within its boundaries; hence, instead of saying that he is in all things it were better to say that all things are in him. Yet, even when we say that all things are in him, we must be on our guard, for we certainly do not mean that he is space and that as such he contains the objects, for he is not a place. Just as the soul is present in its entirety in the body as a whole and also in every part of the body, just as one and the same truth is acknowledged everywhere, thus, by way of comparison, God is present in all things and all things are present in God. And in the

works of the scholastics these thoughts of Augustine recur. Roman Catholic and Protestant theologians have added no essential element. . . .

It is useless to deny this divine omnipresence. We experience it in our heart and conscience. He is not far from each one of us. The only thing which can separate us from God is sin. It brings about a spiritual, not a physical, separation between God and man, Is. 59:2. Going out from the presence of Jehovah, fleeing away from him, does not indicate physical separation, but spiritual incongruity. "It is not with respect to place but with respect to being unlike him that a man is afar from God." Conversely, approaching God and seeking his countenance does not require a pilgrimage, but penitence and humiliation. Moreover, he who seeks God, finds him; he learns that God is not far distant but close at hand; for in him we live and move and have our being.[13]

NOTES

1. On the earlier affirmation, "Thus saith the high and lofty One that inhabiteth eternity, whose name is Holy: I dwell in the high and holy place" (57:15), Alexander remarks that "the idea of habitual or perpetual residence is implied." On the whole, however, one is surprised to find no modern commentator giving any adequate attention to the words for *habitation* in these Isaianic passages.
2. For *El Elyon* see the article in James Hastings, *Dictionary of the Bible* (New York: 1902), I, 682; and "Most High," III, 450. On Nebuchadnezzar's use of this term, see Charles Boutflower, *In and Around the Book of Daniel* (London: 1923), pp. 98-101. Possibly a complete classification of such terms would be in order here. *The God of Heaven* in Daniel 2:18-19, 37, 44; 5:11-12; 6:9-10; 7:12, 21, 23; Ezra 1:2; Nehemiah 1:4-5; 2:4, 20; Jonah 1:9; II Chronicles 36:23; Psalm 136:26; Revelation 11:13; 16:11. For *God Most High*, Daniel 3:26; 4:2; 5:18, 21; for *Most High*, Daniel 4:17, 24-25, 32, 34; Psalm 57:2; 9:3; 18:13. More recently, Ulrich Simon, *Heaven in the Christian Tradition* (New York: 1958), pp. 58-62.
3. On 2:37: "As we find by the succeeding verse, *the* kingdom here is not mere royalty or kingship, but the special royalty of practically universal empire . . . so far as the knowledge of the time went" (J. E. H. Thomson, *Daniel*, in *Pulpit Commentary* [new ed.; New York: 1913], p. 69).
4. J. M. Creed, *Gospel According to St. Luke* (London: 1960), p. 35.
5. It is *very* significant, a matter I have not seen referred to in commentaries, that the titles used by evil spirits in addressing or referring to Christ are the same titles used by angels in referring to Christ.

6. On Acts 7:48-49: R. J. Knowling, in *Expositor's Greek Testament* (London: n.d.), II, 197-99.
7. For a profound discussion of this verse, see Marcus Rainsford, *The Lord's Prayer for Believers* (London: 1895), pp. 473-85.
8. H. C. Leupold, *Exposition of Genesis* (Columbus, Ohio: 1942), p. 214.
9. Leupold, *ibid.*, p. 78.
10. Artur Weiser, *The Psalms* (Philadelphia: 1962), p. 566.
11. Weiser, *ibid.*, p. 189.
12. Stephen Charnock, *Discourses upon the Existence and Attributes of God* (New York: 1868), pp. 366, 369, 374-75, 386-87.
13. Herman Bavinck, *The Doctrine of God* (Grand Rapids: 1951), p. 163.

❖　❖　❖

On heaven as a place, a locality, the following references may be found helpful: A. H. Strong, *Systematic Theology* (rev. ed.; New York: 1907), p. 1032; William Branks, *Heaven Our Home* (3d ed.; Boston: 1864), pp. 19-37; L. N. Dahle, *Life After Death* (Edinburgh: 1896), p. 149; Karl Barth, *Church Dogmatics* (1958), III, 432-37; Ralph E. Knudsen, *Theology in the New Testament* (New York: 1964), pp. 408-9. Unexpectedly, but with common sense, the late Professor Douglas Clyde Macintosh correctly remarked, "There are places enough in God's Universe where He might be" (*Theology as an Empirical Science* [London: 1919], p. 212).

UNIQUENESS OF CHRISTIAN ESCHATOLOGY

While other religions merely looked back upon a lost paradise, upon a golden age which had vanished and disappeared, without presenting anything future, the Christian Church begins with a grand revelation of future realities. She is redeemed in hope, and accordingly she measures and judges of the whole present activity of this world, by the standard and in the light of the future. While heathen and gnostic speculation resorts to questions regarding the constitution of things, cosmogony, and the origin of evil, Christian thought ever inquires about the end of this world and the consummation of all things, kindles her light from historical and prophetical contemplation, and thus shows her practical and ethical character. Christian Eschatology is, therefore, quite different from what is nowadays called the doctrine of immortality. What in modern times has been called the immortality of the soul, is only a meagre and faint reflection of the rich hope of Christianity. Christian hope does not merely expect immortality, which is a negative thing, but eternal life, including not only the resurrection of the soul and spirit, but the resurrection of the body. . . . Christian hope, therefore, takes the form of an apocalyptic vision, embracing in its view Christ and His fellowship, the Church and the world, history and nature, death and Hades, resurrection and judgment, heaven and hell.*

*H. Mortensen, *Christian Dogmatics* (Edinburgh, 1898), pp. 450-51.

5 The Relationship of the Incarnate Christ to Heaven

If it were not for the intimate and eternal relationship of the Lord Jesus Christ to heaven, books on Heaven would hardly be written, and the subject itself, however rich the Biblical data might be, would not assume anything like the importance that attaches to it. Indeed heaven would hardly be a place longed for or desired were it not that this is where Christ is and forever will be in all of His glory. Unless one has given this subject considerable thought, it will come as somewhat of a surprise to most Christians that there are so many different aspects of Christ's relationship to heaven, some of them involving real difficulties and, concerning which, men of equal orthodoxy are found to be in disagreement.

Christ Was in Heaven from the Eternities Before His Incarnation

I believe there is not in the New Testament an actual specific statement that Christ in His preincarnate life was "in heaven" but there are many passages with slightly varying phraseology that can only be interpreted as implying this truth. Indeed the very opening statement of the gospel of John that the eternal Word was with God certainly implies that if God is in heaven, Christ was in heaven with Him. In the same gospel, St. John declares that before His advent Christ was "in the bosom of the Father," a passage that Westcott has illuminated in the following words:

> The image is used of the closest and tenderest of human relationships, of mother and child (Numbers 11:12), and of husband and wife (Deuteronomy 13:6), and also of friends reclining side by side at a feast (cf. John 13:23), and so describes the ultimate fellowship of love. The phrase is not strictly "in the bosom" but "into the bosom." Thus there is the combination (as it were) of rest and motion, of a continuous relation, with the realization of it.[1]

In the great high priestly prayer, our Lord in addressing the Father spoke of "the glory which I had with thee before the world" (John 17:5). All the passages which we are about to consider, affirming that Christ came down from heaven at the time of His advent, certainly imply that Christ was in heaven before the incarnation.

CHRIST CAME DOWN FROM HEAVEN AT THE TIME OF HIS ADVENT

In the very first year of His ministry, our Lord used terms that most emphatically declared the truth of His eternal residence in heaven in referring to Himself as "he that descendeth out of heaven" (John 3:13). This is followed by the enigmatical phrase "even the Son of man who is in heaven." Some believe this is a late insertion, and it is not found in many of the earlier manuscripts. And thus I do not feel that I need to enter into a lengthy discussion concerning the problem which it raises, except to quote the profound statement of Godet: "The Lord had two lives parallel to each other, an earthly life and a heavenly life. He lived in His Father and while thus living with the Father, He gave Himself unceasingly to men in His human life" (see also v. 31).

Six times in the great discourse on the bread of life, our Lord refers to Himself as that bread which came down from heaven (John 6:33-51). It is interesting to note that the Greek word here translated "come down" is the same word used in the LXX in the early account of the giving of the manna (Exodus 16). Lenski in interpreting Christ's statements regarding His coming down out of heaven reminds us that "the present participle does not mean a constant descent out of heaven but describes the quality of this Bread as something constant. Jesus having descended out of heaven by having become incarnate and by assuming His saving mission is the Bread that has this wonderful quality of being derived from heaven." Westcott, with his keen insight, calls attention to the fact that in verse 38 the preposition (*apo*) expresses the idea of leaving and in verse 42 the preposition (*ek*) expresses the idea of proceeding out of; then he makes a statement which some may think is exaggerated: "In the one case the thought is of sacrifice; in the other that of divinity." Declaring the same truth, our Lord affirmed, "I am from above" (8:23) and in the same discourse, "I came forth and am come from God" (8:42; see also 13:3). Again quoting Westcott: "The words can only be interpreted of the true divinity of the Son."

With characteristic insight Hendriksen remarks that what Christ was teaching in the John 6 discourse "was the counterpart or complement of the doctrine of the *virgin birth*. One who is born of a virgin—and who, accordingly, never had a human father (in the ordinary sense of the term), and is not a human person (though he has a human nature)—must have come down out of heaven!"

A number of problems, important in themselves, relating to the incarnation of our Lord need not be discussed in this volume on Heaven, but there is one aspect of the incarnation which at least requires recognition. The descent of Christ from heaven must be acknowledged as something quite different from His later ascent into heaven. Our Lord ascended after the resurrection in bodily form, and visibly. This is not the way He descended. His entrance into the world of humanity was through being conceived by the Holy Spirit in the womb of the Virgin Mary and born of her. At exactly what moment we might affirm that Christ came down from heaven, one would not wish to declare dogmatically. It is a subject which most theologians are inclined not to develop.

THE THREE UTTERANCES FROM HEAVEN CONFIRMING THE CLAIMS OF THE INCARNATE CHRIST

The three Synoptic Gospels all record the fact that as Christ came up out of the water at the time of His baptism, "the heavens were opened unto him," and a voice was heard from heaven acknowledging Him to be the Son of God (Matt. 3:16-17; Mark 1:10-11; Luke 3:21-22). "Never once since the fall of Adam and Eve had the Maker of men been able to say these words till He said them to Jesus Christ that day at the Jordan. . . . Here at last is a man after God's own heart. Here at last is the second Adam with whom God is well pleased."[2]

In a similar manner all three of the Synoptic Gospels state that a voice was heard "out of the cloud" declaring that Christ was indeed the Son of God (Matt. 17:5; Mark 9:2; Luke 9:35). While the word *heaven* does not appear in these synoptic sentences, it does appear in the later account of the transfiguration, written by an eyewitness, St. Peter himself, when he declared, "This voice we heard borne out of heaven" (II Peter 1:18).[3]

The third occasion for an announcement from heaven giving divine approval upon the ministry of our Lord is recorded exclusively in the fourth gospel: "There came therefore a voice out of heaven saying, I have both glorified it and will glorify it again" (John 12:28). In each case, such a voice was heard not only announcing God's total approval of Christ, but doing so in three crises of His life as He faced and consented to death.

Christ Ascended into Heaven

The subject of Heaven is inextricably identified with the ascension of our Lord; and how one interprets the full meaning of the ascension will depend in large part upon his conception of heaven itself, whether it is merely a state or a place. Perhaps we should first of all have before us the New Testament data for this great event found in all of the Gospels, the book of Acts, many of the epistles of Paul, as well as in the epistles of St. Peter, extensively in the epistle to the Hebrews, and a basic assumption in the Apocalypse. Our Lord Himself in more ways than one clearly foretold the fact that He would ascend again to His Father from whence He had come. While the larger portion of these announcements is to be found in the fourth gospel, the actual ascension itself is not recorded by the Apostle John. It is significant that at the conclusion of His great discourse on the bread of God coming down from heaven, He asks the question "What then if ye should behold the Son of man ascending where he was before?" (6:62). With different phraseology but the same connotation, soon after this the Lord said to the Pharisees, "Yet a little while more I am with you and I go unto him that sent me" (7:33). On Thursday of Holy Week, our Lord not only declared that He was going to prepare a place for us (John 14:2) but He again used the clause "I go again unto the Father" (vv. 12, 28). During that same hallowed

Thursday evening fellowship with His disciples, our Lord seemed under compulsion almost as though it were a truth bringing profound comfort to His own soul, when He stated that He would go unto the Father who sent Him (16:5, 10, 17), and then finally, with more detail, "I came out from the Father, and am come into the world: again I leave the world and go unto the Father" (v. 28).

The final statement of our Lord occurred on Easter after the resurrection in His words to Mary Magdalene: "Touch me not; for I am not yet ascended unto the Father: but go unto my brethren, and say to them, I ascend unto my Father and your Father, and my God and your God" (20:17). Two different interpretations of this passage may be found in works on the gospel of John. Some have thought that our Lord here was informing Mary Magdalene that that very morning He would ascend into heaven and, therefore, could not tarry for such an act of worship as she was about to offer, and such an interpretation is generally accompanied by one insisting that our Lord ascended to heaven more than once during His forty days of occasional communion with His disciples; but it is only on the last of these appearances that the event of the ascension occurred. More generally, however, the church has held that our Lord did not mean that on that very day He was ascending to heaven. As Milligan has remarked, neither need we understand our Lord's words to mean that He would ascend at some future date:

> The use of the present is to be explained by the consideration that the resurrection of our Lord was really the beginning of His ascension. At that point earth ceased to be the Saviour's home as it had been; and He Himself was no longer in it what He had been. Thus it might be said by Him "My ascent is begun and shall be soon completed."[4]

If the concluding words of Mark's gospel are to be acknowledged as a later addition, and such is not insisted upon here, we can rightly say that the ascension of our Lord is clearly set forth as a historical event witnessed to by the disciples only in the writings of St. Luke. He concludes his gospel with the words "It came to pass while he blessed them, he parted from them and was carried up into heaven" (Luke 24:51). The closing events of Luke's gospel are also placed at the beginning of Luke's second work where we read, after a brief survey of our Lord's final words, "When he had said these things, as they were looking, he was taken up and a cloud received him out of their sight" (Acts 1:9). Twice St. Luke in the same chapter clearly refers to this epochal event. In his very first sentence, in referring to Christ, he speaks of "the day in which he was received up" (v. 2). And he records for us the very confirmatory word of the angels that Jesus at this hour "was received up from you into heaven" (v. 11).

One cannot understand how such a contemporary as James D. Smart, author of many textbooks for Bible study for use in the Presbyterian church, should state that "the ascension seems to play no more in the thought of St. Paul."[5] Not only does the apostle speak of "our Master who is in heaven" (Eph. 6:9; Col. 4:1), but he specifically writes to the Ephesians of Christ having "ascended far above the heavens that he might fill all things," even quoting Psalm 68:18 to support His assertion (Eph. 4:10). Near the end of his life in writing to Timothy in that profound theological hymn on the Mystery of Godliness, after references to the incarnation, he refers to Christ as having been received up in glory (I Tim. 3:16). Every statement of the apostle's in which he speaks of Christ being exalted or sitting at the right hand of God clearly implies an ascension. I would like to consider the many passages in the epistle to the Hebrews concerning the ascension later in this chapter, when we will be discussing the present heavenly priesthood of the ascended Lord. St. Peter refers to Christ as One "who is on the right hand of God having gone into heaven; angels and authorities and powers being made subject unto him" (I Peter 3:22).

The Greek word translated "ascend" in the New Testament Scriptures is *anabaino,* and we may well be reminded that the opening sentence in Kittel's great *Theological Dictionary of the New Testament,* beginning an extended discussion of this word, affirms: "The basic meaning is spatial, that is, 'to rise from the depths to the heights.' Geographically, it denotes mounting from a plain to a city, from the coast inland, from the lower story of a house to the upper."[6] The word is used in frequent references to going up to Jerusalem or to the temple. It is most interesting to note that in the Greek Old Testament, the word is used of the cloud being taken up from the tabernacle (Exodus 40:36-37), of the glory departing (Exodus 9:3; 11:23), of God returning to Heaven (Gen. 17:22; 35:14). This is the word found in the record of our Lord's utterance to Mary Magdalene: "I ascend unto my Father and your Father" (John 20:17; see also 6:62). A compound of this word occurs in Mark's reference to the ascension and in three places in reference to the ascension in Acts 1, generally translated "received up" (Mark 16:19; Acts 1:2, 11, 22). This is the word used by the Apostle Paul in his great passage in the Ephesian letter regarding the ascension of our Lord (4:8-10). When the Apostle Peter refers to Christ as the One "who is gone into heaven" (I Peter 3:22) he uses a word not found elsewhere in the New Testament, *poreuomai.* St. Luke made an interesting statement: "When the days were well-nigh come that he should be received up, he stedfastly set his face to go to Jerusalem" (9:51). The word here is *analepsis.* When the same writer tells us at the beginning of his second book that Christ was "taken up" (Acts 1:9), he uses the same word that is found in the Septuagint for the taking up of Elijah into heaven, *epairo* (II Kings 2:11).

A recent scholar reminds us that the verb likewise used in speaking of the ascension, *hupsuo,* expresses the idea of a movement from a lower to a higher level as an eagle soaring into the sky (Job 39:27) and "may be taken as the equivalent of *anabaino* and may therefore, if the context warrants it, be understood to refer to the ascension."[7] (See Acts 2:33.) This is the word used to describe action for going up onto a housetop, going up to a mountain, going up to Jerusalem (Acts 10:9; Matt. 5:1; 14:23; Mark 10:32-33).

Before discussing criticisms and denials of a literal ascension, we might have before us a classic expression of the faith of the church in a literal ascension as found in that great work of Bishop John Pearson, *An Exposition of the Creed*:

> Had he been there before in body, it had been no such wonder that he should have ascended thither again: but that his body should ascend unto that place where the majesty of God was most resplendent; that the flesh of our flesh, and bone of our bone, should be seated far above all angels and archangels, all principalities and powers, even at the right hand of God: this was that which *Christ* propounded as worthy of their greatest admiration. Whatsoever heaven then is higher than all the rest which are called heavens; whatsoever sanctuary is holier than all which are called holies; whatsoever place is of greatest dignity in all those courts above, into that place did he ascend, where in the splendour of his Deity he was, before he took upon him our humanity. As therefore when we say *Christ* ascended, we understand a literal and local ascent, not of his Divinity (which possesseth all places, and therefore being every where is not subject to the imperfection of removing any whither), but of his humanity, which was so in one

place that it was not in another: so when we say the place into which he ascended was heaven, and from the expositions of the apostles must understand thereby the heaven of heavens, or the highest heavens, it followeth that we believe the body with the soul of *Christ* to have passed far above all those celestial bodies which we see, and to look upon that opinion as a low conceit which left his body in the sun.[8]

Inasmuch as the subject of the ascension of Christ has been given a great deal of attention during the last few years by New Testament scholars, it may not be out of place to supplement our brief discussion with two contemporary statements. The first is from the late Dr. Klaas Schilder, whose three great volumes on the sufferings and death of Christ proved an epochal contribution to that inexhaustible event:

> The ascension of Christ is therefore of special meaning in the history of heaven. It reveals anew that the history of heaven is closely bound up with that of the earth. The diastase and the conjunction are clearly revealed. For Christ withdrew from the dwelling place of His people. The Greek puts it thus: He made *diastase* between Himself and them. But there is conjunction also; Christ carried His physical body to heaven, a pledge of the coming union between heaven and earth. And He sent His Spirit as a counterpledge—the Spirit who utters that longing of men with unutterable groaning, crying out, "How long, O Lord?" And heaven, too, awaits that consummation; the Son intercedes for the church, straining toward that end, that great moment of time. And the blessed cry out also, "How long, how long, O Lord?" How long before we shall reach that "moment of time when earth and heaven shall be drawn together, as they ought to be"?[9]

Recently Professor J. G. Davies has written an entire volume on this subject, the most thorough treatment that we have from which we take the opportunity of quoting but a single paragraph:

> The Resurrection accomplished the vanquishing of death, and through it the humanity of Christ was transformed so that it was no longer subject to the conditions of mortality; hence the Resurrection was the necessary pre-condition of the Ascension when that transformed humanity entered upon new conditions of existence in heaven. The one established the hope of immortality, the other the certainty of reconciliation through the Lord Jesus. Hence we may agree with H. Sasse that "it is of profound significance that the New Testament distinguishes the resurrection from the exaltation of Christ. As the Risen One, Christ would only be the firstfruit from the dead, the firstborn among many brethren. His resurrection would thus only be the beginning of the general resurrection of the dead. There would be no fundamental difference between His resurrection and ours. His 'Lordship' would be inconceivable apart from the resurrection, but it would not be accounted for by it alone. For this reason the New Testament draws a logical distinction between the resurrection and the exaltation." It is indeed one thing to say that Christ is risen, meaning that death and corruption no longer hold Him: it is another thing to say that He has ascended, meaning that He is not only alive but sovereign.[10]

THE INTERCESSORY WORK OF OUR LORD

The profoundest statements concerning Christ's present ministry in heaven are to be found in the epistle to the Hebrews, particularly in chapters 8-10. In referring to our Lord's ascension, the text reminds us that He "passed through the heavens" (4:14) or "entered . . . into heaven" (9:24), which is supplemented by a later statement that He was "made higher than the heavens" (7:26). As Westcott reminds us, "He not merely ascended up to heaven in the language of space, but He transcended the limitations of space." The verb in the Latin text is suggestive—*penetravit*. Three times in this same epistle we are told that when Christ ascended, He was seated at the right hand of God (8:1; 10:12; 12:2), a state referred to earlier in the epistle as "crowned with glory and honor" (2:9). Lenski remarks that "no Jewish high priest ever *sat* when executing his office. He was not a king who may sit in state, and his office permitted no sitting. Our exalted High Priest is both King and Priest, and thus sits at the right of the throne of Majesty 'as ministrant of the Holy Place and of the true Tabernacle.' Throne and Sanctuary are not in conflict, nor is sitting as a ministrant."[11]

It is necessary to give careful consideration at this point to the actual terms found in the epistle referring to the locality or, if one will, the environment of that place in which Christ is carrying on His present ministry of intercession. All the terms used for designating this particular aspect of our Lord's ministry in heaven are derived from and typified by the tabernacle of the Old Testament, referred to as "a sanctuary of this world" (9:1), or simply "the tabernacle" (8:5; 9:21). The reference to "the first tabernacle" (9:6, 8) refers to the holy place where the priests ministered, while "the second" (v. 7) refers to the holy of holies in which "the high priest alone once in the year not without blood" fulfilled the divinely revealed ritual. (This is no doubt the tabernacle referred to in Revelation 15:5.) It is generally acknowledged that "a holy place made with hands" (9:24-25) embraces both areas—the holy place and the most holy. At the beginning of this inexhaustible ninth chapter, the writer enumerates the various major objects once within the tabernacle, and, as Westcott has beautifully said, "He seems indeed to linger over the sacred treasures of the past; and there is a singular pathos in the passage which is unique in the New Testament."[12]

The relationship of the earthly tabernacle to the heavenly one where our Lord is the "minister of the sanctuary" (8:2) is set forth most elaborately in three different words, all found within one sentence, where we are told the earthly tabernacle "is a copy and shadow of the heavenly things, even as Moses is warned of God when he is about to make the tabernacle: for, See, saith he, that thou make all things according to the pattern that was showed thee in the mount" (8:5, referring to Exodus 25:40). The word translated "pattern" is *tupos*, from which, of course, comes our word *type*, a word originally meaning a mark or trace, a copy, or image (as a child of his parents), and thus, a figure, and, finally in some cases, an example. (For other occasions when this word is used, see Acts 7:44 and 23:25; I Peter 3:21; 5:3.) The word translated "pattern" in 9:24 is a compound of this word—*antitupos*. The word translated "shadow" is *skia*, which means "the dark outline figure cast by an object contrasted with the complete representation produced by the help of color and sound mass" (Westcott). (For other occasions when this word is used, see Mark 4:32; Luke 1:79; Matt. 4:16.) Finally, the word translated "copy" is *hupodeigma*, which is "not only the image which is made by imitation but also the model which is offered for imitation" (see also 4:11 and 9:23). The question of this *pattern* shown to Moses has been excellently set forth by Delitzsch:

> We cannot suppose either that Moses was left to translate his vision of the heavenly world into the architectural and other visible forms of the earthly sanctuary; nor that that vision, when accorded him, consisted of an actual insight into the very essences of the things themselves. Such insight has never yet been vouchsafed to mortal man; and in the case of Moses as mediator of the legal dispensation, we are the more compelled to assume

that the super-sensual, if exhibited to him, must have taken sensuous and visible forms of manifestation.[13]

We are now ready to consider the terms used for defining the environment in which our Lord is carrying on His high priestly ministry. First of all, as we have said before, we are told that our Lord "entered in once for all into the holy place" (9:8, 12). As to what this holy place was, there have been a number of answers; but it seems to me that we can interpret it as nothing else but the heaven of heavens where God dwelleth. Such is almost definitely determined by the phraseology of verse 24: "For Christ entered not into a holy place made with hands, like in pattern to the true; but into heaven itself, now to appear before the face of God for us" (v. 24), in which "a holy place," "heaven" and "before the face of God" must be taken as synonymous. It is into this holy place that we have boldness to enter by the blood of Jesus (10:19). The words of the great Puritan scholar John Owen in his magnificent commentary on Hebrews will be found helpful for the deeper understanding of this passage:

> Now, in that most holy place were all the signs and pledges of the gracious presence of God,—the testimonies of our reconciliation by the blood of the atonement, and our peace with him thereby. Wherefore, to enter into these holies, is nothing but an access with liberty, freedom, and boldness, into the gracious presence of God, on the account of reconciliation and peace made with him. This the apostle doth so plainly and positively declare, Hebrews 10:19-22, that I somewhat admire so many worthy and learned expositors should utterly miss of his meaning in this place. The "holies," then, is the gracious presence of God, whereunto believers draw nigh in the confidence of the atonement made for them, and of acceptance thereon. . . .
> For he was himself both the priest and the sacrifice,

the offerer and the lamb. And as that blood was sprin-
kled before the ark and the mercy-seat, to apply the
atonement made unto all the sacred pledges of God's
presence and good-will; so from this representation of
the offering of Christ, of himself as "a Lamb that had
been slain," in this his appearance before God, doth all
the application of its benefits unto the church proceed.
. . .

There is more in it than merely *for our good.* It is as it
were the appearance of an advocate, a law-appearance
in the behalf of others. So is it declared, I John 2:1, 2.
He will at the end of all present his whole church unto
God, with the whole work of his love and grace accomplished towards them. He first so presents it unto himself, and then to God, Ephesians 5:26, 27. Now he presents them as the portion given unto him of God out of
fallen mankind to be redeemed and saved; saying, "Behold I and the children which thou gavest me; thine they
were, and thou gavest them to me. I present them unto
thy love and care, holy Father, that they may enjoy all
the fruits of thine eternal love, all the benefits of my
death and sacrifice."[14]

Another phrase used for this same locale is found in an
earlier passage in this epistle, when we are told that it is within the veil that Christ has entered for us as a forerunner
(6:19-20; 10:20). Bruce has excellently summarized the
meaning of this much debated passage when he says:

It can scarcely be doubted that the "veil" of which
our author is thinking is the inner veil which separated
the holy place from the holy of holies, the "second veil"
of Ch. 9:3, through the heavenly archetype of which
Jesus has already passed as His people's forerunner
(Ch. 6:19 f.). Here it is natural to ask whether these
words contain an implicit allusion to the rending of the
temple veil from top to bottom at the moment of Jesus's

death (Mark 15:38; cf. Matthew 27:51; Luke 23:45).
For the veil which was then rent in two was also probably
the inner veil, and its rending is recorded not as a natural
portent but as an event of theological significance: in the
death of Jesus, we are to understand, God Himself is
unveiled to us and the way of access to Him is thrown
wide open. . . . It is by His sacrifice that the way of
approach to God has been opened up. The veil which,
from one point of view, kept God and man apart, can be
thought of, from another point of view, as bringing them
together; for it was one and the same veil which on one
side was in contact with the glory of God and on the
other side with the need of men. So in our Lord Godhead and manhood were brought together; He is the
true "daysman" or umpire who can lay His hand upon
both because He shares the nature of both. And by His
death, it could be added, the "veil" of His flesh was
rent asunder and the new way consecrated through it by
which man may come to God.[15]

There is one more passage to which we must give consideration: "But Christ having come a high priest of the good
things to come, through the greater and more perfect tabernacle, not made with hands, that is to say, not of this creation" (9:11). The truth of this passage was introduced in a
preceding chapter when the writer, after telling us that
Christ as a high priest has sat down at the right hand of the
throne of the Majesty in the heavens, added that He has become "a minister of the sanctuary and of the true tabernacle
which the Lord pitched, not man" (8:1-2). As to what this
actual tabernacle might be, there have been a number of different views. Some have insisted that it is the church, as have
many of the early Greek Fathers. Others hold that this tabernacle was Christ's own human nature, which Owen argues
for so elaborately. Delitzsch is right when he identifies this
heavenly sanctuary with heaven itself, but he warns us that

"at the same time we are not to transfer with literal exactness to the heavenly word the local boundaries and partitions of the earthly type." The adjective here used, true (*alethinos*), "is applied to that which answers to its name and notion in the fullest, deepest and most unlimited manner to that which is not merely outward and material, but inward and spiritual. . . . The 'true' tabernacle, in which our High Priest now ministers, is the original, essential, and archetypal one; not a work of human hands; not constructed of perishable materials, but a supra-mundane work of God Himself, the product of an immediate divine operation."[16]

Once again I feel compelled to quote extensively the words of John Owen:

> The apostle expresseth these things by that notion of them which was received under the old testament and in the church of the Hebrews, namely, the "good things to come;"—that is, they were so from the beginning of the world, or the giving of the first promise. Things which were fore-signified by all the ordinances of the law, and which thereon were the desire and expectation of the church in all preceding ages; the things which all the prophets foretold, and which God promised by them, directing the faith of the church unto them; in brief, all the good things in spiritual redemption and salvation which they looked for by the Messiah, are here called the "good things to come." . . . These, therefore, are the "good things to come," consisting in the bringing forth and accomplishing of the glorious effects of the hidden wisdom of God, according unto his promises from the beginning of the world, in the sacrifice of Christ, with all the benefits and privileges of the church, in righteousness, peace, and spiritual worship, which ensued thereon. . . .
>
> This tabernacle, whereby he came a high priest, was his own human nature. The bodies of men are often

called their tabernacles, 2 Corinthians 5:1; 2 Peter 1:14. And Christ called his own body the temple, John 2:19. His flesh was the veil, Hebrews 10:20. And in his incarnation he is said to "pitch the tabernacle among us," John 1:14. Herein dwelt "the fulness of the Godhead bodily," Colossians 2:9,—that is, substantially; represented by all the pledges of God's presence in the tabernacle of old. This was that tabernacle wherein the Son of God administered his sacerdotal office in this world, and wherein he continueth yet so to do in his intercession. . . . The human nature of Christ, wherein he discharged the duties of his sacerdotal office in making atonement for sin, is the greatest, the most perfect and excellent ordinance of God; far excelling those that were most excellent under the old testament.— An ordinance of God it was, in that it was what he designed, appointed, and produced unto his own glory; and it was that which answered all ordinances of worship under the old testament, as the substance of what was shadowed out in them and by them. . . .

This is that which the apostle intimates: Whereas Solomon openly affirms that the habitation of God could not be in the temple that he had built, because it was made with hands, and it is a principle of natural light, that he who made the world and all things contained therein could not dwell in such a temple; and whereas it seems to have belonged unto the faith of the church of old that there should be a temple wherein God would dwell that was to be *acheiropoiētos* in comparing the human nature of Christ with the old tabernacle, he affirms in the first place that it was not made with hands.[17]

I would like to make a suggestion here, which I have not seen in any volume on the epistle to the Hebrews, but which has no doubt been suggested before, and that is that we are not to make the pattern shown to Moses of the tabernacle he was to construct identical with the true tabernacle in which our Lord is now ministering. I trust my readers will not object to another extended quotation from the learned Bishop Westcott. His ideas regarding the significance of the blood of Jesus would not be acceptable to most of us, but his interpretation of the significance of this tabernacle is superb:

> The Tabernacle, as we have seen, presented three main ideas, the ideas of the dwelling of God among men, of His holiness, of His "conversableness." It was that through which He was pleased to make His Presence and His Nature known under the conditions of earth to His people Israel. The antitype of the Tabernacle, whether on earth or in heaven, must fulfil the same office, and fulfil it perfectly. Such an antitype we find in the humanity of Christ, realised in different modes and degrees during His life on earth, in His Body, the Church, and in the consummation in "heaven." In each stage, if we may so speak, of the "fulfilment" (Ephesians 1:23), Christ satisfies in actual life more and more completely, according to our apprehension, that which the Tabernacle suggested by figures. His earthly Body was a Sanctuary (John 2:19 ff.). In Him it was the Father's pleasure that "all the fulness should dwell" (Colossians 1:19), and so "in Him dwelleth all the fulness of the Godhead bodily" (Colossians 2:9). Even now "His Body" is that in which God is, and through which He reveals Himself (John 14:16 ff.; 1 John 2:20; Apoc. 21:3). And so it shall be in the end. The saints "who dwell in heaven" are His "tabernacle" (Apoc. 13:6); and when they are revealed in glory, in fellowship with Christ (1 John 3:2), the goal of creation will be reached (Romans 8:19).[18]

CHRIST'S HIGH PRIESTLY MEDIATION

Two great activities of Christ as our high priest in heaven are set forth in this epistle, one of which has given rise to a

great deal of discussion. In what may be called the last
reference to our Lord's heavenly activities occurring in this
epistle we are told, "It was necessary that the copies of the
things in the heavens should be cleansed with these; but the
heavenly things themselves with better sacrifices than these"
(9:23). No one has more concisely and accurately ascertained
the meaning of this unique statement than Alford: "We must
rest in the plain and literal sense: that the heavens itself
needed and obtained purification by the atoning blood of
Christ . . . that unclouded benignity wherewith the Creator
contemplated His creation had become overcast by the divine anger on account of sin but was again restored by Him
in whom the Father was well pleased." F. F. Bruce, in his
recent and truly epochal commentary on this epistle, takes
a different view when he says:

> What required to be cleansed was the defiled con-
> science of men and women; this is a cleansing which be-
> longs to the spiritual sphere. . . . The people of God are
> the house of God and His dwelling place is in their
> midst. It is they who require inward cleansing not only
> that their approach to God may be free from defilement
> but that they may be a fit habitation for Him. By the
> removal of the defilement of sin from the hearts and
> consciences of the worshipers, the heavenly sphere in
> which they approach God to worship Him is itself
> cleansed from this defilement.[19]

This passage is so important that I think a further comment
will not be considered superfluous:

> This is the order of these things: The heavenly things
> themselves were designed, framed, and disposed in the
> mind of God, in all their order, courses, beauty, efficacy,
> and tendency unto his own eternal glory. This was the
> whole mystery of the wisdom of God for the redemption
> and salvation of the church by Jesus Christ. This is that

which is declared in the gospel, being before hid in God from the foundation of the world, Ephesians 3:8-10. Of these things did God grant a typical resemblance, similitude, and pattern, in the tabernacle and its services. That he would make such a kind of resemblance of those heavenly things, as unto their kind, nature, and use, that he would instruct the church by them, was an act of his mere sovereign will and pleasure. . . . And thus their resemblance of heavenly things, which they had not from their own nature, but merely from the pleasure of God, gave them all their glory and worth; which the saints under the old testament did in some measure understand. . . . But in themselves they were all earthly, carnal, perishing, and liable unto all sorts of corruption. . . .

What these things are is not easy to determine. Some say that *heaven* itself is intended, the superethereal heavens; the place of the present residence of Christ, and of the souls of them that are saved by him. But taking the heavens absolutely, especially for that which is called "the heaven of heavens," with respect unto their fabric, and as the place of God's glorious residence, and it is not easy to conceive how they stood in need to be purified by sacrifice. Some say it is *spiritual things*, that is, the souls and consciences of men, that are intended. And they are called "heavenly" in opposition unto the things of the law, which were all carnal and earthly. And it is certain they are not to be excluded out of this expression; for unto their purification is the virtue of the sacrifice of Christ directly applied, verse 14. Yet the whole context, and the antithesis in it between the types and the things typified, make it evident that they alone are not intended. . . .

By "heavenly things," I understand all the effects of the counsel of God in Christ, in the redemption, worship, salvation, and eternal glory of the church; that is, Christ himself in all his offices, with all the spiritual and eternal effects of them on the souls and consciences of men, with all the worship of God by him according unto the gospel. For of all these things those of the law were the patterns. . . .

The sum is: As the covenant, the book, the people, the tabernacle, were all purified, and dedicated unto their especial ends, by the blood of calves and goats, wherein was laid the foundation of all gracious intercourse between God and the church, under the old covenant; so all things whatever, that in the counsel of God belonged unto the new covenant, the whole mediation of Christ, with all the spiritual and eternal effects of it, were confirmed, dedicated unto God, and made effectual unto the ends of the covenant, by the blood of the sacrifice of Christ, which is the spring from whence efficacy is communicated unto them all. And moreover, the souls and consciences of the elect are purified and sanctified from all defilements thereby; which work is gradually carried on in them, by renewed applications of the same blood unto them, until they are all presented unto God glorious, "without spot, or wrinkle, or any such thing."[20]

Before considering one final and very important statement regarding our Lord's high priestly work, we must not forget that as the priest and high priest never approached the tabernacle except they had something to offer to God, so also our Lord presented an offering when, as the high priest, He entered into the tabernacle not made with hands eternal in the heavens. Here too there has been some difference of opinion as to exactly what He offered. Some go so far as to say that He presented His own blood when entering heaven, a view, strangely enough, supported by no less a scholar than Delitzsch. This view was held by a number of church Fathers but by almost no contemporary New Testament scholar. Milligan sums up eloquently in his volume on the ascension and high priesthood of our Lord which is generally believed by the church, namely, that our Lord presented Himself to God as the one who had offered Himself as the one final sacrifice for sin:

> Does the ascended and glorified Lord even now present to His Father in heaven anything that may with propriety be called an offering? Or are His heavenly functions summed up in the idea of Intercession? The latter view is that generally taken. Our Lord's work of offering is supposed to have been finished when He died. . . . He had to place before the Father either the very blood which He had shed, or the ideas involved in that sacrificial act. But this is supposed to have been done only once and for ever. Having done this, the glorified Redeemer entered upon an entirely different part of His priestly work; and Intercession, not offering, is the function in which He always has been and still is engaged in the Heavenly Sanctuary. Is the view thus taken to be accepted as complete? Are we to confine the thought of "offering" on the part of our Lord to His sacrificial death? Or are we so to extend the thought as to include in it a present and eternal offering to God of His life in heaven? . . . As, therefore, the Jewish priest continued his work of offering after he had gone within the veil, so, in similar circumstances, we must connect with Him in whom the economy of Judaism is fulfilled. . . . Our Lord, even in His exalted and glorified state, must have "somewhat to offer." . . . What our Lord was after He sat down at the right hand of the Heavenly Majesty He can never cease to be. The idea of a continuous application of redemption, resting upon what had been done in the past, cannot exhaust the work of the unchangeable and everlasting High-priest. What He had done must penetrate what He always does; and the thought of Offering cannot give place to that of Intercession. . . . Turning, therefore, to this part of our inquiry, it would appear as if the fundamental conception

of that offering of our Lord by which the breach of the broken covenant is healed, and man is restored to the Divine favour, is not death but life. The place held by death in the process of restoration will have to be spoken of immediately. In the meantime it is enough to say that life, not death, is the essence of atonement, is that by which sin is covered.[21]

We must now consider the best known of all the passages in this epistle relating to our Lord's priestly work in heaven. "Wherefore also he is able to save to the uttermost them that draw near unto God through him, seeing he ever liveth to make intercession for them" (7:25). Here too there are differences of opinion as to exactly what this intercession might consist of. This same truth is the one set forth, of course, by St. Paul near the conclusion of that glorious eighth chapter of his epistle to the Romans: "It is Christ Jesus that died, yea rather, that was raised from the dead, who is at the right hand of God, who also maketh intercession for us" (8:34). Indeed our Lord now does for all believers what He promised to do for the Apostle Peter in praying for him (Luke 22:32). And the great high priestly prayer recorded in John 17 helps us to understand something of the present intercessory work of the Lord Jesus.

CHRIST'S HIGH PRIESTLY INTERCESSION

I am certain that the intercessory work of the risen Lord is a subject which is so rarely considered by believers today, and about which almost nothing is said from our pulpits. Tait has reminded us that in the sixteenth century the subject and manner of Christ's intercession aroused a great deal of controversy among the Lutheran and Reformed parties; but here in the twentieth century, except in a few theological works, how seldom we hear any comment on this profound theme. Exactly what our Lord does and the manner in which

He does it has received different interpretations. It is perhaps correct to say basically that this intercessory work takes three forms. Our High Priest represents man before God (Heb. 7:25, etc.); He brings the prayers of believers to God (Heb. 13:15); and He secures access for man to God (Heb. 4:16; 10:19, etc.). Bishop Moule rightly has said:

> Scripture represents Him as interceding, not as a suppliant, but with the majesty of the accepted and glorified Son once slain. He does not stand before the throne, but is seated on it. . . . It is vain, of course, to ask how in detail He thus acts for us. The essence of the matter is His union with His people, and His perpetual presence, in that union, with the Father, as the once slain Lamb.[22]

The comment of H. B. Swete on this intercessory work of our Lord has won the strong approval of most writers who have attempted to enter into the deeper aspects of the subject we are here considering. Swete says that our Lord is not to be thought of "as an orante, *standing* ever before the Father with outstretched arms, like the figures in the mosaics of the catacombs, and with strong crying and tears pleading our cause in the presence of a reluctant God; but as a *throned* Priest-King, asking what He will from a Father who always hears and grants His request. Our Lord's life in heaven is His prayer."[23]

A number of questions arise as to when the atoning work of our Lord was presented in heaven. I would wholly agree with the words of Harm Henry Meeter in his scholarly doctoral dissertation that the epistle to the Hebrews knows of only one entrance into the holiest. And then he adds:

> The entrance of Christ into heaven, His appearance before God's throne, the sprinkling and the purifying of the heavenly tabernacle, and as well, the presentation

of His blood, are in Hebrews represented as performed in a moment. . . . The offering of Christ in heaven consists in nothing else than in the *presentation* to God or, if you will, of the application of His sacrifice on the Cross.

I would wholly go along with Dr. Meeter's conclusion:

To define positively the manner of Christ's intercession is not possible. Not only Hebrews, but the entire Scripture is silent on this theme. All that we can say is that it is an added uninterrupted activity of the enthroned high priest at the right hand of God as high priestly mediator of His covenant people through which He invokes for them from God the Father the blessings of salvation. But further than this we cannot go.[24]

It is inconceivable that after all we have said concerning the ascension of our Lord, we ought not to attempt to understand the fundamental implications which arise from this epochal event which, as it were, terminates our Lord's work on earth during His incarnation and the beginning of His high priestly work in heaven. First of all, it must be almost axiomatic to recognize that the ascension is an absolutely necessary sequence following our Lord's resurrection. There must be some definite, known, revealed destiny for our Lord after His brief appearances during those wonderful forty days following His resurrection. As many have remarked, the ascension of Jesus is made possible by His resurrection, but the resurrection of our Lord stands or falls with the reality of His ascending into glory in His own body. What a mystery forever would hang over our understanding of the person of the incarnate Lord if He simply, as it were, evaporated, or if He disappeared no one knew where or how, or—even more terrible—if He again somewhere, somehow suffered death.

The ascension of course establishes the truth that the redemptive work of Christ is now forever complete, acceptable
unto God and deserving of the exaltation of the Lord to the
right hand of the Father, crowned with glory and honor. In
the ascension we have, as it were, the enthronement of the
King, the fulfillment of the words of the psalmist: "I have set
my king upon my holy hill of Zion," "Lift up your heads, O
ye gates; yea, lift them up, ye everlasting doors: and the King
of glory will come in" (Ps. 2:6; 24:9). It was, says Milligan,
wholly suitable that this coronation of our Lord "should take
place in the particular form of ascension from the earth. A
coronation upon the earth might have confined men's
thoughts of Him to the earth. It was of the utmost importance to teach men that His earthly condition was to come
to an end and that a new era in His history was to be the
beginning of a new experience in theirs. His upward movement from earth to heaven in the sight of His disciples
showed where the real sphere of His existence was henceforth to be."[25]

Finally, we should remember that the One who ascended
into glory was not only the Son of God but the Man Christ
Jesus. If then at the right hand of God there is now enthroned the Man born of Mary as well as the only begotten
Son of God, then believers in the Lord recognize in the ascension the ultimate glorious goal of humanity. We are partakers
with Him, members of His body, identified not only in His
death and resurrection, but united with Him also in His
ascension. So our Lord could say, and the apostles echo
the truth, that where He is there shall we be also. The most
recent writer on the ascension of our Lord, Dr. J. G. Davies,
in his Bampton Lectures for 1958, succinctly summarizes the
triumphal implications of the ascension of our Lord into
heaven in words that may well conclude our present study:

If we accept the Classical theory of the Atonement, we may see in the Ascension the final act which marks the overthrow of the demonic powers and the triumphal procession of the victor; on the other hand, if we prefer the sacrificial theory, then the Ascension is the occasion of the offering to the Father of that perfect humanity which was sacrificed upon the Cross. It marks not only the bringing of humanity to God, but also the conclusion of the days of humiliation and the consummation of the process of glorification whereby man, in whose nature God had become a participant through the Incarnation, was made a participant in the glory of the Godhead.[26]

The ascension of our Lord is so important in Christian doctrine, as well as a subject of great significance in any volume dealing with the matter of Heaven, that I trust I will be pardoned for bringing this chapter to a close with a magnificent statement concerning our Lord's ascension from the concluding chapter of the very important volume by J. C. Davies:

The Resurrection accomplished the vanquishing of death, and through it the humanity of Christ was transformed so that it was no longer subject to the conditions of mortality; hence the Resurrection was the necessary pre-condition of the Ascension when that transformed humanity entered upon new conditions of existence in heaven. The one established the hope of immortality, the other the certainty of reconciliation through the Lord Jesus. Hence we may agree with H. Sasse that "it is of profound significance that the New Testament distinguishes the resurrection from the exaltation of Christ. As the Risen One, Christ would only be the firstfruit from the dead, the first-born among many brethren. His resurrection would thus only be the beginning of the general resurrection of the dead. There would be no fundamental difference between His resurrection and ours. His 'Lordship' would be inconceivable apart from the resurrection, but it would not be accounted for by it alone. For this reason the New Testament draws a logical distinction between the resurrection and the exaltation." It is indeed one thing to say that Christ is risen, meaning that death and corruption no longer hold Him: it is another thing to say that He has ascended, meaning that He is not only alive but sovereign. . . . The Ascension manifests the final condition of those who are in Christ. We may indeed see man's ultimate goal revealed and already attained by Jesus, who has trodden the whole path of human destiny.[27]

Of course, as Christ ascended into heaven, so from the home of the Father in heaven, He will descend again at His second advent. St. Peter in his second sermon referred to our Lord as the One "whom the heaven must receive until the times of restoration of all things" (Acts 3:21). Twice in the first letter to the Thessalonians, the Apostle Paul reminds these new converts from paganism that "Christ himself shall descend from heaven" or, to put it otherwise, believers are "to wait for his Son from heaven" (I Thess. 4:16; 1:10). In the second epistle to the same church, the apostle in referring to the judgment to come reveals that at that time Christ "shall be revealed from heaven with his mighty angels" (II Thess. 1:7-8). In the description of the Battle of Armageddon, it is not specifically stated that Christ comes down from heaven, but it is certainly implied in such phrases as "I saw the heaven opened; and behold, a white horse, and he that sat thereon called Faithful and True." "The armies which are in heaven followed him upon white horses" (Rev. 19:11, 14).

NOTES

1. Brooke Foss Westcott, *The Gospel According to St. John* (London: 1881), p. 15.
2. Alexander Whyte, *The Walk, Conversation and Character of Jesus Christ Our Lord*, n.d., p. 92.
3. On the significance of the voice from Heaven, see my volume *The Supernaturalness of Christ* (Boston: 1940), pp. 172-74.
4. William Milligan and William F. Moulton, *Commentary on the Gospel of St. John* (Edinburgh: 1898), p. 224.
5. James D. Smart, *The Creed in Christian Teaching* (Philadelphia: 1962), p. 169.
6. Johannes Schneider, in Gerhard Kittel, *Theological Dictionary of the New Testament*, I (Grand Rapids: 1964), 519.
7. John G. Davies, *He Ascended into Heaven* (London: 1958), p. 29.
8. John Pearson, *Exposition of the Creed* (London: 1835), p. 399.
9. K. Schilder, *Heaven, What Is It?* (Grand Rapids: 1950), p. 56.
10. Davies, *op. cit.*, p. 170.
11. R. C. H. Lenski, *Interpretation of Hebrews and James* (New York: 1938), p. 252.
12. Brooke Foss Westcott, *The Epistle to the Hebrews* (2d ed.; London: 1892), p. 242.
13. Franz Delitzsch, *Commentary on the Epistle to the Hebrews* (Edinburgh: 1870), II, 34.
14. John Owen, *An Exposition of the Epistle to the Hebrews* (New York: 1855), VI, 239, 384.
15. F. F. Bruce, *The Epistle to the Hebrews* (Grand Rapids: 1964), pp. 246-47.
16. Delitzsch, *op. cit.*, p. 19.
17. Owen, *op. cit.*, pp. 263-64, 266-67, 270.
18. Westcott, *op. cit.*, p. 240.
19. Bruce, *op. cit.*, p. 218.
20. Owen, *op. cit.*, pp. 371-75. The great Puritan devotes 240 pages to his exposition of this ninth chapter.
21. William Milligan, *The Ascension and Heavenly Priesthood of Our Lord* (London: 1892).
22. H. C. G. Moule, *Outlines of Christian Doctrine*, copyright 1889 (London: n.d.), p. 103.
23. H. B. Swete, *The Ascended Christ* (London: 1911), p. 95.
24. Harm Henry Meeter, *The Heavenly Priesthood of Christ* (Grand Rapids: 1917), pp. 174, 177, 184.
25. Milligan, *op. cit.*, pp. 56-57.
26. Davies, *op. cit.*, p. 171.
27. Davies, *ibid.*, pp. 170, 182.

✿   ✿   ✿

For further study of the ascension, see William Milligan, *The Ascension and Heavenly Priesthood of Our Lord* (London: 1892); G. Campbell Morgan, *Crises of the Christ* (New York: 1903), pp. 385-413; W. H. Griffith Thomas, "Ascension," ISBE (Grand Rapids: 1939), I, 263-66.

6 The Present Inhabitants of Heaven

Of all the supernatural beings mentioned in the Scriptures, it is the angels who are constantly depicted as being identified with heaven. When the angel of God called to Hagar in the wilderness, we read that this call was heard "out of heaven" (Gen. 21:17; also of the angel commanding Abraham in Gen. 22:11, 15). When the angel appeared at the time of the vision which Jacob had at Bethel, he saw a ladder reaching to heaven on which the angels of God were ascending and descending. Often the angels are called "the heavenly ones" (Ps. 29:1) or "the heavenly host" (Luke 2:13). When the angelic host had finished their song to the shepherds, we read that "the angels went away from them into heaven" (Luke 2:15). It was an angel "from heaven" that rolled away the stone at the tomb where our Lord was buried (Matt. 28:2; see also Luke 22:43). Our Lord Himself often spoke of "the angels in heaven" (Mark 12:25; 13:32; Matt. 22:30). Then we have such a phrase as "the angels of heaven" (Matt. 24:36), and in a most interesting passage our Lord said, "Angels do always behold the face of my Father who is in heaven" (Matt. 18:10).

THE BASIC WORDS FOR ANGELS

Both in the Hebrew text and in the Greek New Testament, the words translated "angel" primarily mean messenger. In fact, in the Old Testament there are nearly one hundred different occurrences of the Hebrew word *malak* which is translated nearly fifty times as "messenger," the other occurrences being translated "angel." On the contrary, of some 177 New Testament occurrences of the word *angelos* only five of them refer to human messengers. Thus, in the Old Testament, the messenger is a human being appearing in the episode of Jacob's overture to Esau (Gen. 32:3, 6) and in Saul's sending messengers to apprehend David (I Sam. 19:11-21). Priests are sometimes referred to as messengers (Mal. 2:7), and often prophets are so designated (II Chron. 36:15; Isa. 44:26; Hag. 1:13). In a famous passage on the last page of the Old Testament, the word *malak* refers to John the Baptist: "Behold, I send my messenger, and he shall prepare the way before me: and the Lord, whom ye seek, will suddenly come to his temple; and the messenger of the covenant, whom ye desire, behold, he cometh, saith Jehovah of hosts" (Mal. 3:1, quoted in Mark 1:2 and Matt. 11:10). Only in Luke's gospel is this word *angelos* used in reference to human messengers, two of them referring to John the Evangelist (Luke 7:24, 27), and another in the statement that as Jesus set His face to go to Jerusalem He "sent messengers before his face" (Luke 9:52).

A word often used for angel, generally in reference to a large group of them, is the word *hosts,* as toward the end of the Psalter: "Praise ye him, all his angels: praise ye him, all his hosts" (Ps. 148:2). A phrase is used in an earlier psalm in reference to the hosts of Jehovah that is practically identical with the one quoted at the beginning of the epistle to the Hebrews. "Bless Jehovah, all ye his hosts, ye ministers of his, that do his pleasure" (Ps. 103:21; cf. Heb. 1:7, 14).

Once they are called "holy ones" (Jude 14). Occasionally the word *hosts* does refer to heavenly bodies, the stars (Neh. 9:6), but generally the reference is to heavenly beings.

Exclusively in Job and Psalms the angels are called sons of God (Job 1:6; 2:1; 38:7; Ps. 89:6). It has been well said that "angels bear a relationship analogous to sonship because of having their origin from him and because of their particular propinquity enjoying his most special friendship and love." One would think that this closeness of relationship is implied in such a phrase as "his angels" (Ps. 91:11; 104:4).

When we read of "the holy ones," it is generally assumed that the reference is to angelic beings (Job 5:1; 15:15; Zech. 14:5), concerning which we read of an individual as "a holy one" as an interpreter for Daniel (Dan. 4:13). Probably also the word translated "watcher" in this same passage refers to these divine beings (Dan. 4:17; see also Dan. 8:15 ff.). All would agree that though neither the word *angel* nor any synonym is found, yet in such a statement as "thousands of thousands ministered unto him" the reference certainly is to these angelic beings (Dan. 7:10; Rev. 5:11).

THE ANGEL OF JEHOVAH

It is at this point that we should give consideration to the problem of "the angel of Jehovah." We might first examine the passages in which it occurs and then attempt to ascertain the nature of the person to whom this refers. The Angel of Jehovah appears first in the divine record in the experiences of Hagar in the wilderness. "The angel of Jehovah found her by a fountain of water in the wilderness" (Gen. 16:7; cf. vv. 9-11). We should carefully note the statement in verse 13: "She called the name of Jehovah that spake unto her, Thou art a God that seeth." The word of the angel, "I will greatly multiply thy seed," certainly does not belong to a mere angelic being. So also in the later experiences of this same grieving woman, when we are told, "God heard the voice of the lad; and the angel of God called to Hagar out of heaven, and said unto her. . . ." In the rest of the passage we read that God heard the lad's voice, God opened her eyes, God was with the lad, all of which would imply a revelation of God Himself (Gen. 21:14-21). At the time when Abraham was offering up Isaac, we read that "the angel of Jehovah called unto him out of heaven, and said. . . ." (Gen. 22:9 ff.). And here also the angel says, "By myself have I sworn, saith Jehovah" (Gen. 22:11-15). This same being appeared to Jacob just before his reconciliation with Esau (Gen. 31:11-12) to which Jacob refers many years later in speaking of "the angel who hath redeemed me from all evil" (Gen. 48:16). Delitzsch has well said regarding this passage, "This triple reference to God in which the angel is placed on an equality with Ha-Elohim cannot possibly be a created angel but must be the Angel of God, that is, God manifested in the form of the Angel of Jehovah."

The Angel of Jehovah appears with greatest frequency in the book of Exodus in relation to the deliverance of the Israelites from Egypt. It was the Angel of Jehovah who appeared to Moses in a flame of fire out of the midst of the bush (Exodus 3:2), which is followed by the statement that "when Jehovah saw that he turned aside to see, God called unto him. . . ." Once the march began out of Egypt, we read in one passage that "Jehovah went before them by day" (Exodus 13:21), while elsewhere this divine leading is referred to in the reference to "the angel of God, who went before the camp of Israel" (Exodus 14:19, 24). For later references to the Angel of Jehovah in the Exodus, see Exodus 23:20-24; 32:34; 33:2 and Numbers 20:16.

It was the Angel of Jehovah who so constantly appeared in the strange prophetic ministry of Balaam (Num. 22:22-35). Just as the Israelites were to enter upon the promised land, there appeared to Joshua one who identified himself as "prince of the hosts of Jehovah" (Joshua 5:13–6:5). A similar experience was that of Gideon on the threshold of his courageous plan for the deliverance of his troubled people from the Midianites (Judges 6:11-24; see also 2:1-5; 5:23). Finally, in this early period of Israel's history, the words of the Angel of Jehovah are interwoven in the entire narrative regarding Manoah (Judges 13:1-23).

The question now must be asked, With whom is the Angel of Jehovah to be identified? Some have held the view that this is none other than the second Person of the Godhead, and by those who hold this view, these appearances are called theophanies.

Dr. Theodore Laetsch, in his valuable commentary on the Minor Prophets, excellently summarizes the identity of the Angel of the Lord in these words:

> This Angel of the Lord, who is I AM THAT I AM (Exodus 3:2-14), is just as truly Jehovah's Messenger, His Angel sent by the Lord. Though One with Jehovah in the undivided and indivisible unity of God's Essence and Being, He is a second person. He is Jehovah sent by Jehovah as Jehovah's Messenger. We have here the same unsearchable mystery of the unity in Essence and the duality of Persons to which Christ refers in the New Testament when He says, I and the Father are One (John 10:30; cp. 14:9; 17:11, 21 f.), while just as clearly He states that the Father has sent Him into the world (John 17:18, 23, 25) and that He is coming to the Father (v. 11; cp. John 3:16 f.; 5:17-23; 8:16-18; 16:28, etc.). . . . Malachi calls this Messenger of the Covenant "the LORD coming to His temple," the Church of the New Covenant, as the long-expected Redeemer, the Refiner of His people, the Judge of the world, the Messenger of the New Covenant, who by His work gave to the Old

Covenant whatever power of forgiveness, life and salvation it possessed.[1]

THE NATURE OF ANGELS

In an attempt to briefly summarize the Biblical teaching regarding angels, we are reminded of the words of Barth that the only authority for data concerning the angels is the Holy Scriptures of the Old and New Testaments: "We must not accept any other authority and must listen exhaustively to what this guide has to tell us and we must respect what it says and what it does not say." What is probably the best known single passage regarding the nature of angels is by the author of the epistle to the Hebrews, that all angels are "ministering spirits, sent forth to do service for the sake of them that shall inherit salvation" (Heb. 1:14, from Ps. 103:20-21; 148:2). As spirits they are normally without bodies, but they often assume bodily form, and could at times actually be mistaken for men (Ezek. 9:2; Gen. 18:2, 16). Probably the characteristic most often thought of in relation to angels is that they are holy (Mark 8:38; Luke 9:26), though the book of Job would seem to tell us that even the holiness of angels was not absolute (Job 4:18; 15:15). Of course, in the well-known words of our Lord in reply to the foolish question of the Sadducees regarding marriage and the world to come, He clearly taught that angels are without sex (though always the pronouns used when speaking of angels are masculine and never feminine). Both the Old and the New Testaments tell us that the angelic host is an innumerable company (Heb. 12:22; Dan. 7:19), our Lord even speaking of the possibility of calling upon twelve legions of angels, which would be 72,000 (Matt. 26:53). Angels, Christ has said, do not know the time of the second advent (Matt. 24:36).

KARL BARTH ON THE SUBJECT OF ANGELS

The whole concept of angels in most contemporary religious thinking is reduced to a minimum, if not wholly excluded. And, at times, it is ridiculed. As Dr. Bernard Ramm has said,

> The omission of a discussion of angels in almost every book on the philosophy of religion reveals the gulf between modern mentality and the biblical revelation. Philosophers of religion discuss God, the soul, and nature, but stop short of any serious discussion of angels. Skeptics will spend much time in refuting the proofs of the existence of God and the immortality of the soul, but will not even wet the pen to refute the existence of an angelic host. In contrast to this treatment of angels on behalf of philosophers (religious or skeptical) are the profuse references to angels in sacred Scripture . . . . In the universe of electrons and positrons, atomic energy and rocket power, Einsteinian astronomy and nuclear physics, angels *seem* out of place. They *seem* to intrude upon the scene like the unexpected visit of the country relatives to their rich city kinfolk. Atoms *seem* at home in our contemporary thinking, but not angels! The prospect of some interplanetary *Beagle* cruising among the planets gathering scientific data surprises no educated man of today. But if such a man were called upon to comment upon angels, he would either act very nervous or else he would pompously deny that angels existed. He knows the principles whereby he can reasonably imagine a scientific cruise of the planets by a space-age Darwin, but he has no principles whereby he may discuss angels. So he prefers to dismiss the concept of angels as mythological.[2]

However, just at a time when the whole idea of angels was about to be dismissed even from contemporary theological works, none other than Karl Barth himself suddenly appeared on the stage of theological debate, exercising an influence that could not be denied, and brought back into living reality and significance this whole subject of Angelology. Barth devotes thousands of words to the subject of Angels in the third volume of his *Church Dogmatics: The Doctrine of Creation.* Personally I feel that some of his statements are so important that rather than attempt to condense them myself I am taking the liberty of placing before my readers an extended single passage:

> Obviously their being and function is everywhere presupposed, but they actually appear, and are described as active, only when it is a matter of declaring the Word and work of God Himself as fulfilled in speech or action. They are as it were the luminous border of this Word and work, marking it off from world-occurrence generally. This is how they appear, for example, on the margin of the events of Advent and Christmas, or of the Easter incidents during the forty days, or of the prospective *parousia.* On this margin, or as they themselves form this margin, they are watchers, calling and speaking and singing, and when the time comes sounding the trumpet to awaken all those who are asleep or half-asleep. But they are all this as the sign and testimony of the One who is the Lord and Master of all things and over all things. And they are the primary witness because they belong to this higher cosmos, and belonging to it, in their being and function they take precedence over the lower, over all the prophets and apostles, over the whole Church, over the Jews, over ourselves and our witness to ourselves. The other signs and testimonies are there only because they are there first. Therefore we cannot really compare any of the divine constants in world-occurrence with this constant, this chorus of angels in heaven which accompanies the Lord on his way.

It is true, of course, that we can miss the angels. We

can deny them altogether. We can dismiss them as
superfluous, or absurd and comic. We can protest with
frowning brow and clenched fist that, although we might
admit that there is a God, it is going too far to allow
that there are angels as well. They must be questioned
or completely ignored. There are, therefore, even Christian and theological systems in which there is no place
for angels. . . . If we cannot or will not accept angels,
how can we accept what is told us by the history of
Scripture, or the history of the Church, or the history of
the Jews, or our own life's history? And since it depends
upon our acceptance of these secondary signs and testimonies whether or not our own system includes within
it the living God, we have to ask ourselves whether a
system in which there is no place for angels, and therefore for the primary sign and testimony, will not at bottom be a godless one. Where God is, there the angels of
God are. Where there are no angels, there is no God.
And whatever our system may be, it is comforting and
good that the world and its occurrence should not be
without God and the angels of God, that our lower cosmos should not be without the encounter and contact
with the higher cosmos set in motion by the Word and
work of God. . . . But a dogmatics which tried to escape
the task of angelology would be guilty of an indolent
omission which might well jeopardise the whole Church.
On the contrary, we are summoned to ponder what the
witness of Scripture presents for our consideration in
this respect.[3]

The General Activity of Angels

Fundamentally the function of angels is of a dual nature,
toward God and toward man. The writer of the epistle to
the Hebrews reminds us that "when he again bringeth in the
firstborn into the world he saith, And let all the angels of
God worship him" (Heb. 1:6, quoting the LXX of Deut.

32:43). This is echoed again and again by the psalmist: "Bless Jehovah, ye his angels, that are mighty in strength, that fulfil his word, hearkening unto the voice of his word. Bless Jehovah, all ye his hosts, ye ministers of his, that do his pleasure" (Ps. 103:20-21; see also 148:2). It is not without significance that this basic function of angels will also be one of the great eternal privileges of the redeemed when they are in glory with the angels, namely, ministering to the Lord (Rev. 22:3).

The Activity of Angels in the Old Testament

While we must acknowledge that the Scriptures choose to give us comparatively little specific information about the nature of angels, they give us abundant material regarding the activity of these heavenly creatures. We will find that as messengers, they first of all communicate a word from God to men, these men invariably being the children of God. Furthermore, they give guidance, protection and deliverance, and sometimes they are sent as angels of judgment upon the disobedient. It was the Angel of the Lord who ministered to the despondent Hagar (Gen. 16:7-11; 21:17). It was an angel who pointed out the ram in the thicket which was to be a substitute for the sacrifice of Isaac (Gen. 22:11, 15). It is interesting that the words of Abraham to his son Isaac, and those of Jacob to Joseph and his sons, are almost identical. "Jehovah, the God of heaven, who took me from my father's house, and from the land of my nativity, and who spake unto me . . . saying, Unto thy seed will I give this land; he will send his angel before thee" (Gen. 24:7, 40; cf. 48:15-16). Of course, all Bible readers remember the famous scene of Jacob at Bethel when in a dream he beheld "a ladder set up on the earth, and the top of it reached to heaven; and, behold, the angels of God ascending and descending upon it" (Gen. 28:12; John 1:51). Not only did an angel com-

municate God's message to Moses at the time of the burning
bush (Acts 7:30, 35), but God also promised Moses that
He would send an angel to guide him in the difficult tasks
and long journeys that were ahead of him (Exodus 23:20,
23). An angel protected the Hebrew people at the cross-
ing of the Red Sea (Exodus 14:19). The New Testament
in three different passages informs us that angels participated
in the giving of the law on Mount Sinai (Acts 7:53; Gal.
3:15; Heb. 2:2, referring to the LXX of Deut. 33:2). Sometimes angels are sent to interpret prophetic messages, as
especially for Daniel (8:15-16; 9:21), and particularly in
that remarkable passage in Job which many take to be a
Messianic prophecy: "If there be with him an angel, an
interpreter, one among a thousand, to show unto man what
is right for him" (Job 33:23). There is of course the darker
aspect of angelic activity in the Old Testament in executing
divine judgment on the disobedient as at the time of the
destruction of Sodom and Gomorrah (Gen. 19:13) and the
destruction of the host of Sennacherib (II Kings 19:35). It
is such activity that probably justifies the title "angels of
evil" (Ps. 78:49).

The Ministry of Angels During the Life of Our Lord

The greatest concentration of angelic activity in the historical narratives of the New Testament is to be found at
the time of our Lord's birth, where angels are prominent on
six different occasions, requiring nineteen occurrences of the
word *angel* in four separate chapters, fifteen of which are in
the gospel of Luke. There are three annunciations by angels,
first to Zacharias (Luke 1:11, 13, 18-19), then to Mary (Luke
1:26, 28, 30, 34-35, 38), and finally, after some months had
elapsed, to Joseph (Matt. 1:20, 24; Luke 2:21). After the
birth of our Lord, angels appeared to the shepherds on the
plains of Bethlehem (Luke 2:9-10, 13, 15), then as the mes-

sengers of warning to the holy family (Matt. 2:13), and finally, again to the holy family in prompting them to return to Palestine. When our Lord was at the threshold of His ministry, angels ministered to Him after the exhausting experience of the temptation in the wilderness (Matt. 4:6, 11; Luke 4:10). While Jesus frequently referred to angels in His teaching, at no time in His life, after the temptation, did angels apparently participate until that dark night of agony in Gethsemane when Luke tells us "there appeared unto him an angel of heaven, strengthening him" (Luke 22:43). Incidentally, this particular statement has been considered as an interpolation by such distinguished conservative scholars as Westcott and Hort, but they go on to say that this and Luke 23:34 "may be safely called the most precious among the remains of the angelic tradition which were rescued from oblivion by the scribes of the second century." Finally, angels appeared, not to the Lord but to His followers, early in the morning of Easter Sunday (Matt. 28:2; Luke 24:23; John 20:12). The historic sequence in this point is not without difficulties, and it is true that these angels are referred to as men. But as Langton has said,

> Could anything be more appropriate than that the fact of this supreme event should have been announced by angels? Such an announcement would seem to be demanded in order to assist the Apostles' faith in the fact of the resurrection. . . . It does not seem to us that the mere presence of a human being in the tomb of Jesus is sufficient to account for the amazement and trembling of the women and their hasty flight from the tomb.[4]

OUR LORD'S TEACHING CONCERNING ANGELS

It is only a testimony to the great skill of our Lord in His teaching ministry that His statements are so well remembered by all readers, while most of the other references to angels in the New Testament are not so familiar to us. In the great chapter on the parables of the finding of the lost, our Lord said to the publicans and sinners as well as to the Pharisees and scribes, "I say unto you, there is joy in the presence of the angels of God over one sinner that repenteth" (Luke 15:10). What a beautiful statement is that of our Lord when in referring to "these little ones," He said, "In heaven their angels do always behold the face of my Father who is in heaven" (Matt. 18:10). There has been some disagreement as to the exact meaning of "these little ones." Generally, the church has interpreted it as referring to little children. The statement of Dr. G. Campbell Morgan could be duplicated many times:

> I believe in the ministry of angels and that for every bairn there is a guardian angel who always beholds the face of God. That is one of my profoundest convictions because He said so; and I believe it in spite of all that skepticism may say to attempt to shake my conviction.[5]

On the other hand, many scholars of an unquestioned conservative view of Scripture, including none other than Benjamin B. Warfield, have concluded that the reference here is not to children but to our Lord's disciples, to those who believe on Him. This is certainly the meaning of the Greek word in Matthew 10:42; Mark 9:42; Luke 17:2.[6]

It is, however, in relation to eschatological matters that our Lord most frequently introduces the subject of Angels. It is angels who are sent for the harvest at the end of the age, when the righteous will be separated from the wicked (Matt. 13:39, 41, 49). Though we seldom think of it, the following words of our Lord certainly belong in such a study as this: "And I say unto you, Every one who shall confess me before men, him shall the Son of man also confess before the angels of God: but he that denieth me in the presence

of men shall be denied in the presence of the angels of God"
(Luke 12:8-9). On two different occasions our Lord refers to
the fact that when He returns to this earth it will be with His
angels, or in detail, it will be an event in which "the holy
angels" are with Him (Matt. 16:27; 25:31; Mark 8:38). Once
again He refers to the fact that "he shall send forth his angels
with a great sound of a trumpet, and they shall gather together his elect from the four winds, from one end of heaven
to the other" (Matt. 24:31). St. Paul emphasizes this aspect
of the ministry of angels when he tells us that "the revelation
of the Lord Jesus from heaven" will be "with the angels of
his power in flaming fire, rendering vengeance to them that
know not God, and to them that obey not the gospel of our
Lord Jesus" (II Thess. 1:7-8).

While the angelic ministry in the book of Acts has received
considerable attention, the data does not particularly add to
what we already know about angelic activity. Twice angels
released an apostle from prison (5:19; 12:7 ff.). It is an angel
that commanded Philip to go down to Gaza (8:26). Cor-
nelius' great experience in being converted to the gospel
began when "he saw in a vision openly, as it were about
the ninth hour of the day, an angel of God coming in unto
him" (10:3). Finally, at the end of that terrible experience
in the storm on the Mediterranean, Paul told the entire
crew of the ship, "There stood by me this night an angel of
the God whose I am, whom also I serve, saying, Fear not,
Paul; thou must stand before Caesar: and lo, God hath
granted thee all them that sail with thee" (27:23-24).

When St. Peter, released from prison, came to the home
of Mary, the mother of Mark, and rapped upon the door, the
maid reported that Peter was at the gate, but they refused
to believe her and remarked, "It is his angel."

This may well be the place to ask the question, Are guardian angels assigned to redeemed individuals? It has been

insisted upon by many that such guardian angels are to be assumed. The passage generally quoted is the famous utterance of our Lord in referring to little children: "I say unto you that in heaven their angels do always behold the face of my Father who is in heaven" (Matt. 18:10). Many decades ago, one of America's most careful scholars, Moses Stuart, in arguing for guardian angels, remarked on this passage:

> In what other way can we reasonably interpret this, except as assigning to little children—it matters not, for our present purpose, whether these are literally children or tropically so—presence-angels, or angels of the highest order (comp. Isaiah 6:2 sq. and Revelation 1:4), as their guardians and protectors? The abuse of this doctrine, in order to inculcate the invocation and worship of angels, is no good argument against the truth of it, as it lies in the Scriptures. That all worship of angels is most clearly proscribed by Christianity, is certain from Revelation 19:10; 22:8, 9; Colossians 2:18. But this is surely no objection against regarding angels as the guardian spirits of good men, in and through whom God operates for their deliverance and their benefit, and sometimes for their chastisement.[7]

The famous German exegete Hermann Cremer even went further into detail in saying, "The angels of God bear their souls thither where Christ has preceded them to heaven, the place of eternal life and of the glory of God, there to be till they and all saints shall be revealed from thence with Christ."[8]

Calvin himself was not sure as to whether there were guardian angels or not, and this would be our own position. These are his words: "Whether or not each believer has a single angel assigned to him for his defence, I dare not positively affirm. . . . This indeed I hold for certain, that each of us is cared for not by one angel merely, but that all with one consent watch for our safety."[9]

ARCHANGELS

Occasionally in the Scriptures we read of archangels who are certainly appointed as rulers of large angelic groups (I Thess. 4:16, etc.). Among these archangels are probably to be placed those two angels who alone have names given to them in the Scriptures. One is Gabriel who is the angel most active in the annunciations to those participating in the glorious advent of the Lord Jesus Christ. The other is Michael who is most prominent in the concluding vision of the book of Daniel which is a prediction of the great and dreadful tribulation which is yet to be experienced by the people of Israel.

At the beginning of this vision there are two different angelic beings introduced. First, the anonymous one who tells Daniel that he has been sent to the prophet to unveil to him the prophecy that is about to be given. And then he makes the remarkable statement: "But the prince of the kingdom of Persia withstood me one and twenty days; but, lo, Michael, one of the chief princes, came to help me: and I remained there with the kings of Persia. Now I am come to make thee understand what shall befall thy people in the latter days; for the vision is yet for *many* days" (Dan. 10:13-14). There is now introduced "one in the likeness of the sons of men" who touched his lips who is probably the same one as referred to in verse 18: "Then there touched me again one like the appearance of a man, and he strengthened me."

Michael appears again in a most comforting passage after the main prophecy has been revealed: "And at that time shall Michael stand up, the great prince who standeth for the children of thy people; and there shall be a time of trouble, such as never was since there was a nation even to that same time: and at that time thy people shall be delivered, every one that shall be found written in the book" (12:1). It is this angel Michael who is referred to in the very enigmatical passage in the book of Jude: "But Michael the archangel, when contending with the devil he disputed about the body of Moses, durst not bring against him a railing judgment, but said, The Lord rebuke thee" (v. 9).

In the early days of the Reformation, Michael was considered as possibly the preincarnate Christ, a view that is now not generally held.[10] Many believed that the archangel referred to in I Thessalonians 4:16 might be the angel Michael. While we are referring to this passage in one of Paul's early epistles, we might consider for a moment this very interesting phrase that at the time of our Lord's return He will "descend from heaven, with a shout, with the voice of the archangel, and with the trump of God: and the dead in Christ shall rise first." The late Professor G. G. Findlay believed that these three phrases refer to the single idea, namely, the voice of the Son of God by which the dead are called forth. Dr. Frame says that it is implied in this passage that God or Christ commands the archangel Michael to arouse the dead.[11] Only here and in Jude 9 does the word *archangel* occur in the New Testament. It is not found in the Old Testament.

CHERUBIM AND SERAPHIM

In the discussion of supernatural, heavenly creatures, we must, of course, give consideration to the mysterious beings known as the cherubim and the seraphim. Cherubim first come before us immediately after the fall of our first parents referred to in the well-known passage where we are told that after driving man out of the Garden of Eden, God "placed at the east of the garden of Eden the Cherubim, and the flame of a sword which turned every way, to keep the way of the tree of life" (Gen. 3:24). Apart from symbolic references, which we will consider shortly, they appear especially prominent in Ezekiel 10 where they are apparently to be identified with the living creatures of the first chapter. It is impossible here to interpret all the complicated details given concerning these creatures in Ezekiel. I have always thought that Moorehead's comment on these supernatural beings was a model of conciseness when he says that they are "hieroglyphs of God's attributes, of the eternal forces and infinite powers of the throne of God. . . . The execution of his will is through the power and forces which He himself has created, angels, natural law, human beings and the animal creation."[12] In addition to the actual appearance of these cherubim, they are depicted prominently as symbols of God's power in the tabernacle (Exodus 25:18-22; 37:7-9) and also in the temple of Solomon (I Kings 6:25-35; II Chron. 3:7-14). God is addressed as the One "that sittest above the cherubim" (Ps. 80:1; 99:1; Isa. 37:16). Except in the description of the ancient tabernacle in Hebrews 9:5, the word *cherubim* is not found in the New Testament. Murphy rightly has said,

> The cherubim are real creatures and not mere symbols. . . . The variety in the figuration of the cherubim is owing to the variety of aspects in which they stand, and of offices or services they have to perform in the varying posture of affairs. . . . Their special office seems to be *intellectual and potential,* rather than moral. They stand related on the one side to the God of Omnipotence and on the other to the universe of created things, in its material, animal, and intellectual departments, and to the general administration of the divine will in this comprehensive sphere.[13]

No doubt the cherubim of Ezekiel are closely related to the seraphim of Isaiah 6 and like them are identified with the throne of Jehovah. Some have called these the chiefest in heaven, though there is no particular data in the Scriptures for giving them this extreme preeminence. The word itself is derived from the Hebrew word *saraph*, to burn, and thus "they are the medium of imparting spiritual fire from God to his prophet."

THE HOSTS OF JEHOVAH

The name Jehovah of Hosts occurs with great frequency in the prophetic literature of the Old Testament (247 times). The word *hosts* itself (*cebhaath*) fundamentally has a military connotation in David's words to Goliath: "Thou comest to me with a sword, and with a spear, and with a javelin: but I come to thee in the name of Jehovah of hosts, the God of the armies of Israel, whom thou hast defied" (I Sam. 17:45). The term is used with great frequency in reference to groups of men organized for war, as an army (Gen. 21:22, 32; Judges 4:2, 7; I Sam. 12:9; II Sam. 3:23; Isa. 34:2). Sometimes the word is used in reference to the service of the Levites in the sanctuary (Num. 4:3, 23, 30, 35, 39, 43). Often the host of heaven is set forth as a group of angels associated with Jehovah in His governmental activities (Gen. 32:1-2; Joshua 5:14; I Kings 22:19).[14]

Frequently we have the concept of Jehovah of hosts sitting above the cherubim (I Sam. 4:4; II Sam. 6:2; Ps. 80:1; 99:1). Later in Israel's history, God is referred to as "Jehovah sitting on his throne, and all the host of heaven standing by" (I Kings 22:19; II Chron. 18:18). In the early days of the conquest of Palestine, it was "the prince of the host of Jehovah" who came to help Joshua (Joshua 5:14-15). It is these hosts who make up the army of God that do His will in heaven (Dan. 4:35; see Joel 3:11).

It is significant that the title Jehovah of Hosts appears in the LXX as *kurios pantokrator*, that is, "the Lord Omnipotent." Of course, the warnings against the worship of the

host of heaven always refer to the worship of stars (II Kings
23:5; Jer. 19:13; Zeph. 1:5; Acts 7:42), with the single exception of the reference in Colossians 2:18, where angels are
implied, not the stars of heaven.

Among these hosts are certainly to be included "the armies
which are in heaven" who, as Christ will descend to the
Battle of Armageddon, will follow Him upon white horses
(Rev. 19:14).

We must now give consideration to that very complicated,
variously expressed group of supernatural beings: principalities, powers, dominions, authorities, etc. These occur in
three well-known passages in Paul's epistles and once in writings of St. Peter. In Romans 8:38 and Ephesians 6:12, these
are antagonistic powers, possibly fallen angels; but in Ephesians 1:21 and Colossians 1:16, as well as in I Peter 3:22,
these supernatural beings are closely identified with the
preeminence of the exalted Christ, and they communicate
power to the believer. In this chapter, of course, we will
confine ourselves only to those passages in which the heavenly beings are referred to. Probably the most important word
is authority, a translation of the Greek word *exousia*, a word
that has been examined with great detail in the famous Kittel *Theological Dictionary of the New Testament:*

> The specific role played by *exousia* in the NT world
> of thought rests on three foundations. First, unlike ex-
> pressions for indwelling, objective, physical or spiritual
> power, it denotes the power which decides, so that it is
> particularly well adapted to express the invisible power
> of God whose Word is creative power. The *exousia* of
> Jesus and the apostles is of the same character. Sec-
> ondly, this power of decision is active in a legally ordered
> whole, especially in the state and in all the authoritarian
> relationships supported by it. All these relationships are
> the reflection of the lordship of God in a fallen world

where nothing takes place apart from His *exousia* or authority. They are based upon this lordship. Thus the word *exousia* can refer to the fact that God's will is done in heaven. It can also denote the fact that His will prevails in the sphere of nature as an ordered totality. Indeed, *exousia* is given to Antichrist for his final activity, so that nothing takes place apart from the *exousia* or will of God. Especially in the community the word is indispensable to express the fact that we cannot take anything, but that it has to be given to us. Thus *exousia* describes the position of Jesus as the Head of the Church to whom all power is given and who gives it to His disciples. This *exousia* which is operative in ordered relationships, this authority to act, cannot be separated from its continuous exercise, and therefore thirdly *exousia* can denote the freedom which is given to the community. . . . The word *exousia* is important in understanding the person and work of Christ. It denotes His divinely given power and authority to act. If He is the Son, this authority is not a restrict commission. It is His own rule in free agreement with the Father. *Exousia* is well adapted to denote this freedom too, as in John 10:18.[15]

Closely related to this word is the one generally translated "power," *dunamis* (Rom. 8:38; Eph. 1:21; I Peter 3:22). This has been by many translated by the word *virtue*, which is the word used by our Lord when He said He perceived that virtue had gone out of Him (Mark 5:30). The word *virtue* is akin to the word *virile*. As Heinrich Schlier reminds us, "These creatures have their being in Christ. In fact, their very origin is in Christ, 'and through Him and for Him.' Their source and their final end is not in themselves but in Jesus Christ who is God."[16] The word generally translated "rule" or "principality" is the Greek word *arche* meaning "that which is first," the leader. This would imply, of course, that there are various degrees of authority and position among these heavenly hierarchies. Closely related to these words is the word generally translated "dominion," *kuriotes*, simply meaning "one who possesses power"; and finally, in Colossians 1:16, we have the word *throne* which of course immediately communicates the idea of sovereign power. As others have said, the names in themselves do not give us too much actual information about the various inhabitants.

Eadie has excellently said in summary:

> All we know is that there is no dull and sating uniformity among the inhabitants of heaven; that order and freedom are not inconsistent with gradation of rank, that there are glory and a higher glory, power, and a nobler power, rank and a loftier rank to be witnessed in the mighty scale . . . there are bright and majestic chieftains among the hosts of God, nearer in position and liker God in majesty possessing and reflecting more of the divine splendor than their lustrious brethren around them. But above all, Jesus is enthroned—the highest position in the universe is His.[17]

Many of these groups we have here referred to are no doubt to be included in the famous passage on the council of Jehovah (Jer. 23:18-22). This may be what the psalmist has in mind when he affirms that "God standeth in the congregation of the mighty" (Ps. 82:1, AV).

The most extensive treatment of the subject of angelic activity in the heavens is, of course, to be found in the book of Revelation, and in our chapter on the Rule of Heaven in the Apocalypse, the relevant data will be fully discussed.

NOTES

1. Theodore Laetsch, *Bible Commentary: The Minor Prophets* (St. Louis: 1956), p. 408.
2. Bernard Ramm, in *Basic Christian Doctrines*, ed. Carl F. H. Henry (New York: 1962), pp. 63, 65.
3. Karl Barth, *Church Dogmatics*, Vol. III: *The Doctrine of Creation*, pp. 238, 374.

4. For a full discussion, see Edward Langton, *The Angel Teaching of the New Testament* (London: n.d.), pp. 31, 35.
5. G. Campbell Morgan, *The Teaching of Christ* (New York: 1913), p. 86. See Edward Langton, *The Supernatural* (London: 1934), pp. 127-32.
6. See B. B. Warfield, "Little Ones," *Dictionary of Christ and the Gospels*, ed. James Hastings, II, 36-37.
7. Moses Stuart, "Sketches of Angelology in the Old and New Testaments," *Bibliotheca Sacra* (New York: 1843), p. 104.
8. Hermann Cremer, *Beyond the Grave* (New York: 1886), p. 85. On the general subject of Angels, see in addition Edward Langton, *The Angel Teaching of the New Testament* (London: n.d.), p. 224; G. Kittel (ed.), *Theological Dictionary of the New Testament*, Eng. trans. (Grand Rapids: 1964), I, 74-87; William George Heidt, *Angelology of the Old Testament* (Washington, D.C.: 1949); J. P. Lange, *Life of Our Lord Jesus Christ*, I, 259-72.
9. John Calvin, *Institutes of the Christian Religion*, Book I, chap. 14.
10. A. C. Gaebelein, *The Angels of God* (New York: 1924), and *Gabriel and Michael the Archangel* (New York: 1945).
11. G. G. Findlay, *The Epistles to the Thessalonians* (Cambridge: 1891), p. 100; J. E. Frame, *The Epistles to the Thessalonians* (Naperville, Ill.: 1960), p. 174.
12. Wm. G. Moorehead, *Outline Studies of the Old Testament* (New York: 1893).
13. J. G. Murphy, *Critical and Exegetical Commentary on the Book of Genesis* (new ed.; Andover, Mass.: 1866), pp. 135-37.
14. See B. W. Anderson, in *Interpreter's Dictionary of the Bible*, II, 654-56.
15. G. Kittel, *op. cit.*, II, 566, 568.
16. Heinrich Schlier, *Principalities and Powers in the New Testament* (Edinburgh: 1961), p. 37.
17. John Eadie, *Commentary on the Greek Text of the Epistle of Paul to the Ephesians* (London: 1854), pp. 94-95.

✿   ✿   ✿

There is an interesting chapter on "The Society of Heaven" in Ulrich Simon, *Heaven in the Christian Tradition* (New York: 1958), pp. 126-51.

7 The Kingdom of Heaven

In a volume attempting to consider all the major passages in the Scriptures that relate to heaven as the abode of God and the home of the redeemed, it would hardly be right to pass by the teachings of our Lord concerning "the kingdom of heaven," even though these teachings do not directly relate to the heaven of heavens. For this reason we shall only consider the phrase with brevity. Significantly, the term "the kingdom of heaven" occurs thirty-four times in the gospel of Matthew and nowhere else in the New Testament. Twenty-two statements of Christ connected with His teaching on the kingdom of heaven are unique for Matthew's gospel. Four of them (8:11; 13:11, 31; 19:14) are found in Mark's gospel where, as also in Luke, the phrase invariably is "the kingdom of God." Four times in Matthew's gospel Jesus does use the phrase "the kingdom of God" (12:28; 19:24; 21:31, 43). More frequently He refers simply to "the kingdom" as in the parables of the kingdom (13:19, 38, 43); and in the discourses and utterances of the last week (24:7, 14; 25:34; 26:29; cf. 4:23; 8:12; 12:25).

There has been a great deal of discussion, especially in the twentieth century, as to why Matthew uses the phrase "the kingdom of heaven" and the other evangelists invariably use "the kingdom of God." The Scofield Reference Bible, and many who are of that dispensational school, insist that there is a basic difference intended by Christ in the use of these two phrases. Most scholars, however, would agree with Dr. George Ladd that "no difference is to be seen between kingdom of God and kingdom of heaven. The difference of expression is linguistic, reflecting the Semitic and Greek elements in the Gospel tradition. 'The kingdom of the heavens' is a Semitic idiom which would be meaningless to the Greek ear. Probably Jesus favored the Semitic form of the expression, thus following the usual rabbinic form." However, in the same paragraph, Dr. Ladd says that "the phrase 'the kingdom of the heavens' may place somewhat more emphasis upon the transcendental source and character of the kingdom."[1]

One finds it difficult to believe there was any great difference in our Lord's thinking between the kingdom of heaven and the kingdom of God when, for example, in discussing the subject of wealth, in one verse He talks about the rich man entering the kingdom of heaven, and in the very next verse, He talks about this same man as entering the kingdom of God (Matt. 19:23-24). In a volume on the subject of Christ's teachings concerning the future, William Strawson suggests that Christ "filled this idea with such a richness of thought that more than one phrase would be needed to convey His meaning. . . . It is indeed fortunate that we have both titles of the reign of God, for together they show the divine sovereignty and the beyond-the-earth implications of His teachings."[2] Inasmuch as this chapter is in a book attempting to unfold what the Scriptures say about heaven, and does not attempt a full discussion of all the eschatological teachings of Jesus, it is not necessary to discuss here the vast subject of the kingdom of God; but we will confine ourselves to what Jesus said in regard to the kingdom of heaven mentioned exclusively in the first gospel.

Basically the idea of a kingdom involves a group of men and women, generally a large multitude, who are under one sovereign power, at the head of which is the king. In itself the term does not have any particular moral or ethical implications. It has to do principally with power, and the exercise of that power; and if the kingdom is what it ought to be, it involves the loyalty and glad obedience of those who are embraced within that sovereignty. Normally a kingdom is identified with a certain geographical area, which will not be true, as we shall see, in relation to the kingdom of heaven. The fact that it is the kingdom of *heaven* seems to mean that its principles and ideals are those derived from heavenly standards, whose conduct and activities are according to the direction of Heaven, which of course means the direction of God. On the other hand, as we shall see in this chapter, this kingdom is not located in heaven, but only and continuously here on earth. "The earth transformed into the inheritance of the meek would be its scene."

The kingdom of heaven in the teachings of our Lord is something at hand and at the same time has reference to the future. Both John the Baptist and our Lord at the beginning of His ministry exhorted the people of Palestine to repent, for, said they, "the kingdom of heaven is at hand" (Matt. 3:2; 4:17). The twelve apostles when commissioned to preach were told to say, "The kingdom of heaven is at hand" (10:7). While most of the Beatitudes look to the future for the ultimate fulfillment and are expressed in future tenses, the one that embraces the phrase that we are here studying is in the present tense: "Blessed are the poor in spirit: for theirs is the kingdom of heaven." "Blessed are they that have been persecuted for righteousness' sake: for theirs is the kingdom of heaven" (5:3, 10).

The kingdom of heaven is consistently presented as something that involves continuity, that is, it extends through the centuries down to the very end of this age. This is vividly set forth in the parable of the wheat and the tares (13:36-43), in the parable of the mustard seed (13:31-32), and, whatever our interpretation of it might be, in the parable of the leaven (13:33). Some of these parables cover all that period from the time of our Lord's own ministry down to the end of the age. In the parable of the tares and the wheat, the end of the age is expressed in the idea of harvest; in interpreting the parable, our Lord definitely refers to "the end of the age" when He will send forth His angels to gather out of His kingdom all that practice iniquity. The parable of the ten virgins has exclusive reference to the time when the bridegroom will return, also the parables setting forth a reckoning scene and a banqueting scene initiated by a king (18:21-35; 22:1-13) can only be interpreted as they are made to relate to the King of kings Himself.

Everything our Lord said about the kingdom of heaven has an ethical emphasis. The kingdom of heaven is not established by mankind but by the preaching of the gospel.

> The preaching of the kingdom with which, as we have seen, His ministry began must be regarded as the first step towards its establishment in the world.... This is the teaching likewise of the parable of the sower (Matthew 13:1-23). The seed, it is said, is the word of God. Spoken by the Saviour, it takes no effect in some who hear it, it finds no entrance; in others it produces only a superficial and short-lived change of feeling; but in the case of another class still, it not only effects a lodgment, but finding a prepared soil, a heart above all uncorrupted by insincerities, it yields large and permanent fruit; and so far as this takes place, the Kingdom of God may be said to arise, "the good seed are the children of the kingdom,"

the word spoken by Jesus becoming the generative principle of a new life.[3]

While men themselves do not establish the kingdom or create its statutes, by their relationship to Jesus Christ and obedience to His will they enter it. In the Sermon on the Mount our Lord laid down the principle "Except your righteousness exceed the righteousness of the scribes and Pharisees, ye shall in no wise enter into the kingdom of heaven" (5:20). Toward the end of the same inexhaustible discourse, our Lord seems to summarize all that is required for entrance into the kingdom in His warning and promise: "Not every one that saith unto me, Lord, Lord, shall enter into the kingdom of heaven; but he that doeth the will of my Father who is in heaven" (7:21). Of course, the moment we read these words we are reminded of the close parallel in the prayer which He taught His disciples to pray: "Thy will be done, as in heaven, so on earth" (6:10). Toward the end of His ministry our Lord gave another ideal necessary for entrance into the kingdom of heaven. His disciples had asked the silly question "Who then is greatest in the kingdom of heaven?" To answer this He set a little child in the midst of them and said, "Except ye turn, and become as little children, ye shall in no wise enter into the kingdom of heaven. Whosoever therefore shall humble himself as this little child, the same is the greatest in the kingdom of heaven" (18:1-4; 19:14). The final statement of our Lord concerning requirements for entering the kingdom is expressed as a solemn warning: "It is hard for a rich man to enter into the kingdom of heaven" (19:23).

The kingdom of heaven must not be confused with the church. They are not identical. The church simply is not expressed in the nomenclature of a kingdom. True membership in the church involves regeneration and the work of the Holy Spirit, the practice of the sacraments, etc. Nothing

about these holy subjects is mentioned in passages referring
to the kingdom of heaven or even the kingdom of God in
the Synoptic Gospels. We have been well reminded that
"it is remarkable that in the first four centuries of the Christian era, the identification of the church with the kingdom of
God on earth is nowhere made."[4]

Let me conclude this chapter with a summarizing statement which appears in one of the most satisfying treatments
of the kingdom of heaven which I have seen, found in an
important volume which seems to be almost ignored by contemporary students of our Lord's teaching:

> The kingdom of God is an order of things in connection
> with which God reigns in hearts softened by His grace,
> and His will is done. In this form it came into the world
> with Jesus Christ and in His person. . . . At best it exists
> in the present state in a mixed condition. Evil, that which
> does not belong to it, which is its opposite, is meanwhile
> inseparably mingled with it; but it is not to remain thus
> always. The obnoxious and alien element shall be com-
> pletely separated from it in the end. Small in its begin-
> nings, it is destined to a mighty increase; and its growth
> shall be due to the assimilating power of the life main-
> tained within it by its Divine Head. Its franchises, the
> blessings which it brings to its genuine subjects, are of
> the highest value. When men discover these they will-
> ingly sacrifice all for their attainment. Differing from all
> other kingdoms in its nature, it differs from all like-
> wise in its destiny. These shall pass; the gates of Hades
> shall close on them; this endures, indestructible, im-
> perishable—for ever.[5]

NOTES

1. George E. Ladd, *Jesus and the Kingdom* (New York: 1964), p. 106,
   note 2.
2. William Strawson, *Jesus and the Future Life* (Philadelphia: 1959),
   p. 67.

3. John M. King, *The Theology of Christ's Teaching* (London: 1902), p. 208.
4. W. C. Allen, in James Hastings, *Dictionary of the Apostolic Church*, I, 676.
5. J. M. King, *ibid.*, pp. 227-28.

Beloved, now are we the children of God, and it is not yet made manifest what we shall be. We know that, if he shall be manifested, we shall be like him; for we shall see him even as he is.

—I John 3:2

8 The Possibilities of a Heavenly Life Now

While it is true that hope in itself exercises a tremendous power in the lives of those who have assurance of the hope of good things to come, the Scriptures clearly tell us that the concept of Heaven is for the Christian more than a mere hope. There is the tremendous possibility of heavenly life now. If life in heaven is one of holiness, worship, service, and an overwhelming love for our Redeemer, life here on earth should be, as it were, a preparation for such an eternal environment—a true vestibule leading from this life to the life to come.

A heavenly life on earth now for believers was announced at the very beginning of our Lord's public ministry, when in the prayer He taught His disciples to pray we find the all-embracing petition "Thy will be done, as in heaven, so on earth" (Matt. 6:10; Luke 11:2). In any study of the Biblical doctrine of Heaven, this verse deserves most careful attention. First of all, basically, is the truth set forth that the will of God is done in heaven. This is not in a future tense referring to the redeemed who are to be in heaven, but in the present tense, and must refer to angels in heaven. The psalmist gives expression to this in the famous words "Bless

Jehovah, ye his angels, that are mighty in strength, that fulfil his word, hearkening unto the voice of his word. Bless Jehovah, all ye his hosts, ye ministers of his, that do his pleasure" (Ps. 103:20-21). (The Authorized Version contains the more familiar clause "who keep his commandments.") Of course the angels do the will of God quickly, understandingly, gladly, unquestioningly. What that will might be for them, we are not told; and of course it would be different for different periods, for different occasions, and toward different realms of the universe. The late Adolph Saphir, in his excellent work on the Lord's Prayer, comments on angels obeying God:

> The angels obey God, because they see His face continually. Their obedience is implicit, but not blind. God's authority is perfect light and love. Thus ought our obedience to be in knowledge and meditation: work is prayer acting!

> The obedience of the angels, as we have seen, is very varied and comprehensive. Some watch over little children; some take charge of believers in danger; some seem to have assigned to their care mighty empires, and the various elements of the world. But their motive is always love to God, their object is God's glory. Thus may we serve the Lord in our daily duties, in our most common occupations, in every ministry of charity, in the conversation of social life.

> As God is their centre, the utmost harmony and union prevail among them. Thus they who serve the Lord are to serve Him in brotherly love. . . . The angels behold the glory of God in Christ. In Him they see the manifestation as well as the central object of the Father's purpose. As they took the most profound interest in the Saviour's life on earth, so they are now waiting for the marriage of the Lamb.[1]

Our text does not say that what the angels do in heaven is exactly what the redeemed should be doing on earth, but it does say that we here on earth should be as zealous in seeking to do the will of God while we live here in this environment as the angels are in doing the will of God in a heavenly environment. Perhaps we ought to ask, What is this will of God in a general way? There is an interesting passage at the beginning of Romans 12 that should be considered at this point: "And be not fashioned according to this world: but be ye transformed by the renewing of your mind, that ye may prove what is the good and acceptable and perfect will of God" (v. 2). Note carefully here the contrast between being fashioned according to this world and being transformed by the renewing of our mind. Such a contrast will occur again in another passage we will shortly be studying. Professor John Murray in his commentary on the epistle to the Romans has the most helpful interpretation of this particular passage on the will of God that I have been given the privilege of quoting:

The will of God is regulative of the believer's life. When it is characterized as "good and acceptable and perfect," the construction indicates that these terms are not strictly adjectives describing the will of God. The thought is rather that the will of God is "the good, the acceptable, and the perfect." In respect of that with which the apostle is now dealing the will of God is the good, the acceptable, and the perfect. The will of God is the law of God and the law is holy and just and good (cf. 7:12). We may never fear that the standard God has prescribed for us is only relatively good or acceptable or perfect, that it is an accommodated norm adapted to our present condition and not measuring up to the standard of God's perfection. The will of God is the transcript of God's perfection and is the perfect reflection of his holiness, justice, and goodness. When we are commanded to be perfect as God is perfect (cf. Matthew 5:48), the will of God as revealed to us in his Word is in complete correspondence with the pattern prescribed, namely, "as your heavenly Father is perfect." Hence, when the believer will have attained to this perfection, the criterion will not differ from that now revealed as the will of God. Consummated perfection for the saints is continuous with and the completion of that which is now in process (cf. Colossians 1:28; 4:12; Psalm 19:7-11).[2]

So this very statement regarding the will of God when understood ushers us into our eternal state.

Before we consider what this will might be for the redeemed, we should remember that the Gospels frequently remind us that the entire life of Christ, every moment, every day and every year, was nothing else but doing the will of God. In the early part of His ministry, He could say, "I can of myself do nothing: as I hear, I judge: and my judgment is righteous; because I seek not mine own will, but the will of him that sent me" (John 5:30; see also 6:38-40). At the end of His ministry in those dark hours of His suffering, this was still the overruling force in His life, as in the garden He cried out to His heavenly Father, "Thy will be done" (Matt. 26:42; Luke 22:42). The writer of the epistle to the Hebrews emphasizes this in applying Psalm 50 to the incarnate life of our Lord: "Wherefore when he cometh into the world, he saith, Sacrifice and offering thou wouldest not, but a body didst thou prepare for me; in whole burnt offerings and *sacrifices* for sin thou hadst no pleasure: then said I, Lo, I am come (in the roll of the book it is written of me) to do thy will, O God" (Heb. 10:5-7). And then the writer adds, "By which will we have been sanctified through the offering of the body of Jesus Christ once for all."

While doing the will of God is generally in the New Testament a comprehensive idea, without particularizing details, because the will of God for different people on different occasions will necessarily manifest many variations, still it is interesting to note what ideas are here directly related to the will of God in the New Testament. Two of the most important statements appear significantly in Paul's first letter, that to the Thessalonians, and all would probably agree that this first reference just about embraces everything else in the will of God: "This is the will of God, even your sanctification" (I Thess. 4:3). Later he says, "In everything give thanks: for this is the will of God in Christ Jesus to youward" (I Thess. 5:18; see also I Peter 2:15). Our Lord Himself once said, "It is not the will of your Father who is in heaven, that one of these little ones should perish" (Matt. 18:14). A corollary would be the words of the Apostle Paul when he speaks of Christ as one who gave Himself for our sins "that he might deliver us out of this present evil world, according to the will of our God and Father" (Gal. 1:4). The will of God can only be that which corresponds with the character of God—His holiness, His love, His separation from all sin, His compassion. What this will of God is for each of us must be separately sought and ascertained. Writing to the Ephesians, Paul reminded them that they should "understand what the will of the Lord is" (5:17) where this is contrasted with walking unwisely. To the Colossians the apostle went even a little further and said that he was praying for them that they might "be filled with the knowledge of his will in all spiritual wisdom and understanding, to walk worthy of the Lord unto all pleasing, bearing fruit in every good work, and increasing in the knowledge of God" (Col. 1:9-10). He then added at the end of this epistle that not only was he praying but Epaphras was striving for them in his prayers "that ye may stand perfect and fully assured in all the will of God" (4:12).

If we are true servants of the Lord, we cannot do anything

else but obey His will, as Paul himself reminded us that we
are not to be men pleasers but "as servants of Christ, doing
the will of God from the heart" (Eph. 6:6). A prayer such
as this, taught us by the Lord Jesus, certainly must be one
that can be fulfilled. We *can* do the will of God on earth
as it is in heaven, or the prayer is mockery. Indeed we ought
not to pray this prayer, as so often we might carelessly do,
unless we really mean it, unless we really want to do on earth
that which is in accord with the will of God as is the ministry
of angels in glory. For this we need divine help, and such
help is available. The prayer at the end of the epistle to the
Hebrews reminds us that the God of peace is able to make
us "perfect in every good thing to do his will, working in us
that which is well-pleasing in his sight, through Jesus Christ;
to whom be the glory for ever and ever" (Heb. 13:21).

The Apostle John at the end of the first century gives us
the promise that we are to have boldness in approaching
God knowing that "if we ask anything according to his will,
he heareth us" (I John 5:14).

St. Paul in his letter to the Philippians has one of the most
pregnant statements regarding our present relationship to
heaven to be found anywhere in the Scriptures, in which he
connects the heavenly influence upon our life now with the
great truth of the fact that some day in heaven we will be
clothed in a body conformable to the glorious body of the
Lord Jesus: "For our citizenship is in heaven; whence also
we wait for a Saviour, the Lord Jesus Christ: who shall fashion anew the body of our humiliation, *that it may be* conformed to the body of his glory, according to the working
whereby he is able even to subject all things unto himself"
(Phil. 3:20-21). The Greek word here translated "citizenship" is *politeuman*, which meant, first of all, a common-
wealth or a state, and then it came to mean a colony of
foreigners who in the environment of their present residence

outside of their native country were living according to the laws of the country of which they were citizens, not according to the laws of the country in which they were living. One form of this word is actually translated "citizenship" in Acts 22:28. Finally, in its verbal form the word came to mean a way of living, of conduct, as in Acts 23:1, when Paul says, "Brethren, I have lived before God in all good conscience until this day." (See also Philippians 1:27.)

There is a beautiful meditation on this text by Dr. John Henry Jowett, exquisitely entitled "The True Patriotism of the Soul," from which I would like to quote the following:

> Our relationship to it constitutes our highest patriotism. All other forms of patriotism must bow to this, and from this they must borrow their spirit and their aims. When the earthly citizenship is out of harmony with the heavenly citizenship it becomes a minister of moral discord and disaster. Indeed, patriotism which is harshly divorced from the heavenly citizenship is only a deadly form of selfishness, and it is creative of unlimited bitterness and strife. But the local patriotism which is pervaded by the large inspiration of the heavens is as beautiful as some local rose bush which has breathed in the wider air of Devonshire or in the golden climate of California. In these matters everything depends upon relationship. Our patriotism can be of the earth earthy, or it can be nourished by the atmosphere of heaven. . . .
>
> The patriotism of the soul finds its ideals in heaven. Our Master approached everything from the loftiest standpoint. "I am from above." And therefore He brought the things from above to the things that are below. He brought the heavenly type to the earthly commonplace. And that is the counsel which is given to His followers in His Word. "See that thou make all things according to the pattern shown to thee in the mount." The ideal of the upper world is to determine the move-

ment of the lower world. That is an essential part of all healthy patriotism. Our eyes are to be filled with the light of the heavenly vision when we set ourselves to an earthly task. When we are beginning to reconstruct society, or to build a wall that is in ruins, we are to have before our minds "the holy city, the new Jerusalem coming down out of heaven before God." That is the governing standard of the heavenly citizenship. So long as that vision fills our minds and hearts, we cannot possibly build into our structures anything that is hay or wood or stubble, and still less anything that is rotten or unclean.[3]

Another famous passage in which Paul calls upon believers living in the very midst of this pagan environment to seek those things which are above is in Colossians. The entire passage is packed with profound truth: "If then ye were raised together with Christ, seek the things that are above, where Christ is, seated on the right hand of God. Set your mind on the things that are above, not on the things that are upon the earth. For ye died, and your life is hid with Christ in God. When Christ, *who is* our life, shall be manifested, then shall ye also with him be manifested in glory" (3:1-4). One asks, What are the things which are above? One is often compelled to ask himself the hypothetical question What would have happened to mankind if the Bible had not been written and if Christ had not come? Certainly, the thoughts and intents of the heart of the natural man perpetually gravitate earthward. What great themes because of God's divine revelation have been given to us as faithful magnets to lift our thoughts into the higher regions of the things that are pure and true and honest and eternal, sacred and beautiful. The attributes of God, the grace and goodness and mercy of God, the love of God in Jesus Christ, the unselfishness, the kindness, the goodness of Jesus Christ and

His ultimate sacrifice, the atonement and all of its implications, the resurrection, the ascension, the high-priestly work of Christ, His second advent, the judgment to come, our eternal home with the Father, the promise of resurrection bodies, of a renewed earth and a renewed heaven, the work of the Holy Spirit, the obligation to proclaim the gospel, the fact that man is in the image of God—a hundred great subjects relate to the things that are above. Now, of course, we have our daily employment here on earth, the work of our hands, transactions in business, contact with unbelievers and believers also, the disappointments and sufferings of life. Jesus did not pray that we were to be taken out of the world but that we were to be kept from evil. In the midst of all these necessary earthly occupations, we are still to seek the things that are above. Dr. G. Campbell Morgan stated:

> The very way in which we conduct our business is a method by which we co-operate with God toward the bringing in of His kingdom. Do we share the risen life of Christ? Then we seek the things above, the spiritual things, the true things, the abiding things when we touch the material, incomplete, transient things of the day. To us there is nothing small or merely dust; to us there is nothing only of the hour. For us upon every winged moment there flames the light of all the abiding eternity.
>
> How are we to seek the things that are above? By setting our mind upon them. There we immediately recognize the principle to which attention has so often been drawn, and which is crystallized into the great word of the Bible concerning man, "As he reckoneth within himself, so is he," or as the Authorized Version has it, "As a man thinketh in his heart, so is he." Here the apostle passes from the outer activity to the inward conception. "Set your mind on the things that are above" is a command suggesting the concentration of attention, and intensity of consideration. Set your minds upon those

upper things; not upon the material and transient, but upon the spiritual, the true, the abiding. Set your mind upon these things as you go forth to seek them. Do not look to rebuild the ruined world out of its own debris. Do not hope to set up a great social order by organizing men who are in themselves poisoned with the virus of sin. Not on the things on the earth, let your mind rest, or your hope, but on the things that are above, where Christ sitteth, the Redeemer, Ransomer, Renewer; the One who is able to touch the most bruised, broken, withered life into new glory and new power, and so to reconstruct society.[4]

Canon Liddon, in a powerful sermon on this text which he rightly entitled "The Risen Life," pleaded with his great congregation in St. Paul's Cathedral, London:

Why not make an effort of strong purpose, that "whatsoever things are true, honest, pure, lovely, of good report," we *will* think of these things? A passage of Holy Scripture committed to memory; some sentence of a great author consecrated by the recognition of ages; some lines of an ancient hymn, or, if you will, of a modern one—these may give wings to thought. But for your own sakes, brethren, for God's sake, let your thought rise. Bid it, force it to rise. Think of the face of Jesus, of your future home in heaven, of those revered and loved ones who have gone before you, and who beckon you on toward them from their place of rest in Paradise. Think of all that has ever cheered, strengthened, quickened, braced yourselves. In such thoughts, to such thoughts, Jesus will assuredly and increasingly reveal Himself. As He reveals Himself, thought will take a new shape, it will melt insensibly into the incense of a prayer that shall greet His presence.[5]

We must now turn to one final passage or a group of statements in what has been called the Heavenly Epistle or the

Epistle of the Heavenlies, of course, Paul's letter to the Ephesians. He begins by saying, "Blessed *be* the God and Father of our Lord Jesus Christ, who hath blessed us with every spiritual blessing in the heavenly *places* in Christ" (1:3). In the subsequent prayer, Paul asks the Lord that his Ephesian converts might have a knowledge of the hope of their calling, the riches of God's inheritance in the saints, and the greatness of His power to us "which he wrought in Christ, when He raised him from the dead, and made him to sit at his right hand in the heavenly places [heavenlies]" (1:20 and 2:6). The word here translated "heavenlies" is *epouranios* and the particular phrase "in heavenly places" is found exclusively in this one epistle. The word *heavenlies* in itself is once used by our Lord in reference to God (Matt. 18:35). It is used by the Apostle Paul in reference to the heavenly bodies (I Cor. 15:40) and frequently in reference to Christ (I Cor. 15:48-49; Heb. 11:16; 12:22; II Tim. 4:18). Sometimes it is used in reference simply to heavenly things (Heb. 8:5; 9:23).

Before we try to ascertain exactly what Paul meant by our now being in heavenly places in Christ, it will be helpful to have before us a suggestive paragraph of that inimitable devotional writer, Alexander Smellie:

> It is a wonderful tribute to Christ and Christianity that a prisoner should live and move and have his being "in the heavenlies." When he wrote the Epistle, Paul was a captive in Rome, confined to his own hired room, watched over day and night by the legionaries of Caesar, his left hand fettered to the wrist of one of Nero's guardsmen. But the narrow little chamber could not shut him in. It seemed as if its solid and rigid walls dissolved into thin air, and he walked at liberty through a spacious land, with wide horizons and fruitful fields and a thousand beauties and grandeurs. Its citizens crowded round

him. Its Golden Prince was his intimate Friend. From
the restrictions and discouragements of his immediate
surroundings he escaped to the freedom, the dignity,
and the power of the heavenlies, and none was so rich or
so glad as he. And that is what Christ has done, and is
doing still, not for royal souls like Paul's alone, but for
multitudes of humbler men and women.[6]

The particular phrase "in heavenly places" is found only
in the epistle to the Ephesians in five different passages (1:3,
20; 2:6; 3:10; 6:12). In all these places the idea of locality
is certainly implied, but this does not help us actually to
understand what the apostle means when he says that we are
the recipients of all spiritual blessings in the heavenly places
in Christ. Actually the word *place* is supplied in these sentences, the Greek simply reading *ta epourania,* which led
Chrysostom and Luther to translate the words "in heavenly
things" and more or less this would control, I think, most
modern thought on these passages. Westcott's interpretation
of this phrase deserves study: ". . . the supra-mundane, supra-
sensual eternal order, or as we should say generally, 'the spiritual world' which is perceived by thought and not by sight.
This is not distant or future but present, the scene even now
of the Christian's struggle where his life is already centered
and his strength is assured to him and his triumph is already
realized." Westcott calls attention to similar phraseology
in John 3:12 and Hebrews 8:5. A more recent commentator
affirms that "the blessing originates in heaven, it is as it were
at home there, and is bestowed on us Christians here on
earth."[7]

This life marked by heavenliness while we are here on
earth in the midst of trials and temptations is not something
that will occur automatically. It will certainly mean effort,
a real battle. The apostle says that we are to set our mind
on these things. He does not say that automatically that is

the direction our thoughts will take. I like the words of Bishop Hall, written in a different age than ours, but still relevant:

> And, above all, propose unto thyself and dwell upon that purest, perfectest, simplest, blessedest object, the Glorious and Incomprehensible Deity: there, thou shalt find more than enough, to take up thy thoughts to all eternity. Be thou, O my soul, ever swallowed up in the consideration of that Infinite Self-being Essence, whom all created spirits are not capable sufficiently to admire. Behold, and never cease wondering at, the Majesty of his Glory. The bodily eyes dazzle at the sight of the sun; but, if there were as many suns as there are stars in the firmament of heaven, their united splendor were but darkness to their All-glorious Creator. Thou canst not yet hope to see him, as he is: but, lo, thou beholdest where he dwells, in light inaccessible; the sight of whose very outward verge, is enough to put thee into a perpetual ecstasy. It is not for thee, as yet, to strive to enter within the vail: thine eyes may not be free, where the angels hide their faces. What thou wantest in sight, O my soul, supply in wonder. Never any mortal man, O God, durst sue to see thy face, save that one entire servant of thine, whose face thy conference had made shining and radiant; but even he, though inured to thy presence, was not capable to behold such glory, and live. Far be it from me, O Lord, to presume so high. Only let me see thee as thou hast bidden me; and but so, as not to behold thee, after thy gracious revelation, were my sin. Let me see, even in this distance, some glimmering of thy divine Power, Wisdom, Justice, Mercy, Truth, Providence; and let me bless and adore thee, in what I see.[8]

Similarly Richard Baxter cries out of a heart of need:

> But, ah! my Lord, thy feast is nothing to me without an appetite; thou must give a stomach as well as meat.

Thou hast set the dainties of heaven before me, but alas! I am blind, and cannot see them; I am sick, and cannot relish them; I am so benumbed, that I cannot put forth a hand to take them. What is the glory of sun and moon to a clod of earth? Thou knowest I need thy subjective grace, as well as thine objective, and that thy work upon mine own distempered soul, is not the smallest part of my salvation; I therefore humbly beg this grace, that as thou hast opened heaven unto me in thy blessed work, so thou wouldest open mine eyes to see it, and my heart to affect it; else heaven will be no heaven to me. Awake, therefore, O thou Spirit of life, and breathe upon thy graces in me; blow upon the garden of my heart, that the spices thereof may flow out. Let my Beloved come into his garden, and eat his pleasant fruits; (Cant. 4:16); and take me by the hand, and lift me up from the earth thyself; that I may fetch one walk in the garden of glory, and see by faith what thou hast laid up for them that love thee and wait for thee.[9]

Our continuous relationship to heaven, even while we are here on earth, is set forth in our Lord's words reminding us that we who belong to Him have our names written in heaven (Luke 10:20). The hope that sustains us is laid up for us in heaven (Col. 1:5). The writer to the Hebrews speaks of believers as "partakers of a heavenly calling" (3:1), and in the difficult passage we have discussed elsewhere he speaks of those who have "tasted of the heavenly gift" (6:4).

One cannot truly believe that at death he will at once enter into heaven and the presence of the Lord without determining deep in his soul that he will make this life, by the grace of God, to be, as it were, a vestibule of heaven to come, even now partaking of the holiness of that eternal state.

NOTES

1. Adolph Saphir, *The Lord's Prayer* (4th ed.; London: 1872), pp. 215-16.
2. John Murray, *Commentary on Epistle of Paul to the Romans* (Grand Rapids: 1960), I, 115.
3. John Henry Jowett, *Life in the Heights* (New York: 1925), pp. 188-90.
4. G. Campbell Morgan, in *The Westminster Pulpit*, IX (London: 1914), 119-20.
5. H. P. Liddon, *University Sermons* (first series; New York: 1880), pp. 277, 280-81.
6. Alexander Smellie, *Ephesians*, in *The Speaker's Bible*, p. 20.
7. G. Stoeckhardt, *Commentary on St. Paul's Letter to the Ephesians* (St. Louis: 1952), p. 37. For an older discussion, see Robert S. Candlish, *The Epistle to the Ephesians Expounded* (Edinburgh: 1875), pp. 1-17.
8. Joseph Hall, "The Soul's Farewell to the Earth and Approaches to Heaven," *Bishop Hall's Works* (Oxford: 1837), VIII, 306.
9. Richard Baxter, *Practical Works* (London: 1830), XXIII, 423.

O the depth of the riches both of the wisdom and the knowledge of God! how unsearchable are his judgments, and his ways past tracing out!

—ROMANS 11:33

For we know in part.

—I CORINTHIANS 13:9

For now we see in a mirror, darkly; but then face to face: now I know in part; but then shall I know fully even as also I was fully known.

—I CORINTHIANS 13:12

Not that I have already obtained, or am already made perfect: but I press on, if so be that I may lay hold on that for which also I was laid hold on by Christ Jesus.

—PHILIPPIANS 3:12

9 The Intermediate State

However abundant the Scriptural data might be regarding the resurrection of believers and their life in heaven, the state of the soul between death and resurrection is rarely referred to in the Bible. This is no doubt due to the fact that the hope of the believer is not centered upon an intermediate state, which necessarily would be one of incompleteness, but upon the glorious fact of resurrection and eternal life in communion with the redeemed and in the presence of the Lord Jesus. Because this data is so fragmentary and, as it were, incidental, a number of theories have arisen in the Christian church regarding what is called the Intermediate State. There are actually seven different conceptions regarding the Intermediate State held by various groups of which only three might be called basically important; and of those three, most Evangelicals believe two are erroneous, namely, purgatory and the theory of soul sleep.

I have not felt it was necessary to discuss in this volume the doctrine of purgatory, for three reasons. In the first place, it does not have a Biblical foundation, and this volume confines itself strictly to Biblical data. In the second place, the idea of purgatory is rejected by practically all Protestant groups throughout the world, with the single exception of a few who are of the high church party among Anglicans. In the third place, if, as we shall see, the soul of the believer enters at once into the presence of the Lord upon death, then, of course, there is no place whatever for purgatory. Many arguments have been developed to disprove purgatory, but it is not necessary to repeat them here.

Some theologians of the early church, occasionally other groups in succeeding centuries, and today especially the Seventh-Day Adventists, have held and do hold the view that between death and the coming of Christ the soul sleeps, that is, it is without any consciousness whatever. Now it is true that "sleep" is used as a synonym for death in the New Testament. Our Lord said to His disciples, "Our friend Lazarus is fallen asleep; but I go, that I may awake him out of sleep" (John 11:11). And similarly, He said concerning the daughter of the ruler of the synagogue, "The damsel is not dead, but sleepeth" (Matt. 9:24). St. Luke says that when St. Stephen was martyred "he fell asleep" (Acts 7:60). The Apostle Paul twice uses this figure: "We all shall not sleep, but we shall all be changed" and "If we believe that Jesus died and rose again, even so them also that are fallen asleep in Jesus will God bring with him" (I Cor. 15:51; I Thess. 4:14; see also I Cor. 15:18). It is interesting to note that all occurrences of this word *sleep* are in relation to those in some way identified with the work of the Lord Jesus.

All occurrences in the New Testament of this concept of sleep in relation to death have in mind not the sleep of the soul but *the sleep of the body*. This is emphatically brought out in Matthew's account of the resurrection of some of the saints after our Lord's resurrection, in which He says, "Many bodies of the saints that had fallen asleep were raised" (Matt. 27:52). If the New Testament teaches that a believer at the time of death enters immediately into the presence of his Lord, then, of course, soul sleep is out of the question and this is the conviction held by almost the entire Protestant church.

May I quote here from a work of many years ago that excellently sets forth the true meaning of the sleep of the body following death:

> The leading idea, however, intended to be suggested by the figurative view of death before us, seems plainly to be, complete rest from labor, and freedom from suffering. "The life of the saint," as I have observed elsewhere, "is always in some degree, often in a high degree, a scene of toil and suffering, and the closing part of it is sometimes remarkably characterized by restlessness and agony. His passage over the sea of life is frequently stormy throughout, and sometimes becomes peculiarly tempestuous toward its termination. But at death, 'God maketh the storm a calm, and the waves thereof are still.' Then is the Christian mariner glad because he is quiet. His weather-beaten vessel is moored in a safe haven, never more to return to the tossing of the wasteful ocean. 'There the wicked cease from troubling, and there the weary are at rest.' The Christian 'enters into peace—he rests in his bed—each one that walketh in his uprightness.' His 'end' is, emphatically, 'peace.'"
>
> The figurative expression describes the state of departed Christians, as to both parts of their complex nature—their bodies and souls—now united—then disjoined—ultimately to be reunited.
>
> Their bodies are destitute of sense, and incapable of labor. They sleep in the dust, free from pain and fatigue themselves, and incapable of being the means of affecting, with weariness or suffering, the spirit with which they were once so closely conjoined.[1]

In the second century of our era, Justin Martyr summed up the view held at that time in his statement that "the souls of the pious remain in a better place, while those of the unjust and wicked are in a worse, waiting for the time of judgment. Thus some which have appeared worthy of God never die; but others are punished so long as God lets them to exist and to be punished."[2]

Irenaeus in his epochal work, *Against the Heresies*, develops this idea with greater detail:

> For as the Lord "went away in the midst of the shadow of death," where the souls of the dead were, yet afterwards arose in the body, and after the resurrection was taken up [into heaven], it is manifest that the souls of His disciples also, upon whose account the Lord underwent these things, shall go away into the invisible place allotted to them by God, and there remain until the resurrection, awaiting that event; then receiving their bodies, and rising in their entirety, that is bodily, just as the Lord arose, they shall come thus into the presence of God. . . . As our Master, therefore, did not at once depart, taking flight [to heaven], but awaited the time of His resurrection prescribed by the Father, which had been also shown forth through Jonas, and rising again after three days was taken up [to heaven]; so ought we also to await the time of our resurrection prescribed by God and foretold by the prophets, and so, rising, be taken up, as many as the Lord shall account worthy of this [privilege].[3]

Gregory the Great in his invaluable *Dialogues* set forth the view that is commonly held in the Roman Catholic Church: "It is clearer than daylight that the souls of the perfectly just are received into heavenly thrones as soon as they go forth from the bonds of the flesh. . . . They receive the joys of eternal recompence from the very moment of the dissolution of the flesh."

In his *Enchiridion*, Augustine says, and the passage had a tremendous influence over later views: "During the time

which intervenes between a man's death and the final resurrection, the soul dwells in a hidden retreat where it enjoys
rest or suffers affliction just in proportion to the merit it has
earned by the life which it led on earth." While Augustine
taught that martyrs at once see God face to face, at the time
of death, here he seems to imply a sort of purgatory. Yet as
a recent authority on Augustine's teaching has said, "In no
passage in all his works does St. Augustine explicitly teach
that man cannot see God face to face until after the restoration of the body."[4]

Luther was never very clear in his teachings concerning
the intermediate state. On one occasion in referring to the
use of the word *sleep* in relation to the child of the ruler and
Lazarus, Luther enigmatically said, "Death and grave mean
nothing more than that God neatly lays you as a child in His
cradle or soft little bed where you sweetly sleep until the
day of judgment." A recent scholar has rightly said that how
sleep is to be conceived by Luther "whether unconscious or
in some way consciously expectant remains vague in his writings; likewise it is not clear whether the souls of the pious
sleep in the grave with the body or whether carried aloft by
angels they already rest in the bosom of God in heaven. But
Luther does not mean that the soul lives while the body is
dead."[5]

Calvin, on I Corinthians 13:7, sanely remarks: "Although
we attain the full vision only on the day of the Lord's appearing, yet already in death which releases our soul from
the fetters of the flesh, we are now drawn nearer to the vision
of God." Enlarging upon this, Calvin in a lesser known
treatise says:

> But even though departed souls are conscious they still
> lack their consummate glory . . . for our blessedness is
> always at stake until that day which will finally terminate
> our course; thus it is a question of holding in view the

ultimate glory of the elect and the goal of all our hopes—
that day when all will be fulfilled. For we are all agreed
that there can be no fulfilment of blessedness and glory
unless we are perfectly united with God. To that end we
all aspire and hasten, to that all the texts and promises
of God point us.[6]

Even in the Solomonic period of Israel's history, we have
a hint of what we are unfolding here, found at the end of the
book of Ecclesiastes: "The dust returneth to the earth as it
was, and the spirit returneth unto God who gave it" (12:7).
In general, the words of our Lord "Whosoever liveth and
believeth on me shall never die" (John 11:26) would certainly
seem to contradict any idea of soul sleep. Closely related to
this are our Lord's words in answer to the Sadducees regarding the resurrection: "But as touching the resurrection of the
dead, have ye not read that which was spoken unto you by
God, saying, I am the God of Abraham, and the God of
Isaac, and the God of Jacob? God is not *the God* of the dead,
but of the living" (Matt. 22:31-32). Nothing else can be
drawn from our Lord's words to the thief on the cross, "Verily
I say unto thee, today shalt thou be with me in Paradise"
(Luke 23:43), than that the soul upon death enters into the
presence of the Lord. When our Lord said to the Father in
glory, "Father, into thy hands I commend my spirit: and
having said this, he gave up the ghost" (Luke 23:46; Matt.
27:50), it is impossible to interpret this in any other way
than what the text clearly implies, that while the body of
Jesus was sleeping in the tomb of Joseph of Arimathea, His
spirit went to God. This was possibly the belief of St.
Stephen who, as he died, cried, "Lord Jesus, receive my
spirit" (Acts 7:59). Most would agree that Dr. Ryder Smith
is correct in stating that when our Lord promised Peter that
he would "follow him afterwards" (John 13:36) "this does
not mean that Peter will meet Christ at the Parousia, for this

is not 'following,' but as soon as he is martyred (John 21:28, 29)." Professor Smith goes on to say that in the promise regarding the many mansions of John 14:2, 4, "Jesus does not mean He will prepare a place for the disciples after the Parousia, but that He was going away to do this *now*."[7]

Surely the idea that the soul goes immediately into the presence of the Lord upon death is implied in the famous words of the apostle: "But I am in a strait betwixt the two, having the desire to depart and be with Christ; for it is very far better: yet to abide in the flesh is more needful for your sake" (Phil. 1:23-24). Some of the very words used in the New Testament imply the conscious continuance of the soul after death has separated it from the body. Those appearing to our Lord on the mount of transfiguration spoke to Christ concerning His decease (Luke 9:31). The Greek word used here, *exodos*, is also used by the Apostle Peter, referring to his coming death (II Peter 1:15). The word is used of the actual exodus of the children of Israel from Egypt (Heb. 11:22). They certainly did not go into a state of slumber when they entered into the wilderness of Sinai. When the Apostle Paul says that the time of his departure has come (II Tim. 4:6), he cannot possibly mean the death of entering into sleep. Twice in the New Testament, death is referred to as a dissolution of the body, indicated by the word *tabernacle* (II Cor. 5:1; II Peter 1:13-14). But there is nothing here about the sleeping of the soul.

We cannot of course attempt a fairly comprehensive study of what is known as the intermediate state without giving very careful attention to a passage of the Apostle Paul in his second letter to the Corinthians that probably has had more different interpretations than any other extended eschatological passage in all of Paul's writings. After speaking of having been in a state of danger, perplexed but not despairing, smitten down but not destroyed, bearing about in the body the dying of Jesus, he was nevertheless fully assured that God who "raised up the Lord Jesus shall raise up us also with Jesus, and shall present us with you." He then concludes with one of his most glorious utterances: "Wherefore we faint not; but though our outward man is decaying, yet our inward man is renewed day by day. For our light affliction, which is for the moment, worketh for us more and more exceedingly an eternal weight of glory; while we look not at the things which are seen, but at the things which are not seen: for the things which are seen are temporal; but the things which are not seen are eternal" (II Cor. 4:16-18). It is in this context that we find this passage on the intermediate state, if it is such, concerning which so many interpretations have been offered. "For we know that if the earthly house of our tabernacle be dissolved, we have a building from God, a house not made with hands, eternal, in the heavens. For verily in this we groan, longing to be clothed upon with our habitation which is from heaven: if so be that being clothed we shall not be found naked. For indeed we that are in this tabernacle do groan, being burdened; not for that we would be unclothed, but that we would be clothed upon, that what is mortal may be swallowed up of life. Now he that wrought us for this very thing is God, who gave unto us the earnest of the Spirit" (II Cor. 5:1-5).

Fundamentally the apostle is certainly talking about death. He is emphasizing the matter of a body in relation to death. He speaks of the body he was in as "the earthly house of our tabernacle" in which we groan (repeated twice). He then speaks about another "building from God, a house not made with hands, eternal, in the heavens." The question is To what period in the future is Paul referring when he talks about this heavenly body which we will receive? He shrinks from the idea of his soul living through a period of, as it were, nakedness, without an enveloping body. Of the numerous interpretations of this passage, two may be dismissed with scarcely any discussion. Careful exegete as he was, the great Calvin said that the new garment which Paul is speaking of here is the righteousness of Christ, with which, of course, elsewhere we are clothed. But this is a view that has won very, very few supporters, and certainly it is not evident. The text must be strained to allow for any such interpretation. Closely related to this is the view of some that this is the garment which is raised at baptism when we "put on the new man, that after God hath been created in righteousness and holiness of truth" (Eph. 4:24). Even in the fourth century this view was held by some, but here once again the death Paul is speaking of in this Corinthian passage is not death to sin but the death to the body.

Lenski, in a long discussion of this passage, when, with unjustified bitterness and sarcasm he speaks of all commentators who hold views different from his, says that Paul is simply referring here to an earthly *existence* and a heavenly *existence*. "The old earthly life and mode of existence is taken down and folded away like a tent; the new heavenly life and existence is put on like a glory-garment." This new life was given to us at the time of our new birth and "at our death will swallow up our earthly existence and will leave nothing but itself." Here, like others, Lenski ignores the clear teaching of this passage that it has definite relationship to the death of the body; the Christian's body does not die at the time of regeneration. Dr. Charles Hodge, whose commentary on Second Corinthians is one of the very best, and who can generally be depended upon for careful exegesis, devotes twelve pages to developing a theory that almost no one today would accept, and that is that the house not made with hands, which the apostle knows some day will be his, is nothing less than heaven itself. It is true that the mansions which Christ has gone to prepare for His people are in

heaven, but that is not identical with saying that heaven itself is this body made without hands. "A mansion in heaven
into which believers enter as soon as their earthly tabernacle
is destroyed . . . the soul when it leaves its earthly tabernacle will not be lost in immensity nor driven away houseless
and homeless, but will find a house and home in heaven."[8]
It should be noted that Hodge says nothing here about the
resurrection body still to come which, of course, he certainly
believes is the ultimate destiny of the Christian. Most commentators take the verb translated "we have" as a futuristic
present "simply equivalent to there awaits us as a sure possession" this future body of glory. This would be the view of
the author of this volume. The sensible interpretation with
which the greater number of commentators would agree is
that set forth by the late Professor J. E. McFadyen:

> The earthly body shares the frailty and temporariness
> of the *tent,* the heavenly body partakes of the stability
> and permanence of a *building,* especially as it is a build-
> ing whose maker is God. The contrast recalls that be-
> tween the tent and the city in Hebrews 11:9, 10. The
> *house* to which Paul looks forward is not heaven itself,
> it is *in* heaven: it is the heavenly body *not made with
> hands.* The same epithet could also be fairly applied to
> the natural body, as this too is from God (1 Corinthians
> 12:24); but the resurrection body is divine in a special
> sense (cf. 1 Corinthians 15:38), and the epithet here is
> something like our "supernatural." This body is *eternal,*
> the tent-body *upon the earth* is transient, dissolved at
> death. . . . One thing is certain, Paul distinctly contem-
> plates the possibility of his own death before the coming
> of Christ. He longs indeed to be among those who will
> not die but he changed (1 Corinthians 15:51); but recent
> experience has brought him so close to death (2 Corin-
> thians 1:8), that he feels that his "daily deliverance unto

death for Jesus' sake" (4:11) may well issue in death itself.[9]

One more view needs to be mentioned, and that is that Paul is not only referring to a body to be given him after death, but actually he is implying here that he will have a body before his resurrection body, that is, a temporary and intermediate body. This is the view held in a former generation by Beyschlag and, more recently, by the late Dr. Lewis Sperry Chafer, who gives it as his view that "lest the believer at death should be bodiless or disembodied, there is provided a body from heaven which may serve the believer until the resurrection, when he receives his body from the grave. That provided body will be heavenly in character."[10] This view also has not been commonly accepted, and if there is an intermediate body, such as is here suggested, it is something about which all the rest of the Scriptures are absolutely silent.

Whatever be the interpretation of this Corinthian passage, we would repeat that the church throughout the ages normally has held the view that the soul at the time of death enters into the presence of the Lord. St. Gregory the Great, to go back to the time of the church Fathers, uttered what the entire church of his time would have agreed to: "It is clearer than daylight that the souls of the perfectly just are received into heavenly thrones as soon as they go forth from the bonds of the flesh."[11] To this later he adds a corollary: "They receive the joys of eternal recompense from the very moment of the dissolution of the flesh." The well-known statement of the *Westminster Confession of Faith* (chap. XXXII) reads as follows:

The bodies of men after death return to dust, and see corruption; but their souls, (which neither die nor sleep,) having an immortal subsistence, immediately return to God who gave them. The souls of the righteous, being then made perfect in holiness, are received into the highest heavens, where they behold the face of God in light and glory, waiting for the full redemption of their bodies; and the souls of the wicked are cast into hell, where they remain in torments and utter darkness, reserved to the judgment of the great day. Besides these two places for souls separated from their bodies, the Scripture acknowledgeth none.

In reference to the Confession of Faith, one of the most important commentaries on this precious document, that by Professor A. A. Hodge, has a statement that many would not quite agree with, that is, not even Calvin: "The souls of believers are at their death made perfect in holiness . . . and are immediately introduced into the presence of Christ, and continue to enjoy bright revelations of God and the society of the holy angels."[12] Nearly all would agree with each phrase of this statement except that, upon death, entering into the presence of Christ, the souls of believers "are made perfect in holiness." Concerning this, there is no specific statement in Scripture.

Paul, in bringing this second letter to a conclusion, gives us a rare insight into an unusual spiritual experience which had been granted to him a few years after his conversion. This is the passage: "I must needs glory, though it is not expedient; but I will come to visions and revelations of the Lord. I know a man in Christ, fourteen years ago (whether in the body, I know not; or whether out of the body, I know not; God knoweth), such a one caught up even to the third heaven. And I know such a man (whether in the body, or apart from the body, I know not; God knoweth), how that he was caught up into Paradise, and heard unspeakable words, which it is not lawful for a man to utter" (II Cor.

12:1-4). The late Professor McFadyen begins his interpretation of this passage with words worth repeating:

> The story is told with a certain solemn and rhythmic repetition, and curiously enough, Paul speaks of himself in the third person, suggesting that his part in the matter was purely passive. It was as if the man who enjoyed that unutterable experience could not be himself, the Paul who was so acutely conscious of his weakness.[13]

We have here two expressions in relation to the environments to which Paul was introduced, "the third heaven" and "Paradise." Professor Denney reminds us that the word here translated "even to" (*heos*) "suggests that an impression of vast spaces traversed remained on the apostle's mind."[14] There are two different views regarding these two terms, "the third heaven" and "Paradise." Some, such as Waite and Denney, believe that there are two stages of a translation referred to here. First, Paul was caught up to the third heaven and then beyond that into Paradise. But normally, and this is the view we would take here, these terms in this passage both refer to the same environment. Frequently in non-Biblical literature, and especially in Jewish apocryphal literature, the idea of seven heavens is often expressed, but this is not a Biblical term. In fact, this is the only place in the Scriptures where we find the phrase "the third heaven," which must mean the heaven of heavens, the abode of God. As an authority on the literature of the first century has remarked, "For a triple division of the heavens, we look in vain in contemporary Jewish thought. Such a division appears to have been the creation of the Christian Fathers and to have been deduced from this passage of Second Corinthians."

I myself believe, following Hodge, McFadyen, Hughes and other commentators, that Paul is here referring to one single experience. As Professor Denney has aptly said:

It was the most sacred privilege and honour he had ever known; it was among his strongest sources of inspiration; it had a powerful tendency to generate spiritual pride; and it had its accompaniment, and its counter-weight, in his sharpest trial. The world knows little of its greatest men; perhaps we very rarely know what are the great things in the lives even of the people who are round about us. Paul had kept silence about this sublime experience for fourteen years; and no man had ever guessed it; it had been a secret between the Lord and His disciple; and they only, who were in the secret, could rightly interpret all that depended upon it. There is a kind of profanity in forcing the heart to show itself too far, in compelling a man to speak about, even though he does not divulge, the things that it is not lawful to utter. The Corinthians had put this profane compulsion on the Apostle; but though he yields to it, it is in a way which keeps clear of the profanity.[15]

What these "unspeakable words which it is not lawful for a man to utter" might have been, we do not know. It is unprofitable to discuss what possible language this may have been in. Certainly Paul understood the words that were spoken to him and he means by this statement that he must not repeat them to the Corinthian church or apparently to anyone else. There is no hint in any of Paul's later letters as to what might have been the content of this revelation.

Both in regard to the subject we are here discussing and all matters pertaining to the life to come, I like the words of Calvin: "It is foolish and presumptuous to institute deeper investigation about unknown things which God has not permitted us to know. . . . So let us be content with the limits which God has prescribed." On the concluding statement of I Corinthians 13, Calvin wisely says the apostle intentionally gives no detailed information about the state of souls after

death because it would not help our piety to know anything
about it.

NOTES

1. John Brown, *The Dead in Christ. Their State: Present and Future* (New
   York: 1885), pp. 35-38.
2. Justin Martyr, *Dialogue with Trypho,* chap. V.
3. Irenaeus, *Against the Heresies,* Book V, chap. 31.
4. Augustine, *Enchiridion,* p. 109.
5. D. L. Lehy, *St. Augustine on Eternal Life* (London: n.d.), pp. 114-16.
6. John Calvin, *Commentary on the Epistles of Paul the Apostle to the
   Corinthians* (Edinburgh: 1849), II, 218.
7. C. Ryder Smith, *The Bible Doctrine of the Hereafter* (London: 1958),
   p. 169.
8. Charles Hodge, *An Exposition of the Second Epistle to the Corinthians*
   (New York: 1860), pp. 110-12.
9. J. E. McFadyen, *The Interpreter's Commentary on the Epistles to the
   Corinthians* (London: 1911), pp. 304-5.
10. Lewis Sperry Chafer, "Populating the Third Heaven," *Bibliotheca
    Sacra* (1951), CVIII, 147.
11. St. Gregory the Great, *Dialogues,* IV, 26.
12. A. A. Hodge, *The Confession of Faith, A Handbook of Christian Doc-
    trine* (New York: 1869), p. 381. I thought this matter of what happens
    to believers at the time of death as set forth in the *Shorter Catechism,*
    questions 37 and 38, deserved a further consideration, and I am tak-
    ing the liberty of quoting from a work on the Shorter Catechism of
    a century ago that was extensively used:
    "In the souls of believers at death, perfection appears in the follow-
    ing respects: They feel themselves at liberty among the spirits of just
    men made perfect; they are delivered from sin, and from all the enemies
    with which they were surrounded in this world; they feel no more pain
    from the commission of sin; they are no longer vexed with the filthy com-
    munication of the wicked; they have now arrived at the full stature of
    perfection in Christ Jesus; they have now reached the summit of holiness
    and perfection; they are now perfect as God is perfect, and pure as he
    is pure; in a word, they are now the image of Jehovah, and conformed
    to Jesus, who is 'the image of the invisible God.' . . . They shall be
    made perfectly blessed, or they shall be completely delivered from all
    sin and misery, and fully possessed of all happiness. Blessedness con-
    sists in freedom from sin and sorrow, from suffering and temptation,
    and from all evil whatever. But there can be no freedom from these
    things till death; nor even at death are believers perfectly blessed, for
    before this can take place, the soul and the body must be united; and
    when these are united, they shall be fully satisfied. 'When Christ, who
    is their life, shall appear, then shall they also appear with him in glory.'
    —Col. 3:4" (Alexander Smith Patterson, *A Concise System of Theology*
    [Edinburgh: 1854], pp. 147, 151).
    Also some worthwhile words from Alexander Whyte:
    "Nor are we without actual examples in Scripture of great and sudden
    changes wrought in the spiritual state of men by the power and grace
    of God analogous, at least, to what is here promised to believers at their
    death. The immense and immediate transformation that the disciples
    underwent on the day of Pentecost, was, if not equal, at least analogous

and initial to that consummating change they underwent at the hour of death. Paul also underwent a more radical change at the gate of Damascus than even that which he passed through at his abundant entrance into glory, 'when, like a northern midnight, the rose of evening became suddenly and silently the rose of dawn.' At the same time there is room both in Scripture and Protestant doctrine for the observation of Calvin: 'Although those who have been freed from the mortal body do no longer contend with the lusts of the flesh, and are, as the expression is, beyond the reach of a single dart, yet there will be no absurdity in speaking of them as in the way of advancement, inasmuch as they have not yet reached the point at which they aspire—they do not enjoy the felicity and glory which they have hoped for, and, in fine, the day has not yet shone which is to discover the treasures which lie hid in hope. And in truth, when hope is spoken of, our eyes must always be directed forward to a blessed resurrection as the great object in view'" (Alexander Whyte, *Handbooks for Bible Classes and Private Students. The Shorter Catechism* [Edinburgh: n.d.], p. 96).

13. McFadyen, *op. cit.*, p. 408.
14. James Denney, *The Second Epistle to the Corinthians* (New York: 1903), p. 348.
15. Denney, *ibid.*, p. 350.

10 Our Wealth in Heaven: By Inheritance and by Reward

As, in our earthly life, most wealth comes to men and women either by inheritance or as a result of their own labor, so also in the New Testament, the believer's wealth in the life to come is set forth in some passages as a reward for faithful Christian service here on earth and, in other passages as ours, by straight inheritance, which means a gift. Our Lord Himself refers to both of these aspects of a wealthy life in glory. We might consider the subject of rewards first, reminding ourselves of the fundamental principle set forth in many portions of the Word of God that "the laborer is worthy of his hire" (I Tim. 5:18). The teachings of our Lord regarding rewards are set forth in direct statements concerning such future conditions and in four of our Lord's famous parables.

REWARDS

In Jesus' direct statements concerning reward, it is significant that in none of them does He speak of faithfulness in our service, which is a prominent theme in the parables, as we shall see, but He specifically mentions those experiences of Christian believers which, when faithfully endured or

171

carried out, will receive a reward in glory. The first is from the Beatitudes regarding the reward which will be granted to those who will be reproached, persecuted and falsely spoken against. The text is worth repeating: "Blessed are they that have been persecuted for righteousness' sake: for theirs is the kingdom of heaven. Blessed are ye when *men* shall reproach you, and persecute you, and say all manner of evil against you falsely, for my sake. Rejoice, and be exceeding glad: for great is your reward in heaven: for so persecuted they the prophets that were before you" (Matt. 5:10-12; see also Luke 6:23). While there is no actual reference to heaven in the next statement of our Lord, it seems to me that the text clearly refers not to a reward in this life, but to one in the life to come, two altogether different situations being presented in two successive verses: "He that receiveth a prophet in the name of a prophet shall receive a prophet's reward: and he that receiveth a righteous man in the name of a righteous man shall receive a righteous man's reward. And whosoever shall give to drink unto one of these little ones a cup of cold water only, in the name of a disciple, verily I say unto you he shall in no wise lose his reward" (Matt. 10:41-42; see also Mark 9:41). A third reference to conduct terminating in reward is found exclusively in Luke's gospel: "But love your enemies, and do *them* good, and lend, never despairing; and your reward shall be great, and ye shall be sons of the Most High: for he is kind toward the unthankful and evil" (6:35). A final direct statement regarding rewards was uttered toward the very end of our Lord's ministry and is found in all three Synoptic Gospels: "And Jesus said unto them, Verily I say unto you, that ye who have followed me, in the regeneration when the Son of man shall sit on the throne of his glory, ye also shall sit upon twelve thrones, judging the twelve tribes of Israel. And every one that hath left houses, or brethren, or sisters, or father, or mother, or children, or lands, for my name's sake, shall receive a hundredfold, and shall inherit eternal life" (Matt. 19:28-29; see also Mark 10:29-30; Luke 18:29-30). In the Matthew passage a time phrase appears not found in the Mark and Luke accounts: "Ye who have followed me, in the regeneration." Whatever this particular statement might mean, and there have been a great many differences of opinion, because it is not found in the other two Synoptic Gospels, I would think that the principle of reward here—receiving a hundredfold—is relevant for every age and is a privilege offered to every believer.

There is an elaborate setting forth of the doctrine of rewards in four of the better known parables of our Lord: in that of the faithful and wise steward (Luke 12:41-47), also repeated later in His ministry (Matt. 24:45-51); in the parable of the pounds (Luke 19:11-28); in the parable of the laborers in the vineyard (Matt. 20:1-16); and the famous parable of the talents (Matt. 25:14-30). The rewards that are to be bestowed as set forth in these parables are all assigned to the time of our Lord's return. In the first we have the phrase "his lord when he cometh," in the second, "trade till I come," and in the fourth, "after a long time the Lord of those servants cometh," while in the parable of the laborers in the vineyard, this truth is only assumed. Jesus said that the faithful and wise steward "he will set over all that he hath"; to the one who faithfully trades with what his lord placed in his hands He will say, "Well done, thou good servant: because thou hast been faithful in a very little, have thou authority over ten cities." In the parable of the talents, the reward is stated in similar terms: "Well done, good and faithful servant: thou hast been faithful over a few things, I will set thee over many things," with this additional statement, "enter thou into the joy of thy Lord."

Our Lord Himself refers to the acquisition of riches for our

possessions in heaven on three occasions. The most famous
is that which occurs in the midst of the Sermon on the
Mount: "Lay not up for yourselves treasures upon the earth,
where moth and rust consume, and where thieves break
through and steal: but lay up for yourselves treasures in
heaven, where neither moth nor rust doth consume, and
where thieves do not break through nor steal: for where thy
treasure is, there will thy heart be also" (Matt. 6:19-21; see
also Mark 10:21). Christ pressed home the same truth in a
later exhortation recorded only by St. Luke. "Sell that which
ye have, and give alms; make for yourselves purses which
wax not old, a treasure in the heavens that faileth not, where
no thief draweth near, neither moth destroyeth. For where
your treasure is, there will your heart be also" (Luke 12:33-
34). It is of interest to note that the word here translated
"treasure" (*thesauros*) meaning "the place in which goods
and precious things are collected and laid up; and hence, a
casket or coffer; and then the things laid up in a treasury"
(Thayer), is the word found in Matthew's account of the
visit of the wise men who "opening their treasures . . . offered
unto him gifts" (Matt. 2:11), and twice in the Gospels in our
Lord's profound teaching regarding the need for storing up
treasures in our own hearts (Matt. 12:35; 13:52; Luke 6:45).
These passages regarding riches in heaven have rarely been
considered with adequate detail by commentators. An exception in this case is Lenski, who on the Lucan passage has
said:

> We cannot place the "purses that age not" in heaven,
> or identify their contents with the "treasure unfailing in
> the heavens." While one verb is used for both, this verb
> merely combines what the disciples are to do with their
> earthly wealth and what they are to secure at the same
> time in heaven. By the way the rich fool in the parable
> treated his wealth he made himself a purse that soon

grew old, worn, with holes, out of which all his wealth dropped. . . . The figure of the purse refers to the way they view and treat their earthly wealth, be it small or great. Instead of becoming its slave, they remain its master and apply it as their divine Master bids them. So it is not lost but made to serve them in their calling as disciples on the way to heaven.

Strange confusion results when the "treasure" is placed in the "purses," the latter in heaven like the former, and the "treasure" is turned into merit of some kind acquired by the disciples in almsgiving or in voluntary poverty. This treasure never gives out, as did that of the rich fool "that night." No thief can even get near it, as is the case with earthly treasures; no moth can spoil it, as was the case even with Solomon's fine garments. The moth is added because of v. 27-28. This marvelous treasure is the one we are bidden to seek in v. 31. Not that the verb means that we are to create this treasure; the verb is used in a zeugmatic way for both "purses" and "treasure." We make for ourselves a treasure in heaven, when our heart is in the Kingdom, yea, in heaven, to which grace leads.[1]

Our Lord presses home the truth expressed in these two brief sermons, in His famous interview with the rich ruler. When, upon coming to Christ, actually kneeling to Him and calling Him "Good teacher," he asked what he might do to inherit eternal life, Jesus first emphasized the necessity of obeying the ten great commandments, to which the young man immediately replied, "All these things have I observed from my youth." It was then that our Lord made the statement which reveals the condition of this young man's heart and the impossibility of his receiving eternal life as long as this condition prevailed: "And Jesus looking upon him loved him, and said unto him, One thing thou lackest: go, sell whatsoever thou hast, and give to the poor, and thou shalt have treasure in heaven: and come, follow me" (Mark 10:21). Once again I would turn to Lenski for an adequate understanding of this passage:

> Abandoning what was hitherto his heart's treasure is only the negative side; the positive side is that now "he shall have treasure in heaven," with his whole heart fixed on that. The future "shall have" means from the moment on when his heart is separated from the earthly treasure. It is the grossest perversion of this word of Jesus to make it mean that by selling and giving away his earthly wealth the man would receive as a reward this treasure in heaven. This treasure is the unmerited grace and pardon of God. For the other side of the one thing the man yet lacked, the one that always goes together with contrition, is *the true and saving faith in Christ*. That is why Jesus adds to the selling and giving away the Gospel call to come and follow him. This would be the evidence of true faith in him. The adverb "hither," is sometimes almost a verb, and is used with or without an imperative, here with the present imperative, for continuous following.[2]

In the well-known powerful parable regarding the foolish rich man who in a miserly manner was living exclusively for the acquisition of more and more property and wealth, Jesus declared that his inadequate preparation for the hour of death summed up all of his plans as total foolishness. Then our Lord adds, "So is he that layeth up treasure for himself, and is not rich toward God" (Luke 12:21). On this, once again, Lenski has the best comment:

> Our versions translate "toward God," trying to make *eis* mean direction or even motion. This blurs the sense and often leads to false interpretations. This *eis* is static, as all the newer grammars show. Any motion must be in the verb, it is never in the preposition, and there is neither direction or motion in being rich. This abolishes the

notion of wealth devoted to (toward) God, or of spiritual excellences held out "toward" God for him to approve. To be rich in God is to have the wealth that is found for us in God. This wealth consists of pardon, peace, and salvation in union with God, and "in God" signifies faith. He is rich in God who has the saving gifts which God gives him and holds them with gratitude by faith as his own. Such a man is truly rich, however little he may have of earthly goods; nor will earthly possessions interfere with his true wealth since he will treat this like Abraham, David, and others did, making it wholly subservient to God.

INHERITANCE

Not only did our Lord speak about rewards for faithful service and, apart from rewards, the assurance of riches in heaven, but He also talked about inheritance in relation to the *future* of believers. In a volume on Heaven, it is probably not necessary to make any comment on the beatitude which tells us that the meek shall inherit the earth (Matt. 5:5). We have already seen in a preceding paragraph the promise of Christ concluding with the phrase "shall inherit eternal life." Toward the end of the great Olivet Discourse, in speaking of the final judgment of those whom He characterized as sheep, Christ declared that at the end of the age, when He returns, "shall the King say unto them on his right hand, Come, ye blessed of my Father, inherit the kingdom prepared for you from the foundation of the world" (Matt. 25:34; cf. James 2:5).

Finally, we ought not to wholly pass by a rather enigmatical utterance of Christ, found exclusively in Luke's gospel in the parable of the unrighteous steward: "Make to yourselves friends by means of the mammon of unrighteousness; that, when it shall fail, they may receive you into the eternal tabernacles" (Luke 16:9). The only satisfactory statement I have ever seen on this particular verse is in Dr. G. Campbell Morgan's superb volume on Luke's gospel, and his comment must suffice for our present purpose:

> Money, which, in itself, is a non-moral thing, can be used to blast or bless. In any case, there comes a day when it fails. Sixty seconds after a man is dead he cannot sign a check! All a man can do is to leave his money behind him, for other people to quarrel over, which they mostly do. Personally, I am a strong believer in the idea that it is a poor thing to hang on to money until we are dead. Make use of it now. How? Make friends by means of it, and when it fails, in that very moment, when your hand is no longer able to sign any check, they, the friends you made, shall greet you in the eternal tabernacles. Put upon your money the measurement, not of your own generation, as these men are doing. It fails, when your generation ends. They are wiser "in their generation." Mark the limit of it. They are clever for today, and fools for ever. You make such use of your money, said Jesus, that when it fails, they shall receive you.
>
> How many investments have we made of that kind? There was a hymn which we used to sing a good deal,
>
> "Will any one then at the beautiful gate,
> Be waiting and watching for me?"
>
> Are there any who have gone on, who are likely to want to see us when we arrive, because of the use we made on their behalf of our wealth? Thus the measurements of the undying ages are placed by Jesus upon the transactions of today, in the market-place, or with our banking account.[3]

Before an examination of the rich data in the New Testament Epistles regarding the Christian's *inheritance*, it might be advantageous if we first of all reminded ourselves of what an inheritance really is. The Greek word translated "inheritance" and, in its verbal form, "inherit," occurs 285 times in the Greek version of the Old Testament, and plays a great part in the concept of the relationship of Israel to Jehovah. It is used normally in reference to a possession, an inheritance, as in Numbers 24:18; 27:7; Deuteronomy 3:20. Palestine is called a possession of the Lord (Jer. 2:7). Significantly, God is sometimes referred to as the inheritance or portion of the Levites (Num. 18:20; Joshua 13:14). The idea of Israel as the inheritance of God extends throughout the Old Testament from Deuteronomy 32:9 through the Prophets, as in Jeremiah 12:7 ff. and Micah 7:14. The finest definition of inheritance I have seen is in Westcott's superb note on Hebrews 6:12, which reads as follows:

> The dominant Biblical sense of inheritance is the enjoyment of a rightful title of that which is not the fruit of personal exertion. The heir being what he is in relation to others enters upon a possession which corresponds with his position. An inheritance answers to a position of privilege and describes a blessing conferred with absolute validity; and an heir is one who has authority to deal with, to administer a portion or a possession. The principle that "inheritance is by birth and not by gift" has a spiritual fulfillment. When God gives an inheritance it is because those to whom it is given stand by His grace in that filial relation which in this sense carries the gift.[4]

In that great doctrinal opening statement of the epistle to the Ephesians, after the enumeration of the amazing spiritual realities which are already ours through Christ, the apostle brings the passage to a close by telling us that our being sealed with the Holy Spirit of promise "is an earnest of our inheritance, unto the redemption of God's own possession" (Eph. 1:14). This is simply a reemphasis of the earlier statement that "in Christ we were made a heritage" (v. 11).

Negatively, toward the end of the epistle, St. Paul enumerates some of the characteristics of those unredeemed men who will not have "any inheritance in the kingdom of Christ and God" (5:5). In the Colossian epistle, this truth is twice set forth, first in the clause declaring that the Father has "made us meet to be partakers of the inheritance of the saints in light" (1:12) and in the more elaborate statement, "Whatsoever ye do, work heartily, as unto the Lord, and not unto men; knowing that from the Lord ye shall receive the recompense of the inheritance: ye serve the Lord Christ" (3:23-24).

This very theme is referred to by the Apostle Paul in his famous farewell to the Ephesian elders: "And now I commend you to God, and to the word of his grace, which is able to build *you* up, and to give *you* the inheritance among all them that are sanctified" (Acts 20:32). In the Galatian epistle, the apostle speaks of believers as "heirs according to promise" (3:29), but in the great eighth chapter of the Roman epistle, we have a more elaborate statement: "The Spirit himself beareth witness with our spirit, that we are children of God; and if children, then heirs; heirs of God, and joint-heirs with Christ; if so be that we suffer with *him*, that we may be also glorified with *him*" (vv. 16-17). The note of Tholuck quoted by Alford is especially helpful:

> It is by virtue of their substantial unity with the father, that the children come into participation of his possession. The Roman law regarded them as continuators of his personality. The *dignity* of the inheritance is shewn (1) by its being God's possession, (2) by its being the possession of the Firstborn of God. By the Roman law, the share of the firstborn was no greater than that of the other children,—and the N.T. sets forth this view, making the redeemed equal to Christ (ver. 29), and Christ's possessions, theirs; 1 Corinthians 3:21-23; John 17:22.

In the *joint-heirship* we must not bring out this point, that Christ is *the rightful Heir*, who shares His inheritance with the other children of God: it is as adoptive children that they get the inheritance, and Christ is so far only the means of it, as He gives them power to become sons of God, John 1:12.[5]

It is probably here that we should include Paul's two statements regarding rewards to be assigned to believers at the time of their being judged before the judgment seat of their Lord, not, of course, the judgment of the great white throne. In the Roman epistle he simply says, "We shall all stand before the judgment seat of God . . . so each one of us shall give account of himself to God." This is more elaborately set forth in Second Corinthians in the famous statement "Wherefore also we make it our aim, whether at home or absent, to be well-pleasing unto him. For we must all be made manifest before the judgment-seat of Christ; that each one may receive the things *done* in the body, according to what he hath done, whether *it be* good or bad" (5:9-10). The words of Chrysostom on this passage have been recognized down through the centuries as one of the most eloquent passages that the golden-mouthed orator ever wrote:

By saying these words, he both reviveth those who have done virtuously and are persecuted with those hopes, and maketh those who have fallen back more earnest by that fear. And he thus confirmed his words touching the resurrection of the body. "For surely," saith he, "that which hath ministered to the one and to the other shall not stand excluded from the recompenses: but along with the soul shall in the one case be punished, in the other crowned." But some of the heretics say, that it is another body that is raised. How so? tell me. Did one sin, and is another punished? Did one do virtuously, and is another crowned? And what will ye

answer to Paul, saying, "We would not be unclothed, but
clothed upon?" And how is that is mortal "swallowed
up of life?" For he said not, that the mortal or corruptible body should be swallowed up of the incorruptible
body; but that corruption [should be swallowed up] "of
life." For then this happeneth when the same body is
raised; but if, giving up that body, He should prepare
another, no longer is corruption swallowed up but continueth dominant. Therefore this is not so; but "this
corruptible," that is to say the body, "must put on incorruption." For the body is in a middle state, being at
present in this and hereafter to be in that; and for this
reason in this first, because it is impossible for the incorruption to be dissolved. "For neither doth corruption
inherit incorruption," saith he, (for how is it [then] incorruption?) but on the contrary, "corruption is swallowed up of life:" for this indeed survives the other, but
not the other this. For as wax is melted by fire but itself
doth not melt the fire: so also doth corruption melt and
vanish away under incorruption, but is never able itself
to get the better of incorruption.

Let us then hear the voice of Paul, saying, that "we
must stand at the judgment-seat of Christ;" and let us
picture to ourselves that court of justice, and imagine it
to be present now and the reckoning to be required. For
I will speak of it more at large. For Paul, seeing that he
was discoursing on affliction, and he had no mind to af-
flict them again, did not dwell on the subject; but having
in brief expressed its austerity, "Each one shall receive
according to what he hath done," he quickly passed on.
Let us then imagine it to be present now, and reckon each
one of us with his own conscience, and account the Judge
to be already present, and everything to be revealed and
brought forth. For we must not merely stand, but also
be manifested. Do ye not blush? Are ye not astonied?
But if now, when the reality is not yet present, but is
granted in supposition merely and imaged in thought;

if now [I say] we perish conscience-struck; what shall
we do when [it] shall arrive, when the whole world shall
be present, when angels and archangels, when ranks
upon ranks, and all hurrying at once, and some caught
up on the clouds, and an array full of trembling; when
there shall be the trumpets, one upon another, [when]
those unceasing voices?[6]

It is, however, in the epistle to the Hebrews that we have
the most frequent references to this theme, some in relation
to the patriarchs in times past, and some in relation to believers now and through the ages. At the beginning of the
epistle, the whole subject of inheritance is placed on a lofty
level by our being told that concerning Jesus Christ, God has
"appointed him heir of all things" (Heb. 1:2). Twice in the
sixth chapter of this epistle the author urges his readers to
avoid sluggish spirituality and instead to be "imitators of
them who through faith and patience inherit the promises."
Once again, with a slight variation, he speaks of believers as
"the heirs of the promise" (vv. 12, 17). Later in the same
epistle, he speaks of all who are followers of the Lord Jesus
as those who will "receive the promise of the eternal inheritance" (9:15). In the great roll call of the faithful, the
writer refers to Noah as one who became "the heir of righteousness according to faith" and immediately uses the same
concept in regard to Abraham who in journeying to Palestine
"obeyed to go out unto a place which he was to receive for an
inheritance" (11:7-8).

The word here translated "recompense of reward" is a com-
bination of two Greek words meaning riches and rewards,
misthapodosia, found nowhere else in the entire Greek Bible
but in this epistle, a word that "emphasizes the exact requital
of either good or evil by a sovereign judge."[7]

There is only one more passage which needs to be discussed here, found at the beginning of St. Peter's first epistle:

"Blessed *be* the God and Father of our Lord Jesus Christ, who according to his great mercy begat us again unto a living hope by the resurrection of Jesus Christ from the dead, unto an inheritance incorruptible, and undefiled, and that fadeth not away, reserved in heaven for you, who by the power of God are guarded through faith unto a salvation ready to be revealed in the last time" (1:3-5; see also a briefer reference in 3:9). All who have read widely in the classics of the Christian faith are unanimously agreed that probably the richest devotional commentary of modern times on this epistle is the one by Archbishop Robert Leighton, which was originally given as a series of discourses in the church of which he was minister from 1642 to 1653. I do not hesitate to give an extended quotation of this rich passage though I am quite thoroughly acquainted with the excellent commentaries that have appeared since:

> God is bountiful to all, gives to all men all that they have, health, riches, honour, strength, beauty, and wit, but these things He scatters (as it were) with an indifferent hand. Upon others He looks, as well as on His beloved children; but the *inheritance* is peculiarly *theirs*. Inheritance is convertible with sonship; Abraham gave gifts to Keturah's sons, and dismissed them, Genesis 25:5; but the inheritance was for the son of the promise. . . .
>
> While the children of God are childish and weak in faith, they are like some great heirs before they come to years of understanding; they consider not their Inheritance and what they are to come to, have not their spirits elevated to thoughts worthy of their estate, and their behaviour conformed to it; but as they grow up in years, they come, by little and little, to be sensible of those things, and the nearer they come to possession the more apprehensive they are of their quality, and of what doth answerably become them to do. And this is the duty of

such as are indeed heirs of glory;—to grow in the understanding and consideration of that which is prepared for them, and to suit themselves, as they are able, to those great hopes. This is what the Apostle St. Paul prays for, on behalf of his Ephesians, ch. 1. ver. 18, *The eyes of your understanding being enlightened, that ye may know what is the hope of His calling, and what the riches of the glory of His inheritance in the saints.* This would make them holy and heavenly, to *have their conversation in Heaven, from whence they look for a Saviour.* . . .

As it is *incorruptible*, it carries away the palm from all earthly possessions and inheritances; for all those epithets are intended to signify its opposition to the things of this world, and to show how far it excels them all; and in this comparative light we are to consider it. . . . We cannot tell you what it is, but we can say so far what it is not, as declare it is unspeakably above all the most excellent things of the inferior world and this present life. . . .

All possessions here are defiled and stained with many other defects and failings; still somewhat wanting, some damp on them or crack in them; fair houses, but sad cares flying about the gilded and ceiled roofs; stately and soft beds, and a full table, but a sickly body and queasy stomach; the fairest face has some mole or wart in it. All possessions are stained with sin, either in acquiring or in using them, and therefore they are called, *mammon of unrighteousness,* Luke 16:9. . . . Foul hands pollute all they touch; it is our sin that defiles what we possess; it is sin that burdens the whole creation, and presses groans out of the very frame of the world, Romans 8:22, *For we know, that the whole creation groaneth and travaileth in pain together until now.* This our leprosy defiles our houses, the very walls and floors, our meat and drink and all we touch, polluted when alone, and polluted in society, our meetings and conversations together being for the greatest part nothing but a commerce and interchange of sin and vanity. . . .

Then, as these earthly inheritances are stained with sin in their use, so, what grief, and strife, and contentions about obtaining or retaining them! Doth not the matter of possession, this same *meum* and *tuum,* divide many times the affections of those who are knit together in nature, or other strict ties, and prove the very apple of strife betwixt nearest friends?

If we trace great estates to their first original, how few will be found that owe not their beginning either to fraud, or rapine, or oppression! and the greatest empires and kingdoms in the world have had their foundations laid in blood. Are not these defiled inheritances? . . .

That fadeth not away. No spot of sin nor sorrow there; all pollution wiped away, and all tears with it; no envy nor strife; not as here among men, one supplanting another, one pleading and fighting against another, dividing this point of earth with fire and sword:—no, this Inheritance is not the less by division, by being parted amongst so many brethren; everyone hath it all, each his crown, and all agreeing in casting them down before His throne from whom they have received them, and in the harmony of His praises. . . .

As it is a rich and pleasant country where it lieth, it hath also this privilege, to be the only land of rest and peace, free from all possibility of invasion. There is no spoiling of it, and laying it waste, and defacing its beauty, by leading armies into it and making it the seat of war; no noise of drums or trumpets, no inundations of one people driving out another and sitting down in their possessions. In a word, as there is nothing there subject to decay of itself, so neither is it in danger of fraud or violence. When our Saviour speaks of this same happiness, in a like term, Matthew 6:20, what is here called an *inheritance,* is there called a *treasure.* He expresses the permanency of it by these two instances, that it *hath neither moth nor rust* in itself to *corrupt* it, nor can *thieves break through and steal* it. There is a worm at the root of all our enjoyment here, corrupting causes within themselves; and besides that, they are exposed to injury from without, which may deprive us of them. How many stately palaces, that have been possibly divers years in building, hath fire upon a very small beginning destroyed in a few hours! What great hopes of gain by traffic hath one tempest mocked and disappointed! How many who have thought their possessions very sure, yet have lost them by some trick of law, and others (as in time of war) been driven from them by the sword! Nothing free from all danger but this *Inheritance,* which is laid up in the hands of GOD, and kept in Heaven for us.[8]

This whole subject of rewards for the believer is one, I am afraid, rarely thought of by the ordinary Christian, or even the average student of the Scriptures. It is both a joyous and solemn theme. Some have said that the whole subject of rewards has in it an element of selfishness and personal gain, which is contrary to the mind of God, and they cannot be so interpreted so as to eliminate the basic concepts of the Lord for service. This is what the Lord intended, and His apostles as well. The late Mr. Walker, who has been quoted above, concludes his article on Reward with a bold statement with which the author of this book would wholly agree. "The idea of reward accompanies almost of necessity belief in a personal God. Viewed as the apostolic writers are taught by our Lord to view it, it is the loftiest and most potent incentive to holiness of life."

Let me conclude this chapter with some words of Dean Alford in a volume long forgotten, but still worth reading:

For the apostles constantly and persistently set before us the aiming at the Christian reward as their own motive, and as that which ought to be ours. Hear St. Paul saying that, if he preached the gospel as matter of duty only, it was the stewardship committed to him; but if freely and without pay, a reward, or wages, would be due to him. Hear him again, in expectation of his departure glorying in the certainty of his reward, "I have fought a good fight, I have finished my course, I have kept the faith: henceforth there is laid up for me a crown of righteousness, which the Lord the righteous Judge shall give me at that day: and not to me only, but to all them also that love His appearing." Listen to St. John, whom we are accustomed to regard as the most lofty and heavenly of all the apostles in his thoughts and motives. What does he say to his well-beloved Gaius? "Look to yourselves, that we lose not the things which we have wrought, but that we receive the full reward." Listen, again, to the writer of the Epistle to the Hebrews, that apostolic man, eloquent and mighty in the Scriptures, and hear him describing the very qualities and attributes of faith, that he who cometh to God must believe that He is, and that He is a rewarder of them that diligently seek Him, and saying of one of the first and brightest examples of faith, that he had respect unto the recompense of reward.[9]

NOTES

1. R. C. H. Lenski, *Interpretation of the Gospel of St. Luke* (Columbus, Ohio: 1944), pp. 440-41.
2. Lenski, *ibid.*, p. 276.
3. G. Campbell Morgan, *The Gospel of Luke* (New York: 1931), p. 186.
4. B. F. Westcott, *The Epistle to the Hebrews* (2d ed.; London: 1892), p. 168.
5. F. A. G. Tholuck, in Henry Alford, *The Greek Testament*, II (7th ed.; London: 1877), 392.
6. John Chrysostom, *Homilies on the Epistles of Paul to the Corinthians* (New York: 1889), pp. 328-29.
7. Dawson Walker, "Reward," in James Hastings, *Dictionary of the Apostolic Church*, II, 368.
8. Robert Leighton, *A Practical Commentary upon the First Epistle of St. Peter* (London: 1870), pp. 40-48. On this passage a comment of an American writer of a century ago is suggestive: "Now, nothing can

be more evident, as already stated, than that the inheritance here spoken of is one thing, and that Heaven is another. The inheritance is explicitly declared to be 'In Heaven.' They are as absolutely distinct the one from the other, as are the planets from the Heaven of infinite space in which they float. It would be an absurdity to speak of an inheritance as being 'in' an inheritance. On the other hand, in view of the doctrine of the intermediate state between death and the resurrection, where the believer, having 'died in faith' of the promised inheritance at the resurrection morn, and where he 'rests' in joyful expectation of its final conferment, it is perfectly consistent to speak of it as 'reserved in Heaven' for him.

"It follows, of course, that this inheritance, in its nature and properties, differs from the Heaven in which it is said to be, just as the orbs of the solar system differ from the aereal region in which they are suspended. Let it be observed, then, that in whatever consists the nature and properties of this inheritance which is the object of the believer's faith and hope, there must necessarily exist a *homogeneity* between them, and the nature and properties of man's resurrected corporeal being" (R. C. Shimeall, *The Unseen World* [New York: 1870], pp. 240-41.

9. Henry Alford, *The State of the Blessed Dead* (new ed.; London: 1870), pp. 67-71. Thomas Goodwin closes his once famous work, *On the Blessed State of Glory Which the Saints Possess After Death*, with an exhortation as relevant now as then: "And because it is probable, yea, and more than probable, that there are degrees of glory in heaven, that God will reward every one according to their works, do not only content yourselves to go to heaven, but endeavour to serve God more, that you may have great glory in heaven; be abundant in good works, hoard up good works, according to which glory shall be weighed to you in heaven. Let not pleasures hinder thee of the least degree of glory, for to have but one pearl added to thy crown is more than the whole world. Commit therefore no sin that might hinder your attaining of glory, for what though God pardon thy sin? Yet thou losest glory which thou mightest have gotten whilst thou wast committing the sin, the least shred of which glory transcends all the glory of the world" (*Works*, VII [Edinburgh: 1863], 464).

11 *Occupations of the Redeemed*
in Heaven

The Scriptures do not give us much specific data regarding the actual occupations of the redeemed in heaven, so that what we do have we must consider as particularly precious and important.

WORSHIP

Perhaps the first great and continuous activity for the redeemed will be worship of the triune God. Significantly, the entire opening part of Revelation 19, the same chapter in which we have the prophecy of the Battle of Armageddon, is devoted entirely (vv. 1-8) to a scene of worship in heaven:

> After these things I heard as it were a great voice of a great multitude in heaven, saying, Hallelujah; Salvation, and glory, and power, belong to our God: for true and righteous are his judgments; for he hath judged the great harlot, her that corrupted the earth with her fornication, and he hath avenged the blood of his servants at her hand. And a second time they say, Hallelujah. And her smoke goeth up for ever and ever. And the four and twenty elders and the four living creatures fell down

190

and worshipped God that sitteth on the throne, saying, Amen; Hallelujah. And a voice came forth from the throne, saying, Give praise to our God, all ye his servants, ye that fear him, the small and the great. And I heard as it were the voice of a great multitude, and as the voice of many waters, and as the voice of mighty thunders, saying, Hallelujah: for the Lord our God, the Almighty, reigneth. Let us rejoice and be exceeding glad, and let us give the glory unto him: for the marriage of the Lamb is come, and his wife hath made herself ready. And it was given unto her that she should array herself in fine linen, bright *and* pure: for the fine linen is the righteous acts of the saints.

No doubt, many of the well-known passages in the Psalms relating to the worship of God will have their perfect fulfillment in those days of eternal bliss (see Ps. 29:2; 95:6; 96:9; 132:7; Heb. 1:6).

Much of this worship will be conducted within the framework of music. The book of Revelation contains more songs than any other book in the Bible, with the exception, of course, of the Psalter—fourteen of them, all sung by groups appearing in heaven, some by the angels, some by the elders, but a number of them by the redeemed. In addition to the two songs of the passage we have just quoted, one should include those recorded in Revelation 7:10; 11:16-18; 15:2-4.

SERVICE

One of the most significant statements regarding the activity of the redeemed in glory is the short but pregnant sentence "His servants shall serve him" (22.3). The word here translated "servant," *doulos*, is the one so frequently used by St. Paul in referring to the present relationship of believers to the Lord Jesus Christ (Eph. 6:6; Phil. 1:1; Col. 4:12), and by the other apostles as well (II Peter 1:1; James 1:1; Jude 1). The word is found with almost unexpected frequency in the book of Revelation (1:1; 7:3; 10:7; 11:18; 15:3; 19:5; 22:3, 6). The concepts of service and rewards for faithfulness are basic themes in our Lord's teaching concerning His return (Matt. 24:45-46; 25:14, 19, 21, 23). Thus we may safely say, as many have, that there will be a number of activities in heaven which will be a continuation of our labor for Christ here on earth, without, of course, exhaustion, weariness or failure. It is, however, to be noticed that the verb in the sentence we are commenting upon, "His servants shall *serve* him," is not the verbal form of the word *doulos* but an altogether different word, *latreuo*, occurring in the book of Revelation only in one other place in the glorious statement that those who have come out of the great tribulation are seen "before the throne of God; and they shall serve him day and night in his temple" (7:15). This is the word that is generally used in reference to service carried on in the house of God, in the temple, or in the church (Matt. 4:10; Luke 2:37; Acts 24:14; 26:7; 27:23; Phil. 3:3; Heb. 9:14; 12:28; 13:10; the noun form is found in Rom. 12:1 and Heb. 9:6).

> It is work as free from care and toil and fatigue as is the wing-stroke of the jubilant lark when it soars into the sunlight of a fresh, clear day and, spontaneously and for self-relief, pours out its thrilling carol. Work up there is a matter of self-relief, as well as a matter of obedience to the ruling will of God. It is work according to one's tastes and delight and ability. If tastes vary there, if abilities vary there, then occupations will vary there.[1]

AUTHORITY

In two of His eschatological parables our Lord speaks of assigning certain authority to His faithful servants upon His return. In the parable of the pounds to two of His servants, He gives, respectively, "authority over ten cities" and "over five cities" (Luke 19:17, 19). In the parable of the talents, He says to the two good and faithful servants, "I will set thee over many things; enter thou into the joy of thy Lord" (Matt. 25:21, 23). Now we must acknowledge that we do not really know specifically how the servants of the Lord will exercise the authority here spoken of, but apparently it refers to activity here on earth during *and after* the millennium. I would at this point like to introduce an idea which I have not seen in any volume. May there not be here some relationship to the idea of what the apostle calls the inheritance of the Christian (Luke 20:32; Eph. 1:11, 14; 5:5; Col. 3:24; 1:12; Heb. 9:15; I Peter 1:4)? Now I realize that this inheritance is first of all something spiritual, immaterial, involving eternal life, righteousness, etc.; but is there not something more here than merely inheriting eternal life? The Apostle Paul in his Roman epistle, speaking of the promises made to Abraham and his seed, says that they involved the fact that "he should be heir of the world" (4:13), and this certainly is not basically something spiritual. In the same epistle, the apostle speaks of Christians as "heirs of God, and joint-heirs with Christ" (8:17). Now certainly Christ was never an *heir* of eternal life or righteousness. These He possessed from eternity. Is not the inheritance here spoken of in relation to Christ somewhat related to the promise in Psalm 2? "Ask of me, and I will give *thee* the nations for thine inheritance, and the uttermost parts of the earth for thy possession" (v. 8).

Closely related to the idea of being given authority over certain cities and areas on the earth (I have never been able to discover anything in the Scriptures that would seem to indicate we would be assigned to other planets or stars in the universe), we are told over and over again that we will *reign* with Christ. We should carefully note that when we are told that the children of God ultimately will "reign upon the

earth," actually the Greek text reads, "We shall reign *over*
the earth" (see also Rev. 19:8, 11-16).

There is one other passage which is closely related to what
we have been discussing and that is the prediction that we
shall in the days to come be found judging the twelve tribes
of Israel: "And Jesus said unto them, Verily I say unto you,
that ye who have followed me, in the regeneration when the
Son of man shall sit on the throne of his glory, ye also shall
sit upon twelve thrones, judging the twelve tribes of Israel"
(Matt. 19:28; see also Luke 22:30).

FELLOWSHIP

Many passages in the New Testament speak of the ultimate fellowship that all believers will have in glory (see, e.g.,
Heb. 12:23; Rev. 19:19). Archbishop Whately has one of the
finest pages on friendship in heaven ever written:

> I am convinced that the extension and perfection of
> friendship will constitute a great part of the future hap-
> piness of the blest. Many have lived in various and
> distant ages and countries, who have been in their char-
> acters—I mean not merely in their being generally *estima-*
> *ble*, but—in the agreement of their tastes, and suitable-
> ness of dispositions, perfectly adapted for friendship
> with each other, but who of course could never *meet* in
> this world. Many a one selects, when he is reading his-
> tory—a truly pious Christian most especially in reading
> sacred history—some one or two favorite characters with
> whom he feels that a personal acquaintance would have
> been peculiarly delightful to him. Why should not such
> a desire be realized in a future state? A wish to see and
> personally know, for example, the apostle Paul, or John
> is the most likely to arise in the noblest and purest mind.
> I should be sorry to think such a wish absurd and pre-
> sumptuous, or unlikely ever to be gratified. The highest

enjoyment doubtless to the blest will be the personal knowledge of their great and beloved Master. Yet I cannot but think that some part of their happiness will consist in an intimate knowledge of the greatest of His followers also; and of those of them in particular, whose peculiar qualities are, to each, the most peculiarly attractive. In this world, again, our friendships are limited not only to those who live in the same age and country, but to a small portion even of those who are not unknown to us, and whom we know to be estimable and amiable, and whom, we feel, *might* have been among our dearest friends. Our command of *time and leisure* to cultivate friendships, imposes a limit to their extent; they are bounded rather by the occupation of our *thoughts,* than of our *affections.*[2]

Melanchthon, in his memorial address on Luther, enlarged upon this idea of fellowship in heaven:

We remember the great delight with which he recounted the course, the counsels, the perils and escapes of the prophets, and the learning with which he discoursed on all the ages of the Church, thereby showing that he was inflamed by no ordinary passion for these wonderful men. Now he embraces them and rejoices to hear them speak and to speak to them in turn. Now they hail him gladly as a companion, and thank God with him for having gathered and preserved the Church.[3]

While it would be difficult to point to any one passage in the Scriptures which could be unequivocally said to teach such a truth, many have remarked, and some in great detail, that in heaven we will be permitted to finish many of those worthy tasks which we had dreamed to do while on earth but which neither time nor strength nor ability allowed us to achieve. Sainted F. B. Meyer once said, "Oh, that the ecstasy of the ardent student of nature might fill our hearts as we

direct our thought to the great works of our Saviour God! . . .
Probably this will be our employment in eternity; ever pass-
ing into deeper and fuller appreciation of the works of God,
and breaking into more rapturous songs."[4]

Professor O. M. Mitchel, the great astronomer, believed
that in the future life he would go on from world to world,
continuing his studies of the heavens.[5] For an extended development of this theme of unfinished tasks being completed
in heaven, a famous French writer glowingly said:

> The brilliant tribute of knowledge, intellect, and
> varied faculties which man has acquired at the cost of so
> many efforts, cannot be taken from him. He will retain
> them when he passes to the farther side of the tomb.
> Mozart died at thirty-five, after amazing and delighting
> his contemporaries by the productions of his precocious
> genius; and shall his genius and his personality vanish
> forever because death prematurely arrested his earthly
> career? We cannot think so; we believe that Mozart,
> risen again, now charms celestial phalanxes by his be-
> wildering melodies. Raphael at thirty-seven dropped
> into the night of the tomb the brush which had created
> so many masterpieces, and must he therefore stop short
> in his sublime career? No! his soul continues, doubt it
> not, to scatter masterpieces among the happy beings who
> people the ethereal fields. . . . Why does the old man,
> near his end, still cherish hopes which seem foolish and
> ridiculous to every one else? Why do bold schemes,
> pleasant projects, dispel the melancholy of his latter
> years? Because he has a vague and secret presentiment
> that after the shadows of the evening of life shall come
> the bright lights of a new dawn, and a hope that the
> plans which he secretly ponders may some day be real-
> ized. It is not in vain that he has labored and suffered
> here below; his experience and his wisdom shall not be
> taken from him. Then let him dream, during his last

days of life, of enterprises to be realized when he has crossed the terrible bridge that leads to eternity.[6]

LEARNING

None other than Sir William Robertson Nicoll, along with others, has frankly confessed his own conviction regarding Christ being our great Instructor in heaven:

> We can penetrate but a very little way into Christ's manner of working and teaching with His saints in Paradise. May we not suppose that He teaches the redeemed to love God as they have never loved Him before? In one of his last articles Dr. Marcus Dods said that very few religious writers had a passionate love for God, and he put St. Augustine higher than the rest in this respect. But God Himself has made Christianity historic in making Himself a Man. Our Blessed Lord, as the poor Scotch girl said, was a real Man, and lived a real life, and died a real death, and behold He is alive for evermore! As Dora Greenwell has said, "Everything in Christianity, even the blessed Cross itself, stops too short, if we stop short at it, and do not let it lead us back to the Father— that *righteous Father*, Whom our Lord declared that He alone knew, and would reveal to a world that knows Him not. It often seems to me that Christianity has still a great advance to make in this direction; when we consider the deep unrighteousness, such as slavery in its various forms, still tolerated in many Christian countries, also in almost all forms of political and commercial thought, what a denial there is of the great primitive principles of justice and morality." Jesus will yet show us the Father, and it shall suffice us. We shall understand then, as we do not understand now, what it meant for God the Father to give His only begotten Son that whosoever believeth in Him should not perish but have everlasting life.[7]

REST

Let me close this chapter with two quotations from older works written at a time when men had abundant leisure and gave days and nights to meditating upon these holy themes. The inimitable Richard Baxter has an exquisite paragraph on the matter of rest in heaven concerning which we so rarely think today under the false impression that anything less than constant activity is wasteful:

> Rest; how sweet a word is this to mine ears! Methinks the sound doth turn to substance, and having entered at the ear, doth possess my brain; and thence descendeth down to my very heart: methinks I feel it stir and work, and that through all my parts and powers, but with a various work upon my various parts. To my wearied senses and languid spirits it seems a quieting, powerful opiate; to my dulled powers it is spirit and life; to my dark eyes it is both eye-salve and a prospective; to my taste it is sweetness; to mine ears it is melody; to my hands and feet it is strength and nimbleness. Methinks I feel it digest as it proceeds, and increase my native heat and moisture; and, lying as a reviving cordial at my heart, from thence doth send forth lively spirits, which beat through all the pulses of my soul. Rest,—not as the stone that rests on the earth, nor as these clods of flesh shall rest in the grave; so our beasts must rest as well as we: nor is it the satisfying of our fleshly lusts, nor such rest as the carnal world desireth: no, no; we have another kind of rest than these: rest we shall from all our labours, which were but the way and means to rest, but yet that is the smallest part. O blessed rest, where we shall never rest day or night, crying "Holy, holy, holy, Lord God of sabbaths:" when we shall rest from sin, but not from worship; from suffering and sorrow, but not from solace! O blessed day, when I shall rest with God; when I shall rest in knowing, loving, rejoicing, and prais-

ing; when my perfect soul and body together, shall in these perfect things perfectly enjoy the most perfect God; when God also, who is love itself, shall perfectly love me; yea, and rest in his love to me, as I shall rest in my love to him, and rejoice over me with joy and singing, (Zeph. 3:17), as I shall rejoice in him![8]

In a later century, Dr. John Howe gave us a penetrating study of life in heaven, and from this I would like to extract one single paragraph for the refreshing of our own souls as we continue to live in this suffocating atmosphere of materialism:

Now, the soul will be equally disposed to every holy exercise that shall be suitable to its state. Its temper shall be even and symmetral; its motions uniform, and agreeable: nothing done out of season; nothing seasonable omitted, for want of a present disposition of spirit thereto. There will be not only an habitual, but actual entireness of the frame of holiness in the blessed soul.—2. Again, this image will be *perfect in degree*; so as to exclude all degrees of its contrary, and to include all degrees of itself. There will be now no longer any colluctation with contrary principles; no law in the members warring against the law of the mind; no lustings of the flesh against the spirit. That war is now ended in a glorious victory, and eternal peace. There will be no remaining blindness of mind, nor error of judgment, nor perverseness of will, nor irregularity or rebellion of affections; no ignorance of God, no aversation from him, or disaffection towards him. This likeness removes all culpable dissimilitude or unlikeness. This communicated glory fills up the whole soul, causes all clouds and darkness to vanish, leaves no place for any thing that is vile or inglorious; 'tis pure glory, free from mixture of any thing that is alien to it. And it is itself full. The soul is replenished, not with airy, evanid shadows; but with substantial, solid glory, a massive, weighty glory: for I know not but subjective glory may be taken in within the significance of that known scripture, if it be not more principally intended; inasmuch as the text speaks of a glory to be wrought out by afflictions, which are the files and furnaces, as it were, to polish or refine the soul into a glorious frame. 'Tis cumulated glory, glory added to glory. Here 'tis growing, progressive glory, we are changed into the same image from glory to glory. It shall, now, be stable, consistent glory; that carries a self-fulness with it: (which some include also in the notion of purity:) 'tis full itself, includes every degree requisite to its own perfection. God hath now put the last hand to this glorious image, added to it its ultimate accomplishments.[9]

NOTES

1. David Gregg, *The Heaven-Life* (New York: 1895), p. 62.
2. Richard Whately, *A Future State* (3d ed.; Philadelphia: 1857), pp. 214-15.
3. Melanchthon, quoted in W. R. Nicoll, *Reunion in Eternity* (New York: 1919), pp. 117-18.
4. F. B. Meyer, *Our Daily Homily* (London: n.d.), p. 111.
5. See Horace C. Stanton, *The Starry Universe* (New York: 1909), p. 198; Abraham Kuyper, *Asleep in Jesus* (Grand Rapids: 1929), pp. 52-58; David Gregg, *op. cit.*, pp. 45-82.
6. Louis Figuier, *Our Joys Beyond the Threshold* (Boston: 1893), pp. 109-11.
7. W. R. Nicoll, *op. cit.*, pp. 85-86. See also L. N. Dahle, *Life After Death* (Edinburgh: 1896), pp. 447-49.
8. Richard Baxter, *Practical Works* (London: 1830), XXIII, 407-8. For a recent statement about rest in heaven, see Ulrich Simon, *Heaven in the Christian Tradition* (New York: 1958), pp. 233-36.
9. John Howe, *The Blessedness of the Righteous Opened*, in *Works* (London: 1832), p. 213.

✶ ✶ ✶

This subject certainly deserves additional data. Isaac Watts, in the great work we have been quoting from time to time, has a long section on the varied occupations of the redeemed in glory, from which I would like to quote the following:

"But to come down to more modern times, is there not a Boyle, (a) and a Ray, (b) in heaven? Pious souls who were trained up in sanctified philosophy; and surely they are fitted beyond their fellow-saints, to contemplate the wisdom of God in the works of his hands. Is there not a More, (c) and a Howe, (d) that have exercised their minds in an uncommon acquaintance with the world of spirits? And doubtless their thoughts are refined and improved in the upper world, and yet still engaged in the same pursuit. There is also a Goodwin, (e) and an Owen, (f) who have laid out the vigour of their enquiries in the glories and wonders of the person of Christ, his bloody sacrifice, his dying love, and his exalted station at the right-hand of God. The first of these, with a penetrating genius, traced out many a new and uncommon thought, and made rich discoveries by digging in the mines of scripture. The latter of them humbly pursued and confirmed divine truth; and both of them were eminent in promoting faith and piety, spiritual peace and joy, upon the principles of grace and the gospel. Their labours in some of these subjects, no doubt, have prepared them for some correspondent peculiarities in the state of glory. For though the doctrines of the person, the priesthood, and the grace of Christ, are themes which all the glorified souls converse with and rejoice in; yet spirits that have been trained up in them with peculiar delight for forty or fifty years, and devoted most of their time to these blessed contemplations, have surely gained some advantage by it, some peculiar fitness to receive the heavenly illuminations of these mysteries above their fellow-spirits.

"There is also the soul of an ancient Eusebius, (g) and the latter spirits of an Ussher (h) and a Burnet, (i) who have entertained themselves and the world with the sacred histories of the church, and the wonders of divine providence, in its preservation and recovery. There is a Tillotson, (k) that has cultivated the subjects of holiness, peace, and love, by his pen and his practice: There is a Baxter, (l) that has wrought hard for an end of controversies, and laboured with much zeal for the conversion of souls, though with much more success in the last than in the first.

"Now though all the spirits in heaven enjoy the general happiness of the love of God and Christ, and the pleasurable review of providence; yet may we not suppose these spirits have some special circumstances of sacred pleasure, suited to their labours and studies in their state of trial on earth? For the church on earth is but a training-school for the church on high, and as it were a tiring-room in which we are drest in proper habits for our appearance and our places in that bright assembly" (*Works* [London: 1812], II, 388-89).

Augustine's expression regarding this subject will be echoed by many of us: "And now let us consider, with such ability as God may vouchsafe, how the saints shall be employed when they are clothed in immortal and spiritual bodies, and when the flesh shall live no longer in a fleshly but a spiritual fashion. And indeed, to tell the truth, I am at a loss to understand the nature of that employment, or, shall I rather say, repose and ease, for it has never come within the range of my bodily senses. And if I should speak of my mind or understanding, what is our understanding in comparison of its excellence? . . . And so, when I am asked how the saints shall be employed in that spiritual body, I do not say what I see, but I say what I believe, according to that which I read in the psalm, 'I believed,' therefore have I spoken.'"

For further material on this subject, see James M. Campbell, *Heaven Opened* (New York: 1924), chap. 19, pp. 119-24; A. C. Thompson, *A Better Land* (Boston: 1859), pp. 199-209; N. A. Woychuk, "What Will We Do in Heaven?" in *Bibliotheca Sacra* (1951), CVIII, 488-502.

12   *The Rule of Heaven in the Apocalypse*

If we omit the references to "the kingdom of heaven" in the gospel of Matthew, then we may rightly say that "heaven" occurs more frequently in the book of Revelation than in any successive twenty-two chapters in the Word of God—fifty-four times to be exact. In Matthew's gospel, the many references to heaven which occur in the teachings of our Lord principally relate to the fact that God is the God of heaven, and that the angels are identified with heaven, whereas in the book of Revelation, not only is God the God of heaven but there is tremendous activity on the part of heavenly beings. In the Gospels the references to heaven are without qualifying or descriptive clauses, whereas in the book of Revelation, John sets down some of the things that he actually saw when taken into heaven in his spirit.

The Celestial Heavens

It is only necessary to consider with extreme brevity the references to the *celestial* heavens in the Apocalypse. Twice we are told that God created the heavens, a truth that on both occasions is an announcement by angels (10:6; 14:7). After the description of the reign of the beast and the false prophet, in a chapter emphasizing the wrath of God toward unrepentant men, the angel said to those that dwell on the earth, "Fear God, and give him glory; for the hour of his judgment is come: and worship him that made the heaven and the earth and sea and fountains of waters" (14:7). Swete has a significant comment on this passage in which he reminds us: "It contains no reference to the Christian hope; the basis of the appeal is pure Theism. It is an appeal to the conscience of untaught heathenism, incapable as yet of comprehending any other." In this very passage, the angel making this announcement was seen "flying in mid heaven." Similarly, in an earlier passage, John says, "I saw, and I heard an eagle, flying in mid heaven, saying with a great voice, Woe, woe, woe, for them that dwell on the earth" (8:13). Lenski echoes most commentators in saying that in the Apocalypse "those dwelling on the earth" is "regularly used as a designation for all those who reject the Gospel and love the earth instead." He then adds that "the eagle flies in mid heaven because his woes pertain to all the dwellers on the earth" (see also a reference to birds flying in midheaven in 19:17). As we have found in many places, in the Old Testament and in the New as well, many ordinary phenomena of the heavens above us are related to these celestial areas, for instance, hail (16:21; 20:9), stars (6:13-14; 8:13), the sun and the moon (6:12), the air (16:17), and a white cloud (1:7; 10:1; 11:12; 14:14-16). The two witnesses in Jerusalem will have power to shut the heavens—that is, to prevent rain (11:6); and the antichrist during his dreadful reign will be able to simulate fire coming down out of heaven (13:13).

HEAVEN AS THE ABODE OF GOD

Once in the Apocalypse God is referred to as "the God of heaven" (11:13), a title that appears, as so much else of this book appears, in the prophecy of Daniel (2:18-19). Men, under the wrath of God, instead of repenting "blasphemed the God of heaven" because of their pains (16:11). While God Himself is not specifically referred to in the opening statement, it is God who is seen sitting on the throne when John beholds "a door opened in heaven" (4:1). Heaven as the abode of God is certainly implied in such a statement as regarding the sins of Babylon, that "her sins have reached even unto heaven" (18:5; see also v. 20).

Thrones in Heaven

Probably of all the phenomena mentioned in the book of Revelation in descriptions of heaven, that which appears most frequently is the *throne*. As with many other words, such as *war, conquer, power, might, kingdom,* etc., we have in the Apocalypse not only the throne of God and of Christ, but we have the thrones of Satan (2:13; 13:2), and of the beast (13:2; 16:10). The throne in relation to God is referred to thirty-six times, from the opening paragraph of the first chapter to the initial statement of the last chapter. The concept of "the throne of God" is not new in the Apocalypse. The psalmist cried out, "Thy throne, O God, is for ever and ever: a sceptre of equity is the sceptre of thy kingdom" (Ps. 45:6, quoted in Heb. 1:8). As revelations to Isaiah are about to terminate, Jehovah declares, "Heaven is my throne, and the earth is my footstool" and then asks the questions "What manner of house will ye build unto me? And what place shall be my rest?" (Isa. 66:1, quoted in Acts 7:49; see also I Kings 8:27). We are sometimes inclined to forget, in spite of the fact that it occurs in the Sermon on the Mount, that our Lord Himself declared that heaven is "the throne of God" (Matt. 5:34), and He speaks of His own throne, "when the Son of man shall sit on the throne of his glory" (Matt. 19:28; 25:31; see also Luke 1:32). The writer of the epistle to the Hebrews speaks of Christ our High Priest as having "sat down on the right hand of the throne of the Majesty in the heavens" (8:1; 12:2).

There are a number of occasions in the Scriptures when we read of heaven being *opened* as at the beginning of the revelations given to Ezekiel (1:1) and at the time of our Lord's baptism (Mark 1:10). We should here remember the promise of our Lord "Ye shall see the heaven opened, and the angels of God ascending and descending upon the Son of man" (John 1:51; see also Acts 7:56). But nowhere else in the Scriptures do we have an account of what someone actually saw as he was allowed to enter heaven, apart from what we find here in this marvelous description of the Apostle John in this fourth chapter of Revelation. There are fourteen occurrences of the word *heaven* in this single chapter. As Alford reminds us, on these occasions when heaven is opened, "the heaven itself parts asunder and discloses the vision to those below on earth: here the heaven, the house or palace of God remains firmly shut to those on earth but a door is opened and the Seer is rapt in the spirit through it. Henceforth usually he looks from the heaven down on the earth, seeing however both alike, and being present in either, as the localities of his various visions require." It is most significant that even such a modern theologian as Karl Barth devotes over nine thousand words to an eloquent and penetrating exegesis of this very chapter. We must give some attention to the rich clauses of this passage in such a work as we are attempting on the subject of Heaven. First of all, there can be no question about it that the One here seated upon the throne must be God the Father. The apostle does not attempt, of course, to give any description of God Himself. He simply tells us what he saw with his own eyes, not anything about the character or holiness or power of God as such. God, he says, was like "a jasper stone and a sardius." Jasper was a beautiful stone of various colors, semiopaque, granulous in texture, used in ancient times for gems and ornaments, of a greenish hue, while sardius was a red stone, generally thought to be the same as our cornelian. These two stones are the first and last of the twelve stones on the breastplate of the high priest (Exodus 28:17-21), the jasper representing Reuben, the firstborn of Jacob, and the sardius representing Benjamin, his youngest son. Furthermore, in the foundation of the New Jerusalem, the jasper is the first stone mentioned, and the sardius is the sixth (Rev. 21:19-20). In addition there was a rainbow round about the throne like an emerald. As Swete has reminded us, "The description vigorously shuns anthropomorphic details." Grace and mercy seem to be set forth as prominent in this opening symbolic description.

Creatures Surrounding the Throne

Elders. There now appears the first of a group of creatures surrounding the throne of God, identified as a group of twenty-four elders. "And round about the throne *were* four and twenty thrones: and upon the thrones *I saw* four and twenty elders sitting, arrayed in white garments; and on their heads crowns of gold" (4:4). Govett summarizes what most commentators have attempted to say: "These are counselors of the throne; conversant with the purposes of the king and able to impart intelligence to John as the servant of God." All attempts to identify these twenty-four elders with angels, or as representatives of the church, as such, have failed. Lang is probably correct in saying that inasmuch as their functions are first of all governmental, they must be placed among the principalities and powers to which the Apostle Paul refers. However, they have a priestly work to perform as well, and practically on every occasion when they are presented to us, they are found worshiping God (see 5:5-8; 7:11, 13; 11:16; 19:4). Some have identified them with the cherubim of the tabernacle (Exodus 25:20; 37:9). It is wise not to speak more dogmatically as to the specific identity of these supernatural beings than the text allows. Barth points out that in their leaving their thrones and casting their crowns before the throne of God they acknowledge "before God and all other heavenly creatures and even earthly creation in the person of the Seer that there can be no question of any rivalry between their being and majesty and greatness and distinction and the rule and the being, activity, and rule of God Himself."[1]

The second group consists of four living creatures "full of eyes before and behind. And the first creature *was* like a lion, and the second creature like a calf, and the third creature had a face as of a man, and the fourth creature *was* like a flying eagle" (4:6-7). Alford's words here are sensible:

> These four living-beings are in the main identical with the cherubim of the O.T. (compare Ezek. 1:5-10, 10:20), which are called by the same name of living creatures, and are similarly described. We may trace however some differences. In Ezekiel's vision, each living-being has all four faces, Ez. 1:6, whereas here the four belong severally, one to each. Again in Ezekiel's vision, it is apparently the *wheels* which are full of eyes, Ez. 1:18; though in id. 10:12, it would appear as if the animals also were included. Again, the having *six* wings apiece is not found in the cherubim of Ezekiel, which have *four*, Ez. 1:6,— but belongs to the seraphim described in Isa. 6:2, to whom also (see above) belongs the ascription of praise here given. So that these are forms compounded out of the most significant particulars of more than one O.T. vision.[2]

After a long discussion of the various interpretations through the ages of these living creatures, Alford rightly concludes, and most scholars would agree, that these forms "are

the representatives of animated creation." To quote one
other, H. B. Swete, whose commentary on Revelation must
be recognized as one of the greatest of our century, "The
four forms suggest what is noblest, strongest, wisest, and
swiftest in inanimate nature. Nature, including Man, is
represented before the throne taking its part in the fulfillment
of the divine will and the worship of the Divine Majesty."

As we would expect, there are also great multitudes of
angels around the throne who play a tremendous part in the
cataclysmic events of this concluding book of divine revelation, and to their activity we will be giving a separate section
in this chapter. They also with the living creatures and the
elders sing praises to the Redeemer, "ten thousand times ten
thousand, and thousands of thousands; saying with a great
voice, Worthy is the Lamb that hath been slain to receive
the power, and riches, and wisdom, and might, and honor,
and glory, and blessing" (5:11-12).

There is a fourth group mentioned, I believe, only once in
this book, participating with the elders and the four living
creatures in singing a new song before the throne, namely,
"harpers harping with their harps" (14:3). This may simply
be a reference to the four living creatures and the elders of
whom we were previously told each one had a harp (5:8),
though most commentators are inclined to believe that of
this group only the elders seem to be intended here. These
are the only two places in the New Testament where the harp
is mentioned, though of course there are many references to
such an instrument in the literature of the Davidic period.
The *kithara* was more like a guitar or lute than a harp.

THE TEMPLE IN HEAVEN

The references in the Apocalypse to a temple in heaven are
exceedingly important. We should note, first of all, that the
Greek word here is in every case *naos*, and never the word

hieron. The initial occurrence of this word is as it were incidental in the promise to overcomers in the Church of Philadelphia: "He that overcometh, I will make him a pillar in the temple of my God," though it is in this verse that we also have the most detailed anticipatory statement regarding the Holy City to be found in the Apocalypse (3:12). We might also say that the later reference to those who came out of the great tribulation and serve God day and night in His temple (7:15) is likewise an incidental reference without any defining terms. It is when we come to one of the great divisions of the book at the end of chapter 11 that we find the most extensive of all references to this phenomenon: "And there was opened the temple of God that is in heaven; and there was seen in his temple the ark of his covenant; and there followed lightnings, and voices, and thunders, and an earthquake, and great hail" (11:19). There are two ways of considering this verse. Many believe that it forms a conclusion to the second division of the book, to be followed by those events that bring our age to a close, especially those episodes which are initiated by Satan and the antichrist, leading to their overthrow. Others look upon this as an introduction to a new series of judgments, suggesting even that in the text it ought not to be placed at the end of chapter 11, but as an opening statement for chapter 12. This is the view, for instance, of Walter Scott. Alford combines the two ideas:

> The ark of the covenant is seen, the symbol of God's faithfulness in bestowing grace on His people and in inflicting vengeance on His people's enemies. This is evidently a solemn and befitting inauguration of God's final judgments as it is a conclusion of the series pointed out by the trumpets which have been inflicted in answer to the prayers of the saints. It is from this temple that the judgments proceed forth (cf. Ch. 14:15, 17, 15:5ff., 16:17); from His inmost and holiest place that those

acts of vengeance are wrought which the great multitude
in heaven recognize as faithful and true, ch. 19:2. The
symbolism of this verse, the *opening* for the first time of
the heavenly temple, also indicates of what nature the
succeeding visions are to be: that they will relate to
God's covenant people and His dealings with them.[3]

Probably the most important commentary on the Greek
text of the book of Revelation, published at the beginning
of our century, is the one by the great scholar Henry Barclay
Swete. One of Swete's most penetrating statements is that
which occurs as he attempts to unfold what is implied in this
verse:

> The purpose of the celestial scenery and the celestial
> agencies which are employed is not to take the attention
> of the reader from contemporary or coming events, but
> to lead him to connect these with the invisible powers
> by which they are controlled, and to let the light of
> heaven fall upon the earthly tragedy. The Throne and
> the Temple in the *epourania* are seen to be the ultimate
> source of the energies by which human history is car-
> ried to its goal. But it is in human history that the
> interests of the prophecy are centred. In the events
> which follow the opening of the Seals, if they have been
> rightly interpreted in this commentary, the Seer depicts
> the conditions under which the Empire, as he knew it in
> Asia, was fulfilling its destiny, and passes from these to
> the great dynastic and social changes which must accom-
> pany or follow its collapse. In the scenes announced by
> the Trumpet-blasts, he works out at great length the
> second of these topics; the revolutions which were in
> the lap of the future, the woes which it held in store
> for the unbelieving and impenitent world, are painted in
> a vivid symbolism borrowed partly from the Old Testa-
> ment, partly from the apocalyptic thought of the time.[4]

There is one more important reference to the temple in heaven, occurring in the description of what John saw in heaven, just before the outpouring of the seven vials of judgment: "And after these things I saw, and the temple of the tabernacle of the testimony in heaven was opened" (15:5). The phrase "the tabernacle of the testimony" is found in Acts 7:44. It was so called because it contained the ark in which rested the law of God, which testifies against sin (Exodus 25:16, 21; 30:36). It is thought by many that the pattern which Moses saw in heaven (Exodus 25:40; Heb. 8:5) was that which the Apostle John now beholds. In 11:19 the temple was opened but here the holy of holies is opened and the veil is withdrawn. That the temple was at this time "filled with smoke from the glory of God and from the power" reminds us, of course, of passages in the experience of Moses (Exodus 19:18) and of the Prophet Isaiah (6:4). It is significant that no temple appears in the opening chapters of Ezekiel describing what was revealed to the prophet concerning him who sat upon the throne. Many find trouble in reconciling the clear statements of a temple being in heaven with the later declaration that when John beheld the Holy City he said, "I saw no temple therein: for the Lord God the Almighty, and the Lamb, are the temple thereof" (21:22). It should be carefully noted that John is here speaking not of heaven itself, but of the Holy City.

THE ACTIVITY OF THE ANGELS

As we might expect in any account of a description of what was seen by the Apostle John, when he was spiritually given access into heaven, angels play a prominent part in the events there recorded. Angels appear with greater frequency in the book of Revelation than in any other portion of the Holy Scriptures. I am not acquainted myself with any specific study of angels in the Apocalypse, and perhaps the following attempt to classify this material may prove helpful. First of all, of course, as we would expect, "John saw and heard a voice of many angels round about the throne" together with the living creatures and the elders (5:11). One of these angels called "a strong angel" asked, "Who is worthy to open the book, and to loose the seals thereof?" (v. 2). Once again these angels are found in the company of the elders and the four living creatures, all falling down and worshiping God (7:11-12). In most of the passages, however, where the activity of angels is described, we find them unrelated to the other supernatural beings in the celestial world. Personally, I would think that there are two major activities on the part of the angels in the Apocalypse in addition to some minor ones.

Major Angelic Activities. First of all, the angels are active in the fundamental matter of revealing things to come, to which activity the very first sentence of the book introduces us. "The Revelation of Jesus Christ, which God gave him to show unto his servants, *even* the things which must shortly come to pass: and he sent and signified *it* by his angel unto his servant John; who bare witness of the word of God, and of the testimony of Jesus Christ, *even* of all things that he saw" (1:1-2). When the Apostle John later wonders at the meaning of Babylon the great, the angel encourages him by saying, "I will tell thee the mystery of the woman, and of the beast that carrieth her" (17:7). An angel constantly accompanies John as he surveys the Holy City.

It is one of the seven angels of the vial judgments who said to John, "Come hither, I will show thee the bride, the wife of the Lamb" (21:9; see also v. 15). When the great vision of the Holy City is complete, and it is time for this book of Revelation to be brought to a close, John writes, "And he said unto me, These words are faithful and true: and the Lord, the God of the spirits of the prophets, sent his angel to show unto

his servants the things which must shortly come to pass"
(22:6; see also vv. 8, 16). Because the angels play such a
prominent part in communicating prophetic truth to the
Apostle John, it is perfectly natural that the little book which
is presented to the Apostle John should be open in the hands
of another strong angel coming down out of heaven "who set
his right foot upon the sea, and his left upon the earth"
(10:2).

Closely related to the matter of interpretation and revelation is the activity engaged in by three different angels announcing the important messages to dwellers on the earth at
the time apparently of the reign of the antichrist. The first
angel of this group, we are told, is "flying in mid heaven,
having eternal good tidings to proclaim unto them that dwell
on the earth, and unto every nation and tribe and tongue
and people; and he saith with a great voice, Fear God, and
give him glory; for the hour of his judgment is come: and
worship him that made the heaven and the earth and sea and
fountains of waters" (14:6-7). The words of Swete here are
more satisfying than any I have ever seen on this passage:

> St. John has in view, as the sequel shews, a particular
> aspect of the Gospel, a Gospel which announces the
> Parousia and the consummation which the Parousia will
> bring. . . . The Angel's call seems to be the reverse of
> a gospel; it announces that judgment is imminent, and
> summons the pagan world to repentance. Like St. Paul's
> speech at Lystra (Acts 14: 15 ff.) it contains no refer-
> ence to the Christian hope; the basis of the appeal is
> pure theism. . . . It is an appeal to the conscience of
> untaught heathendom, incapable as yet of comprehend-
> ing any other. Yet there is a gospel in the implied fact
> that repentance is still possible, and the very judgment
> that impends promises a new order which is the hope
> both of the Church and of the world.[5]

The second of the three angels of this group followed immediately with the cry "Fallen, fallen is Babylon the great, that hath made all the nations to drink of the wine of the wrath of her fornication" (14:8). This is one of those great anticipatory statements announcing the fall of Babylon before the event actually takes place, and may be looked upon as a word of warning, somewhat like the warning of the angels to Lot before the destruction of Sodom and Gomorrah. The last of these three angelic messages is neither an exhortation or warning, but a final word of judgment for those who worship the beast and his image (vv. 9-12), with very contradiction of the proclamation of the beast (vv. 15, 17).

In addition to the work of revealing truth concerning future events, the angels in Revelation are used as executors in carrying out the fearful divine judgments that are to fall upon this earth at the end of the age. The seven trumpets announcing a series of preliminary judgments are in the hands of seven angels (8:1–9:1, 13-14). Of the last we read, "But in the days of the voice of the seventh angel, when he is about to sound, then is finished the mystery of God, according to the good tidings which he declared to his servants the prophets" (10:7). When the seventh angel sounded, one of the greatest announcements of the entire book of Revelation was uttered: "And the seventh angel sounded; and there followed great voices in heaven, and they said, The kingdom of the world is become *the kingdom* of our Lord, and of his Christ: and he shall reign for ever and ever" (11:15). Between the trumpet judgments and the vial judgments, two angels are seen coming out from the temple which is in heaven and participating in the harvest of the souls of men (14:7-8). There is a third angel mentioned here as "he that hath power over fire" (v. 18) who, according to Revere F. Weidner, is "evidently the same as the one mentioned in 8:3-5 as presenting the prayers of the saints and as casting some of the fire of the altar upon the earth, introductory to the judgments of the trumpets."

As it was the blowing of the trumpets by seven angels that introduced that series of judgments, so are the seven vial judgments also initiated by the pouring out of these separate vials at the command of "a great voice out of the temple" which is, no doubt, the voice of God (16:1-17; 17:1). As one would expect, when the time has come for the destruction of Babylon, it is an angel who makes this announcement as it was an angel who spoke in anticipation of this same event (18:1-3; see 14:8). It is an angel also who was seen "standing in the sun; and he cried with a loud voice, saying to all the birds that fly in mid heaven, Come *and* be gathered together unto the great supper of God; that ye may eat the flesh of kings, and the flesh of captains, and the flesh of mighty men, and the flesh of horses and of them that sit thereon, and the flesh of all men, both free and bond, and small and great" (19:17-18). There are three groups of angels related to specific events that must be mentioned here in conclusion.

Immediately after the occurrence of the seven sealed judgments, John says, "After this I saw four angels standing at the four corners of the earth holding the four winds of the earth that no wind should blow on the earth, or on the sea, or upon any tree" (7:1). Then we are told that John saw another angel ascending from the sunrising, or the East, crying with a great voice to these four angels, "Hurt not the earth." It is not necessary in our study to even attempt to identify here this company of 144,000, for we are simply concerned with the activities of heaven and the angels that are sent down from heaven. Heaven is not specifically mentioned here, but certainly these are angelic beings descending from glory. They are sent on a particular errand relating to a specific event. As we have seen above, in this very section of the Apocalypse, we saw seven angels standing before God to whom were given the seven trumpets by the blowing of which they introduced this second series of judgments upon earth.

At the time of the blowing of the sixth trumpet, a voice from the horns of the golden altar was heard to say to the sixth angel, "Loose the four angels that are bound at the great river Euphrates . . . who had been prepared for the hour and day and month and year that they should kill the third part of men" (9:14-15). A question has arisen as to the character of these angels. Are they from among the good angels of heaven or the wicked angels that are in the employ of Satan? Many would agree with the most recent commentator on the book of Revelation, John F. Walvoord:

> The four angels bound in the Euphrates River are evil angels who are loosed on the occasion of the sounding of the sixth trumpet in order to execute this judgment. It is another instance of the loosing of wicked angels similar to the release of the demonic locusts earlier in the fifth trumpet. They all are prepared for their hour of activity much as the whale was prepared to swallow Jonah and effect divine discipline upon the prophet. These are wicked angels designated to execute the great judgment of the sixth trumpet but prevented from doing so until the proper moment. . . .
>
> The judgment here depicted, that of slaying the third part of men, is one of the most devastating mentioned anywhere in the book of Revelation prior to the second coming. Earlier in the fourth seal, a fourth of the earth's population is killed. Here an additional third is marked out for slaughter. These two judgments alone account for half of the world's population, and it is clear that in addition to these judgments there is widespread destruction of human life in other divine judgments contained in the seals, trumpets, and vials. Never since Noah has such a substantial proportion of the

earth's population come under God's righteous judgment. The fact that the third part of the population of the world is killed is repeated in verse 18.[6]

In this same chapter—and how crowded this section is with angelic activity—we read that when the fifth angel sounded, John saw a star from heaven to whom was given "the key to the pit of the abyss" (9:1). This seems to be an angel designated by God as specially assigned to direct and control events occurring on earth in the dark and dreadful days at the close of this age that relate to the underworld. Not only does he on this occasion open the bottomless pit to release these demon forces, but after the Battle of Armageddon we see one who must be this angel who has not only the key of the abyss but a great chain in his hand, who lays hold of the dragon and casts him into the same abyss for a thousand years (20:1).

There are some incidental angelic activities in this book which do not need any elaborate consideration. There are the angels under the directorship of Michael who aid him in the great war in heaven (12:7-9). There are twelve angels at the twelve gates of the holy city (21:12), and there is one reference to "the angel of the waters" who at the time of the pouring out of the third vial of judgment affirms the righteousness of these judgments of God. I believe this is the only time in the book of Revelation where such an extended utterance is pronounced by a single angel (16:5-6).

Though we are mainly concerned in this chapter with the activity of the angels in heaven, perhaps a word might not be out of place pertaining to "the angel of the abyss" by the name of Abaddon, who was a king, as it were, over these demon forces. Abaddon means "destroyer" and is used in reference to a place of perdition in the book of Job (26:6; 28:22; 31:12). While we are not expounding the book of Revelation here as such, the words of Milligan identifying these demon forces are well worth quoting. We have here "a great outburst of spiritual evil which shall aggravate the sorrows of the world, make it learn how bitter is the bondage of Satan and teach it to feel, even in the midst of enjoyment, that it were better to die than to live." (Once our Lord referred to these demon powers when He spoke of "everlasting fire prepared for the devil and his angels" in Matthew 25:41.)

In the fifth section of our book (chaps. 17-19), inasmuch as the first two chapters are devoted to the subject of Babylon, we would hardly expect many references either to angels or to heaven, and this is exactly what we find to be true. In fact, in this extended passage of forty-two verses, all we read concerning heaven and the angels is the opening statement, "There came one of the seven angels that had the seven bowls, and spake with me" (17:1). Later John saw "another angel coming down out of heaven, having great authority" (18:1). A voice was heard from heaven calling the people of God to come out of Babylon (18:4), and once we read of a strong angel who symbolically lifted a great stone and cast it into the sea as a symbol of the fall of Babylon. Once the word *heaven* appears in the exhortation "Rejoice over her, thou heaven, and ye saints, and ye apostles, and ye prophets; for God hath judged your judgment on her" (18:20).

The twelfth song in the book is sung by a great multitude in heaven: "Hallelujah; Salvation, and glory, and power, belong to our God: for true and righteous are his judgments; for he hath judged the great harlot, her that corrupted the earth with her fornication, and he hath avenged the blood of his servants at her hand" (19:1-2). The thirteenth song consists only of two words: "Amen, hallelujah" (v. 4). The fourteenth is uttered simply by a voice coming forth from the throne: "Give praise to our God, all ye his servants, ye that fear him, the small and the great" (19:5). Finally we have the greatest of all the songs sung by a great multitude, "as the voice of many waters, and as the voice of mighty thunders, saying, Hallelujah: for the Lord our God, the Almighty, reigneth. Let us rejoice and be exceeding glad, and let us give the glory unto him: for the marriage of the Lamb is come, and his wife hath made herself ready. And it was given unto her that she should array herself in fine linen, bright *and* pure: for the fine linen is the righteous acts of the saints" (19:6-8).

As the Battle of Armageddon is about to be introduced, St. John's words remind us of the first passage we have considered in this study. "He saw the heaven opened" (v. 11), and Him called Faithful and True riding upon a white horse with "the armies which are in heaven" (vv. 14, 19). There is one final appearance of an angel upon this occasion who was seen "standing in the sun" and calling to the birds that fly in midheaven to eat of the flesh of the conquered kings and captains and mighty men.

In the final events which introduce us into eternity, we have the opening statement that it was an angel coming down out of heaven who laid hold on the dragon and bound him in the abyss for a thousand years (20.1). After the description of the millennium and the final revolt of Satan, John sees the great white throne at which all the dead, great and small, apart from the redeemed, will be judged and their final destiny begin. The eternal state of believers is then unfolded, beginning with "I saw a new heaven and a new earth," a theme to which an entire chapter in this book has been assigned. Here again John heard a great voice out of the throne (v. 3) followed by an utterance actually from Him who sat upon the throne: "Behold, I make all things new." It is from the throne of God and of the Lamb that John sees the river of water of life proceeding (22:1; see also v. 3). Only once does an angel appear in this entire description of the holy city: "There came one of the seven angels who had the seven bowls, . . . saying, Come hither, I will show thee the bride, the wife of the Lamb" (21:9). The statement concerning the angel of revelation in 22:6 takes us back to the first sentence of the Apocalypse.

Satan has a throne and power and authority and dominion, all acknowledged in the Apocalypse; but only God is almighty. Men have their armies, sometimes led by demonized kings, but they are helpless before the armies of heaven. Apollyon is king over the abyss, but Christ is the Ruler of the princes of this earth and King of kings. Fearful will be the carnage of those last attempts to thwart God—but glorious will be the new heavens and the new earth wherein dwelleth righteousness.

The Bible begins with God the Creator of heaven and earth. The New Testament begins with One coming down from heaven to establish the kingdom of heaven and to give us the promise of life in heaven forever with Him. Appropriately the last book of the New Testament in depicting the final and universal rebellions against Christ, participated in by men, by Satan, by Satan's angels, and by the antichrist, shows heaven and its supernatural citizens as possessing a foreknowledge of all that is to happen on earth, and supernatural power to determine the time and limitations of these outbursts, to announce and execute the judgment of God, and to participate in the final disposition of every power arraigned against God. Here is fulfilled in final and irrevocable reality the oft-heard pronouncement that all power and authority has been given to Christ and He and He alone is able to subdue all things unto Himself and to bring those whom He has redeemed into their eternal habitation, which is the habitation of God.

The basic undertone of all that is revealed in the Apocalypse concerning the activities of heaven may be summed up in this one word *throne*. A throne implies government with power, or to be more specific, government with adequate power. The power of the throne may be disputed, but if the throne abides, it will overcome all antagonistic forces as it does in the book of Revelation. A throne not only must bring about a submission of all personalities and powers within its sovereign realm, but it must also punish the rebellious subjects that attempt to disturb or revolt against its sovereign rule, including men, kings, nations, demons, the antichrist, and Satan himself. The book begins with the triune God upon the throne, and ends with the same triune God in absolute and eternal sway, after having defeated every antagonistic power. Actually the realm over which the throne exercises its power is first of all this entire earth, and then the great universe itself. The kings who oppose our Lord are "the kings of the whole world" (16:14; 17:2, 18; 18:9; 19:19). Antichrist rules and deceives the whole world (12:9). It is indeed acknowledged that "there was given to him authority over every tribe and people and tongue and nation" (13:7). Friedrich Düsterdieck states, "The expression designates the entire number of the inhabitants of the earth who easily appear in opposition to the saints." This beast out of the sea is worshiped by the whole world (13:8). The harlot exercises authority over "peoples and multitudes and nations and tongues" (17:15). And yet at the very beginning of this glorious final book of the Scriptures, our Lord is designated, along with other titles, as "the ruler of the kings of the earth" (1:5). Almost the entire book of Revelation is nothing else but a prophecy of the defeat of all evil forces in the universe as, appearing on this earth, they attempt to thwart the purposes of God and deprive the King of kings of His rightful authority. The final victory and permanent triumph are referred to after all the conflicts are over: "And the nations shall walk amidst the light thereof: and the kings of the earth bring their glory into it" (21:24). Around this throne there is seen a constant movement of supernatural beings, elders, living creatures, angels, harpers, and then the glorious company of the redeemed, offering to Him that sits upon the throne their joyous and unceasing worship, singing praises to God the Creator, to Christ the Redeemer, and to the Spirit of God the Revealer, praising the triune God for what they are and for what they have done. Nowhere is the final victory of heaven and the infinite glory of that eternal state of holiness and joy more clearly revealed than just before the beginning of the series of judgments to be poured out upon this earth: "And I saw, and I heard a voice of many angels round about the throne and the living creatures and the elders; and the number of them was ten thousand times ten thousand, and thousands of thousands; saying with a great voice, Worthy is the Lamb that hath been slain to receive the power, and riches, and wisdom, and might, and honor, and glory, and blessing. And every created thing which is in the heaven, and on the earth, and under the earth, and on the sea, and all things that are in them, heard I saying, Unto him that sitteth on the throne, and unto the Lamb, *be* the blessing, and the honor, and the glory, and the dominion, for ever and ever. And the four living creatures said, Amen. And the elders fell down and worshipped" (5:11-14).

NOTES

1. Karl Barth, *Church Dogmatics*, Vol. III: *The Doctrine of Creation* (Part III; Edinburgh: 1960), p. 468.
2. Henry Alford, *The Greek Testament* (7th ed.; London: 1877), IV, 599.
3. Alford, *ibid.*, p. 666.
4. Henry B. Swete, *The Apocalypse of St. John* (3d ed.; London: 1909), pp. 145-46.
5. Swete, *ibid.*, pp. 181-82.
6. John F. Walvoord, *The Revelation of Jesus Christ* (Chicago: 1966), pp. 14-15.

        o   o   o

On the subject of Angels and Heaven in the book of Revelation, see Hermann Gebhardt, *The Doctrine of the Apocalypse* (Edinburgh: 1878), pp. 36-52.

13 New Heavens and a New Earth

However difficult the subject might be, acknowledging that the Scriptures give no specific details as to the implications of this vast phenomenon, in a book dealing with the Biblical doctrine of heaven we cannot avoid giving some attention to the theme found in both the Old and New Testaments that as time concludes, there will be "a new heaven and a new earth." To begin with, we must not confuse this idea with the other statement regarding celestial phenomena found also both in the Old and the New Testaments, to which our Lord refers in the Olivet Discourse when He says, "Immediately after the tribulation of those days the sun shall be darkened, and the moon shall not give her light, and the stars shall fall from heaven, and the powers of the heavens shall be shaken" (Matt. 24:29; Mark 13:24-25; Luke 21:25a, 26b). (This is a restatement of similar announcements often found in the Old Testament prophetic books, especially in such passages as Isaiah 13:10; 24:23; also Ezekiel 32:7; Jeremiah 4:23-24, etc.) These phenomena are spelled out for us more or less in the book of Revelation as in the judgments of the seven-sealed book, and of the trumpets, and of the seven vials (6:12-14; 8:12; 9:2; 12:4; 16:8). In all of these passages, Old Testament and New Testament, the text

clearly states that a number of other phenomena are to follow, including the second advent of our Lord, the judgment
of Gentiles, the Battle of Armageddon. These passages then
do not bear directly upon our subject of the new heavens
and the new earth.

We are introduced to the theme of a new heaven and a
new earth most appropriately at the conclusion of the inexhaustible book of Isaiah. As the prophet now is about to
finish the recording of the marvelous revelations granted to
him, his prophetic eye is allowed to behold not only the
termination of earthly oppositions to the kingdom of God
but also a glorious transformation of the entire universe embracing the earth and the heavens above. The statement is
brief and we could but wish it had been given to us in great
detail: "For, behold, I create new heavens and a new earth;
and the former things shall not be remembered, nor come
into mind" (Isa. 65:17; see also 66:22). No one could question the accuracy of the comment by the learned Professor
Joseph Alexander a century ago that "the precise nature of
the change and of the means by which it shall be brought
about form no part of the revelation here."[1] Probably in
reading this, we might be prone to too quickly pass over the
second clause of this verse which literally reads, "and it shall
not come up upon the heart." Delitzsch helps us to understand this in saying that "Jehovah creates a new heaven and
new earth which so fascinate by their splendor, so satisfy
every wish, that all remembrance of the first, of wishing
them back again, is utterly out of the question."[2]

It is to this ultimate state that the psalmist probably refers
when, in speaking of God creating the heavens and the earth,
he continues by saying, "They shall perish, but thou shalt
endure; yea, all of them shall wax old like a garment; as a
vesture shalt thou change them, and they shall be changed"
(Ps. 102:26). It is to be noted that all these passages are set

in a context of contrasts. In Isaiah 65:17, temporary trouble is contrasted with eternal joy. In Isaiah 66:22 the sufferings of Israel are contrasted with her ultimate and unchanging blessings. In Isaiah 54:10 the prophet contrasts the temporalness of the hills and the mountains with the everlasting loving-kindness of God. The psalmist repeats this theme as does the writer of the epistle to the Hebrews in quoting this particular passage (Heb. 1:11-12). It is most significant that we wait until we come to the very end of divine revelation to be introduced to that period when the new heavens and the new earth have become realities. This is the consummating and final statement of this truth: "And I saw a new heaven and a new earth: for the first heaven and the first earth are passed away; and the sea is no more" (Rev. 21:1). We must here carefully note that the new heaven and the new earth are not to appear until after the Battle of Armageddon, after the millennial reign of Christ, after the final disposition of Satan, and the judgment of the great white throne!

The key word of this passage, the understanding of which is necessary for a correct idea of what John is here setting forth, is this word *new*. There are two words translated "new" in the Greek New Testament, *neos* and *kainos*. It is the latter which is used throughout the Apocalypse in speaking of various things that are new (as in 3:12 and three times in this particular passage, vv. 1, 2, 5); at other times this same word refers to things that have not been used (Matt. 9:17; 27:60). Sometimes it refers to phenomena that were not previously present, thus remarkable or strange (Mark 1:27; 16:17). It is the word used by the Apostle Paul in speaking of the new creation and of the renewing of a person who has been supernaturally converted (Eph. 2:15; 4:24). This is also the word used in the great Petrine passage which we shall shortly be considering. The explanation of this word by Trench has been quoted for over a century and still stands as indisputably accurate. Trench says,

> The word contemplates the new not under aspects of *time* but of *quality*. The new as setting over against that which has seen service, the outworn, the effete, or marred through age. . . . The word will often as a secondary notion imply praise; for the new is commonly better than the old; thus everything is new in the kingdom of glory, "the new Jerusalem" (Revelation 3:12 and 21:22); the "new name" (2:17; 3:12); a "new song" (5:9; 14:3), and "all things new" (21:5).[3]

Swete aptly says that the word *new* here "suggests fresh life arising from the decay and wreck of the old world," a palingenesia of heaven and earth.

Of the scores of commentaries on the book of Revelation which it has been my privilege to read, I have found the words of the late Professor Lenski to contain the very best interpretation of this famous statement:

> The heaven and the earth as we now see them in the universe, grand and wonderful, indeed, yet sadly disturbed by sin and evil, invaded by the dragon, the beast, the lamb-beast, the whore, full of the kings of the earth and the dwellers of the earth (all having but antichristian earth thoughts), "went away," disappeared; "for, behold I create a new heavens and a new earth, and the former shall not be remembered nor come into mind" (Isaiah 65:17). . . . The newness of the heaven and of the earth shall be like our own. We shall be the same persons and have the same body and the same soul that we now have; but these made entirely new. Our newness begins with regeneration. Already this the Scriptures call a creation of God, Ephesians 2:10; 4:24, so that we are "a new creation," 2 Corinthians 5:17; Galatians 6:15. After body and soul are glorified, we shall be new-

created, indeed. The same will be true with regard to the new heaven and the new earth. This is more than an analogy, for man is the creature for whom the first heaven and the first earth were created, and if he is made new by creative acts without first having been annihilated, he the head of all this creation, shall God annihilate heaven and earth and create *ex nihilo* another heaven and earth?[4]

It would seem that it is this new heaven and new earth to which the Apostle Peter is referring in that very difficult passage concluding his second epistle: "But the heavens that now are, and the earth, by the same word have been stored up for fire, being reserved against the day of judgment and destruction of ungodly men. But the day of the Lord will come as a thief; in the which the heavens shall pass away with a great noise, and the elements shall be dissolved with fervent heat, and the earth and the works that are therein shall be burned up. Seeing that these things are thus all to be dissolved, what manner of persons ought ye to be in *all* holy living and godliness, looking for and earnestly desiring the coming of the day of God, by reason of which the heavens being on fire shall be dissolved, and the elements shall melt with fervent heat? But, according to his promise, we look for new heavens and a new earth, wherein dwelleth righteousness. Wherefore, beloved, seeing that ye look for these things, give diligence that ye may be found in peace, without spot and blameless in his sight" (3:7, 10-14). Let us first of all examine this word translated "elements." We may pass by the actual meaning of the English word to get at the meaning of the word St. Peter here used, *stoicheia*. The famous philologist A. Hermann Cremer, in his monumental *Lexicon of New Testament Greek*, says that from the time of Plato, this word "signifies the first principle, *element*, of which the world and all in the world consists." In the latest

edition of the great Greek-English Lexicon by Liddell and
Scott there is really a most amazing definition in which they
say that in the realm of physics the word refers to "the com-
ponents through which matter is ultimately divisible." Peter
says that in the final conflagration—and we will discuss the
interpretation of this passage as an eschatological pronouncement in the chapter immediately following this—these elements, these *stoicheia*, will be *dissolved*. The word here
translated "dissolved" is the simple Greek word *luo.* It seems
to me to have in it the idea which we find in the modern
splitting of the atom, or, if one will, in nuclear fission; though
of course the idea of such a nucleus was wholly unknown to
the writers of Peter's day, as it was to those of all the nineteen
hundred years that were to follow. At the very threshold of
our Lord's ministry, John the Baptist said, referring to Jesus,
that He was One "the latchet of whose shoe I am not worthy
to unloose" (John 1:27). The verb he used was *luo.* In the
release of atomic energy are we not *unloosing* as it were the
particles that are bound together in the atom? In the raising
of Lazarus from the dead, our Lord gave the command
"Loose him, and let him go" (John 11:44). Some years later,
when Paul had been captured and bound when the Jewish
mob set upon him in the temple at Jerusalem, we read that,
on the following day, the captain "loosed him, and commanded the chief priests. . . ." Here again is the untying and
the releasing of a man bound. In Revelation 5:2 the word is
used in loosing or lifting up a seal. In Acts 27:41 it is used
of a ship being broken up, smashed to pieces by the waves,
when it had run aground. A similar use of the word was on
the lips of our Lord when He challenged His enemies, "*Destroy* this temple, and in three days I will raise it up" (John
2:19). Looking over these various texts, we have the fundamental idea of *setting free that which has been bound.* Is not
this exactly what we have in the release of atomic energy by

the fission of the nucleus? What I am getting at is that when Peter said that at the end of this entire age there would be a great conflagration of the heavens and the earth, he expressed it in language that implied that the elementary particles of matter, which we call atoms, would be dissolved or released, or, as it were, their energies hitherto imprisoned, set free; and that this would cause the fire.

It will be helpful, I believe, if we give a brief historical survey of some of the great Biblical scholars of various ages in the church. St. Augustine, toward the end of his ever inexhaustible *City of God,* says:

> These heavens which are to perish may be understood to be the same which he said were kept in store reserved for fire; and the elements which are to be burned are those which are full of storm and disturbance in this lowest part of the world in which he said that these heavens were kept in store; for the higher heavens in whose firmament are set the stars are safe, and remain in their integrity. For even the expression of Scripture, that "the stars shall fall from heaven," not to mention that a different interpretation is much preferable, rather shows that the heavens themselves shall remain, if the stars are to fall from them. This expression, then, is either figurative, as is more credible, or this phenomenon will take place in this lowest heaven, like that mentioned by Virgil,—
>
>> "A meteor with a train of light
>> Athwart the sky gleamed dazzling bright,
>> Then in Idaean woods was lost."
>
> But the passage I have quoted from the psalm seems to except none of the heavens from the destiny of destruction; for he says, "The heavens are the works of Thy hands: they shall perish"; so that, as none of them are excepted from the category of God's works, none of

them are excepted from destruction. For our opponents will not condescend to defend the Hebrew piety, which has won the approbation of their gods, by the words of the Apostle Peter, whom they vehemently detest; nor will they argue that, as the apostle in his epistle understands a part when he speaks of the whole world perishing in the flood, though only the lowest part of it, and the corresponding heavens were destroyed, so in the psalm the whole is used for a part, and it is said "They shall perish," though only the lowest heavens are to perish. But since, as I said, they will not condescend to reason thus, lest they should seem to approve of Peter's meaning, or ascribe as much importance to the final conflagration as we ascribe to the deluge, whereas they contend that no waters or flames could destroy the whole human race, it only remains to them to maintain that their gods lauded the wisdom of the Hebrews because they had not read this psalm.[5]

Interesting as it might be, we will pass by the subsequent interpretations of this passage until we come down to the eighteenth century when there was published a work which created a great sensation at that time, *The Sacred Theory of the Earth,* by Thomas Burnet, in the second volume of which a great deal of attention is given to this particular prophecy. After devoting many pages to a collation of other Scripture verses which he takes to refer to the same conflagration and giving a number of ethical and spiritual exhortations, he finally comes to a direct examination of the question: What could possibly cause this last, great, consuming fire?

He says that there are three possible sources: the materials on the earth such as volcanoes; the materials in the earth, especially the fire which he takes to be at the center of this globe; and the materials above the earth in the air, specifically the meteors. After repeating this analogy in different ways until it really becomes almost monotonous, he says:

In general there is a great analogy to be observed betwixt the two deluges of water and of fire, not only as to the bounds of them, but as to the general causes and sources upon which they depend from above and from below. At the flood the windows of heaven were opened above and the abyss was opened below; and the waters of these two churned together to overflow the world. In like manner, at the conflagration God will rain down fire from heaven as He did once upon Sodom, and at the same time two subterraneous storehouses of fire will be broken open, which answers to the disruption of the abyss; and these two meeting and mingling together involve all the heavens and earth in flames. . . . If you cast the earth into a new and better mold you must first melt it down; and the last fire, being as a refiner's fire, will make an improvement in it both as to matter and form.[6]

I do not know of any work written in the nineteenth century which gives such a satisfactory interpretation of these words of the Apostle Peter; that is, satisfactory to us after a century of remarkable scientific advance, as the amazingly suggestive and almost prophetic words of the English Biblical scholar, Dr. Adam Clarke. I think the entire passage is worth quoting as an illustration of what a man can do in interpreting the Word of God when abreast of the best thought of his day and taught by the Holy Spirit:

As the heavens mean here, and in the passages above, the whole atmosphere, in which all the terrestrial vapours are lodged; and as water itself is composed of two gases, eighty-five parts in weight of oxygen, and fifteen of hydrogen, or two parts in volume of the latter, and one of the former; (for if these quantities be put together, and several electric sparks passed through them, a chemical union takes place, and water is the product; and, vice versa, if the galvanic spark be made to pass through water, a portion of the fluid is immediately decomposed into its two constituent gases, oxygen and hydrogen;) and as the electric or ethereal fire is that which, in all likelihood, God will use in the general conflagration; the noise occasioned by the application of this fire to such an immense congeries of aqueous particles as float in the atmosphere, must be terrible in the extreme. Put a drop of water on an anvil, place over it a piece of iron red hot, strike the iron with a hammer on the part above the drop of water, and the report will be as loud as a musket; when, then the whole strength of those opposite agents is brought together into a state of conflict, the noise, the thunderings, the innumerable explosions, (till every particle of water on the earth and in the atmosphere is, by the action of the fire, reduced into its component gaseous parts), will be frequent, loud, confounding, and terrific, beyond every comprehension but that of God himself. . . .

It does appear, from these promises, what the apostle says here, and what is said in Revelation 21:27; 22:14, 15, that the present earth, though destined to be burned up, will not be destroyed, but be renewed and refined, purged from all moral and natural imperfection, and made the endless abode of blessed spirits. But this state is certainly to be expected after the day of judgment; for on this the apostle is very express, who says the conflagration and renovation are to take place at the judgment of the great day; see ver. 7, 8, 10, and 12. That such an event may take place is very possible; and, from the terms used by St. Peter, is very probable. And, indeed, it is more reasonable and philosophical to conclude that the earth shall be refined and restored than finally destroyed. But this has nothing to do with what some call the millennium state; as this shall take place when time, with the present state and order of things, shall be no more.[7]

The famous natural scientist of the first half of the nineteenth century, Dr. Edward Hitchcock, professor and later President of Amherst College and the first chairman of the Association of American Geologists and Naturalists (1840), gave this as his opinion:

> We may infer that Peter did not mean to teach that the matter of the globe would be in the least diminished by the final conflagration. I doubt not the sufficiency of divine power partially or wholly to annihilate the material universe. But heat, however intense, has no tendency to do this; it only gives matter a new form. And heat is the only agency which the apostle represents as employed. In short, we have no evidence, either from science or revelation, that the minutest atom of matter has ever been destroyed since the original creation; nor have we any more evidence that any of it ever will be reduced to the nothingness from which it sprang. The prevalent ideas upon this subject all result from erroneous notions of the effect of intense heat. . . .
>
> We may, therefore, conclude that the Bible does plainly and distinctly teach us that this earth will hereafter be burned up; in other words, that all upon or within it, capable of combustion, will be consumed, and the entire mass, the elements, without the loss of one particle of the matter now existing, will be melted; and then, that the world, thus purified from the contamination of sin, and surrounded by a new atmosphere, or heavens, and adapted in all respects to the nature and wants of spiritual and sinless beings, will become the residence of the righteous. Of the precise nature of that new dispensation, and of the mode of existence there, the Scriptures are indeed silent. But that, like the present world, it will be material,—that there will be a solid globe, and a transparent expanse around it,—it seems most clearly indicated in the sacred record.[8]

The greatest commentary on the Greek text of Second Peter that has appeared in our language is the one by the late J. B. Mayor; and here again we find more than hints of a possible relationship existing between that conflagration which St. Peter predicts and electrical phenomena of our day. Mayor's words, being the sober reflection of one of the greatest Greek scholars of modern times, should be carefully pondered by those who today may be inclined to sneer at any interpretation which would imply that the discovery of modern science might be divinely indicated in this ancient prophecy of the early church:

> The guesses of modern science present a curious contrast to those of the ancient naturalists. . . . The accepted theory of yesterday was, that cold, rather than heat, would be the cause of the destruction of life throughout the universe, since it is the tendency of all other forms of energy to change into the form called Heat, which itself gets lost by radiation into space. There being no known cause which could make up for this constant loss of heat from the sun, the radiating centre of our solar system, it was inferred that the life which depends upon heat must gradually disappear from our earth. Today it seems likely that this hypothesis will have to be considerably modified in consequence of the recognition of the stores of energy in the chemical elements, and of the varieties of radiant energy to which attention has been prominently directed by the discovery of radium.[9]

Inasmuch as this book was published in 1907, this passage was probably written as early as 1905, which means that almost forty years before man discovered a way to release atomic energy, Mayor believed that this passage in St. Peter might refer to just such a discovery.

It is interesting to note how this particular passage came

into the mind of many writers and ecclesiastics at the time of the dropping of the atomic bomb. In October, 1945, the Archbishop of York, in an address widely quoted, said, "The biblical declaration that the end of the world will come suddenly is driven home to us with fresh meaning: *The heavens shall pass away with great noise, and the elements shall melt with fervent heat; the earth also, and the works which are therein, shall be burned.* The writing on the wall of threatened doom and destruction can now be read clearly by all thoughtful men."

One must not avoid facing the question: Do these passages regarding a new heaven and a new earth refer to heaven as the abode of God? I cannot help but believe firmly that the abode of God, the third heaven, is not referred to here. The old heaven and the old earth will pass away or be transformed because they are marred by the effects of sin, by corruption and violence. Certainly this is not true of the abode of God. God is not living in some imperfect environment awaiting the consummation of His redemptive program on earth. The earth and the celestial bodies round about it will not themselves be annihilated, but only as Alford once said, in their outward and recognizable form, a renewal to a fresh and more glorious condition. Most modern commentators refrain from going into any detail or from trusting themselves to make a statement even as specific as the one I have attempted in this last paragraph. Perhaps John Gill in his *Body of Doctrinal Divinity* has examined this passage with as much detail as is possible, and I would go along with his conclusion:

> The new heavens must be interpreted of the airy heavens and of a new air in them. The new heavens will be clear of all unhealthy fogs, mists, meteors, storms of hail, storms of snow, blustering tempests, peals of thunder—nothing of this kind will be heard or seen but a pure

serene and tranquil air quite suited to the bodies of raised saints.[10]

NOTES

1. Joseph Addison Alexander, *The Prophecies of Isaiah* (New York: 1869), 1953 ed., II, 452.
2. F. Delitzsch, *Biblical Commentary on the Prophecies of Isaiah* (3d ed.; London: 1890-92), Vol. II.
3. R. C. Trench, *Synonyms of the New Testament* (12th ed.; London: 1894), pp. 220-21.
4. R. C. H. Lenski, *The Interpretation of St. John's Revelation* (Columbus: 1943), pp. 614-15.
5. Augustine, *City of God*, Book XX, chaps. 16, 18.
6. Thomas Burnet, *The Sacred Theory of the Earth* (London: 1719), II, 92, 118-19.
7. Adam Clarke, *The New Testament of Our Lord and Saviour Jesus Christ—with a Commentary and Critical Notes* (new ed.; New York: 1837), II, 892-93.
8. Edward Hitchcock, *The Religion of Geology and Its Connected Sciences* (1851), pp. 371, 375, 497.
9. J. B. Mayor, *The Epistle of Jude and the Second Epistle of St. Peter* (London: 1907), pp. 157, 208-9.
10. John Gill, *A Body of Doctrinal Divinity* (London: 1837), pp. 638-39.

✺   ✺   ✺

For the general idea of the destruction of the world by fire and the appearance of the new heavens and the new earth, see George N. H. Peters, *The Theocratic Kingdom of the Lord Jesus Christ* (Grand Rapids: 1951), pp. 494-509; W. O. E. Oesterley, *Hebrew Religion, Origin and Development* (2d ed.; New York: 1937), pp. 391-93; a very scholarly article by Jacob Cooper, "The End of the Material Universe," in the *Reformed Church Review*, 4th ser. (Oct., 1903), VII, 536-67; and Wilbur M. Smith, *This Atomic Age and the Word of God* (Boston: 1948), pp. 126-63.

Collect for Ascension Day

Grant, we beseech thee, Almighty God, that like as we do believe thy only begotten Son our Lord Jesus Christ to have ascended into the heavens; so we may also in heart and mind thither ascend, and with him continually dwell, who liveth and reigneth with thee and the Holy Ghost, one God, world without end. Amen.

The Burial of the Dead

Unto Almighty God we commend the soul of our brother *departed, and we commit* his *body to the ground; earth to earth, ashes to ashes, dust to dust; in sure and certain hope of the Resurrection unto eternal life, through our Lord Jesus Christ; at whose coming in glorious majesty to judge the world, the earth and the sea shall give up their dead; and the corruptible bodies of those who sleep in him shall be changed, and made like unto his own glorious body; according to the mighty working whereby he is able to subdue all things unto himself.*

FROM THE BOOK OF COMMON PRAYER

14 The Holy City

The most important work done on the book of Revelation in America in the last half of the nineteenth century is to be found in the rich Notes and Excursuses of Dr. E. C. Craven in the final volume of the English translation of the Bible commentary edited by John Peter Lange. At the end of his summary of the teaching of the passage we are about to consider, that is, the Holy City, Craven concludes with words with which I myself would like to begin this chapter: "The study of the Divinely given Revelation has convinced the writer of certain facts concerning this great and glorious subject. These facts, together with certain probable implications, he has stated with trembling, and he trusts with becoming modesty." In Revelation 21:1—22:5 we have the most extensive revelation of the eternal home of the redeemed to be found anywhere in the Scriptures, and most suitably it forms the conclusion of all the revelation of the ages recorded in our Bible. The remaining verses are simply an appendix including an exhortation, warning and promise. Before proceeding to examine the passage in detail, we should carefully keep in mind that this vision of the Holy City is placed in the Apocalypse after the record of stupendous series of eschatological events from the Battle of Armageddon through the millennium, concluding with the judgment of the great white throne.

We should not forget that what John saw was a vision which, as Lenski has said, "God gave in such a manner that he could see it and that can be seen in no other way." Basically we should state at the beginning of this study that the Holy City is not to be identified with heaven. It is seen coming down from heaven, but inasmuch as it is the most detailed account of the ultimate home of the redeemed, it certainly belongs in any treatise of the general subject of Heaven. In this chapter I do not want to consider each minute detail that is here recorded. It will not be necessary for our purpose to identify and interpret each of the stones forming the foundation of the city nor go into elaborate treatment of the supper of the Lamb, etc. What I would like to do here is to take a comprehensive view of the major themes that are introduced into this inexhaustible passage. I think it would be wise to discuss the city itself first, and then to consider the problem as to what era this refers to.

OLD TESTAMENT CONCEPTION OF THE COMING CITY OF GOD

Before attempting to ascertain to what period it is to be assigned, where it might be located, and who will be in the Holy City, perhaps we should first consider the two titles that are given to this soul-satisfying phenomenon—the Holy *City* and the *New* Jerusalem. The idea of a city of God, radiant with His presence and existing forever, goes far back to the very beginning of the patriarchal period when God began to form a people for Himself. While there is no record of this in the book of Genesis, the writer of the epistle to the Hebrews tells us that Abraham "looked for the city which hath the foundations, whose builder and maker is God" (11:10). Carrying out the same idea, the writer refers to all believers as having come "unto Mount Zion, and unto the city of the living God, the heavenly Jerusalem, and to innumerable hosts of angels" (12:22). The comment of the great Puritan divine John Owen is worthy of repeating here:

> It is plain that this was the ultimate object of the faith of Abraham, the sum and substance of what he looked for from God, on the account of His promise and covenant. To suppose that this was only an earthly city, not to be possessed by his posterity until eight hundred years afterward, and then but for a limited time, is utterly to overthrow his faith, the nature of the covenant of God with him, and his being an example unto gospel believers, as he is here proposed to be. This city, therefore, which Abraham looked for, is that heavenly city, that everlasting mansion, which God hath provided and prepared for all true believers with Himself after this life, as it is declared in Hebrews 11:16. . . . With the expectation hereof did Abraham and the following patriarchs support, refresh, and satisfy themselves, in the midst of all the toil and labor of their pilgrimage. For a certain expectation of the heavenly reward, grounded on the promises and covenant of God, is sufficient to support and encourage the souls of believers under all their trials in the whole course of their obedience. . . . Of this city it is said that Abraham by faith looked for it; that is, he believed in eternal rest with God in heaven, whereon he comfortably and constantly sustained the trouble of his pilgrimage in this world. This expectation is an act and fruit of faith, or it is that hope proceeding from faith whereby we are saved; or rather, it is a blessed fruit of faith, trust, and hope, whereby the soul is kept continually looking into and after the things that are promised.[1]

This idea of a holy city is, in the literature of Israel, closely interwoven with the choosing of Jerusalem as the dwelling place of God and the prophecies that relate to the ultimate glory of this city. It is referred to sometimes as Zion: "Ye are come unto mount Zion, and unto the city of the living God, the heavenly Jerusalem" (Heb. 12:22). No doubt an experience of Ezekiel had reference to the city of Zion: "In the visions of God brought he me into the land of Israel, and set me down upon a very high mountain, whereon was as it were the frame of a city on the south" (Ezek. 40:2). Indeed the book of Ezekiel closes with the statement "The name of the city from that day shall be, Jehovah is there" (48:35). (It is interesting to note that neither the word *Zion* nor the word *Jerusalem* occurs anywhere in Ezekiel's concluding nine chapters.) That this city cannot possibly refer to the eternal environment of the redeemed is clear from such facts that here we have actual geographical boundaries. We have an altar and priests and sacrifices and a temple, not one of which is even hinted at in the Holy City of the book of Revelation. Moses Stuart significantly reminds us:

> The mind of the writer must have been imbued with Ezekiel's description, yet he is not so close an imitator as to expose himself as a servile copyist. While Ezekiel, after his usual copious manner, occupies nine chapters with his description of a new Jerusalem, John occupies only twenty-three verses into which he has compressed all that is splendid and striking, while at the same time some portion of it is entirely original.[2]

Here we might do well to remind ourselves of the significance of a *city* itself, which has been so superbly set forth by Dr. C. Anderson Scott in a book on Revelation which he wrote some years ago:

> It is a city in all the moral significance of that idea. A city is first the ambition and then the despair of man. The great lesson of this vision is that it remains the ideal

of God. Babylon in all its incarnations, from the first
on the Euphrates, through that set upon the Tiber, to
those we know on the Seine or on the Thames, stands
for the human instinct of fellowship and mutual cooperation, but also for the reiterated human experience
that a great city is a great evil. In vain do we try to
stem the steady tide of population setting from the country to town. In vain do we deplore the growth of these
enormous communities. "Back to the land" is a kind of
despairing watchword, for the simple reason that so few
wish to go. The instinct of the race is against it. The
city is the great lodestone; men are proud of a city;
they name themselves by its name; they sun themselves
in its power and splendor. And yet in the hands of men
the city has become a monster which devours its children. . . . And God "prepares for them a city." Here is
an amazing antimony, and an eloquent one; an instinct
practically universal, practically ineradicable; an experience of moral and social failure, repeated from age to
age, from country to country, from one civilization to
another; a kind of cry from all who care for the best life
of their fellow men, "God help us to keep our cities
small." Yet the ideal life which God sets before us as
the life of heaven is the life of a city, with streets, and
walls, and gates, and "boys and girls playing in the
streets thereof." For the instinct to seek a common life,
to form a complicated web of mutual sympathy and
dependence, which is represented by a city, is after all
a true one, and the opportunity for its exercise essential
alike to man's true happiness and to the full development
of his powers. "It is not good for man to be alone"; neither
is it good for a family to be alone, nor yet for a group of
families; and this vision shows us "the far-off divine
event" as realized in the corporate life of humanity, in a
society so vast that none of God's children is left out of
it, and yet so compact that it can best be described as
the society of those who dwell in one city.[3]

We are not yet through with the two titles of this eternal home of the redeemed. We read that this is not only a city of glory, of the presence of God, of freedom from pain and tears and death, but it is designated as "the holy city." Here indeed the hopes and expectations of the Old Testament concerning the city of Jerusalem on earth now find their permanent fulfillment (see Neh. 11:1, 18; Isa. 48:2; 52:1). One of the great visions concerning the holiness of Jerusalem is found near the beginning of Isaiah's prophecies: "And it shall come to pass, that he that is left in Zion, and he that remaineth in Jerusalem, shall be called holy, even every one that is written among the living in Jerusalem; when the Lord shall have washed away the filth of the daughters of Zion, and shall have purged the blood of Jerusalem from the midst thereof, by the spirit of justice, and by the spirit of burning" (4:3-4; cf. Joel 3:17; Jer. 31:40). Even in the New Testament, Jerusalem is twice referred to as the Holy City (Matt. 4:5; 27:53). I believe that Jerusalem is the only city on earth characterized as holy in the Biblical revelation though in Isaiah 64:10 occurs the clause "thy holy cities are become a wilderness." Yet even here Zion and Jerusalem are both mentioned in the same verse, and no other city. As we will find so frequently as we carefully examine the passage we are studying, so here the idea of our future home to be named the New Jerusalem is a concept appearing at the beginning of the Apocalypse: "He that overcometh, I will make him a pillar in the temple of my God, and he shall go out thence no more: and I will write upon him the name of my God, and the name of the city of my God, the new Jerusalem, which cometh down out of heaven from my God, and mine own new name" (3:12). Let us return now to this matter of holiness characterizing the eternal city. To begin with, God Himself is everywhere revealed as a God of infinite holiness and it is almost axiomatic that if God is to dwell in actuality in the Holy City, it must be a place suitable in its own holiness for such a residence. Not only is God Himself absolute in His holiness, but the people whom He has chosen for Himself were intended to continually manifest this very holiness.

So likewise the tabernacle was to be a holy structure, and its innermost area was the very holy of holies. The priests were to be clothed with holy garments, the temple likewise was to be holy and the place whereon it stood was a holy place. The very command of God "Let them make me a sanctuary" (Exodus 25:8) clearly emphasizes the concept of holiness. Again and again in the Old Testament and the New Testament the people of God are exhorted to be holy because God is holy. What more natural than that the eternal city where God will dwell with the redeemed is to be a holy city, which means the structures are holy, the conversation and thoughts are holy, the service that is offered is sanctified, the very bodies in which the believers will dwell will be bodies without sin or taint of any kind. Thus the great purpose of God to redeem from sin and sanctify wholly will be eternally displayed in the activity and persons of the Holy City.

The Size and Shape of the City

In verse 16 we are told that when John measured the city, he found the length and the breadth and the height each to be twelve thousand furlongs. Inasmuch as one mile is equivalent to about eight furlongs, this city measured fifteen hundred miles in each direction. It is true that the holy of holies in the temple of Solomon was a perfect cube, twenty cubits in each direction, which led Swete to say that "the Holy City is the Holy of Holies of the future." It may be true as Kelly states that the cubical form "is simply to be understood of its perfectness," but this seems to me rather extreme symbolism. Years ago the well-known German theologian C. E. Luthardt suggested that without doing violence to the text, the city might be considered to be in the form of a pyramid, an idea that has been accepted by many.[4]

Generally I have not cared for attempts to mathematically estimate how many people a city of this size would accommodate, but no less a brilliant and unusually popular essayist and preacher than F. W. Boreham has thought it worth his while to give careful consideration to this very matter, and I feel confident many will want to have for permanent keeping what he has said as he tells the story of an Australian engineer by the name of Tammas, one of his parishioners, with whom he was talking:

> "Did you ever think about the size of the city?" he asked. And without waiting for a reply he proceeded to reveal the significance of his statistics. "Man, it's amazing; it's astounding; it beats everything I ever heard of! John says that each of the walls of the city measures twelve thousand furlongs. Now, if you work that out"— he bent closely over his notebook—"it will give you an area of 2,250,000 square miles! Did you ever hear the like of that? The only city foursquare that I ever saw was Adelaide in South Australia. The ship that brought me out from the old country called in there for a couple of days, and I thought it a fine city. But, as you know, very well, the city of Adelaide covers only one square mile. Each of the four sides is a mile long. London covers an area of 140 square miles. But this city—the City Foursquare! It is 2,250,000 times as big as Adelaide. It is 15,000 times as big as London! It is twenty times as big as all New Zealand! It is ten times as big as Germany, and ten times as big as France! It is forty times as big as all England! It is ever so much bigger than India! Why, it's an enormous continent in itself. I had no idea of it until I went into the figures with my blue pencil here." He would allow no comment at this stage.

"Wait a minute," he pleaded, as Gavin turned to ask a
question, "wait a minute. I've been going into the matter of population, and it's even more wonderful still.
Look at this! Working it out on the basis of the number
of people to the square mile in the city of London, the
population of the City Foursquare comes out at a hundred thousand millions—seventy times the present population of the globe!"[5]

Perhaps before proceeding into a more detailed discussion
of some of the basic factors of the city, we ought to call attention to the opening statement that this is a *new* Jerusalem,
a part of "a new heaven and a new earth." "Two words are
employed in the New Testament to express the idea of new-
ness, the one bringing prominently forward the thought of
a recent introduction into existence (as in the case of young
persons), the other of that freshness or continuing greenness
of quality which may belong even to what is old. In this
latter sense the body of our Lord was laid in a 'new tomb,'
in a tomb not, it may be, recently prepared, but which, because no man had as yet been laid in it, retained that quality
of freshness by which it was fitted for Him who could see no
corruption. In like manner the 'tongues' referred to in Mark
16:17 are described by the same word for 'new.' In one sense
old, they were devoted to a new purpose, enabled to express
the mysteries of a new and higher state of being. The
'heavens,' the 'earth,' and the 'Jerusalem' here spoken of are
in this sense 'new.' They are the 'new heavens and new
earth, wherein dwelleth righteousness' (2 Peter 3:13)."
Lenski brings out a truth generally passed by when he says
that "the old separation of the heaven of God, of angels, and
of saints from our present heaven and earth where the dragon
and all his anti-Christian powers have wrought their vicious
effects is forever ended. God's heaven and the new heaven
and the new earth are joined together and made one."

THE CITY OF GLORY AND LIGHT

Not only is the great purpose of God to sanctify the redeemed here brought into final consummation, but the whole
concept of *glory* in relation to the presence and purpose of
God is also revealed in final perfection. It will be remembered that when the presence of God first filled the holy of
holies upon its final construction according to the divine
plan, "the cloud covered the tent of meeting, and the glory
of Jehovah filled the tabernacle. And Moses was not able to
enter into the tent of meeting, because the cloud abode thereon, and the glory of Jehovah filled the tabernacle" (Exodus
40:34-35).

When our Lord appeared on earth, the Apostle John introduced the idea of the incarnation by the famous statement "And the Word became flesh, and dwelt among us (and
we beheld his glory, glory as of the only begotten from the
Father), full of grace and truth" (John 1:14). Christ Jesus
is called not only "the Lord of glory" (I Cor. 2:8) but He is
said to be "the brightness of God's glory" (Heb. 1:3). Not
only was He "received up into glory" (I Tim. 3:16) but He
will return again with great glory (Luke 21:27) and at that
time "we will be raised in glory" (I Cor. 15:43). As our Lord
was ending His great high priestly prayer, He said to the
Father, "I desire that they also whom thou hast given me be
with me where I am, that they may behold my glory, which
thou hast given me" (John 17:24). It is to this that the Apostle
Paul refers when he says that we will appear with Him in
glory (Col. 3:4) and that the salvation which is granted to us
is "with eternal glory" (II Tim. 2:10).

A third factor in the general concept of the Holy City is
that of sovereignty or power, referred to toward the close of
the description of this vast array of phenomena, namely, that
a river of water of life was seen proceeding out of the throne
of God and of the Lamb. "The throne of God and of the Lamb

shall be therein." This is the last of many references to
thrones in the book of Revelation. Twice do we read of the
throne of Satan (2:13; 13:2), and once we read of the throne
of the beast (16:10), but the beast and Satan and all God's
enemies are now forever defeated and assigned to their eternal abode, and the throne of God symbolizes the omnipotence of God and His ultimate reign throughout the universe.
Thirty-six times in this one book is the throne of God mentioned from the fourth verse of chapter 1 down to this very
description of the Holy City.

A word should certainly be said regarding the illumination
of the city. Not only is John's entire portrayal of the Holy
City somehow interpenetrated with light even though the
terminology might not be specifically referred to, still to
make this clear John says, "The city hath no need of the sun,
neither of the moon, to shine upon it: for the glory of God did
lighten it, and the lamp thereof is the Lamb" (21:23). It is
with the same truth that he concludes the entire description:
"And there shall be night no more; and they need no light of
lamp, neither light of sun; for the Lord God shall give them
light: and they shall reign for ever and ever" (22:5; cf. Isa.
60:19-20; 24:23).

The words of Seiss here surpass anything I have seen on
these verses:

> That shining is not from any material combustion, not
> from any consumption of fuel that needs to be replaced
> as one supply burns out; for it is the uncreated light
> of Him who is light, dispensed by and through the Lamb
> as the everlasting Lamp, to the home, and hearts, and
> understandings of His glorified saints. When Paul and
> Silas lay wounded and bound in the inner dungeon of
> the prison of Philippi, they still had sacred light which
> enabled them to beguile the night watches with happy
> songs. When Paul was on his way to Damascus, a light

brighter than the sun at noon shone round about him,
irradiating his whole being with new sights and understanding, and making his soul and body ever afterward
light in the Lord. When Moses came down from the
mount of his communion with God, his face was so luminous that his brethren could not endure to look upon it.
He was in such close fellowship with light that he became
informed with light, and came to the camp as a very
lamp of God, glowing with the glory of God. On the
Mount of Transfiguration that same light streamed forth
from all the body and raiment of the blessed Jesus. And
with reference to the very time when this city comes
into being and place, Isaiah says, "The moon shall be
ashamed and the sun confounded," ashamed because of
the outbeaming glory which then shall appear in the
New Jerusalem, leaving no more need for them to shine
in it, since the glory of God lights it, and the Lamb is the
light thereof.[6]

Perhaps we should not pass on to a different class of data
without referring to the emphasis upon the abundance of
gold in the Holy City. We are told not only that "the street
of the city was pure gold, as it were transparent glass" (v.
21) but that "the city was pure gold, like unto pure glass"
(v. 18). It is interesting to note that in the description of
the harlot identified with Babylon, she had "a golden cup full
of abominations" (17:4), but as the text later says, this was
gilded gold rather than pure gold, a shabby imitation. Here
again we have the ultimate consummation of the use of this
most precious material because the ark, the table of shew-
bread, and the candlestick of the tabernacle, were all to be
made of pure gold (Exodus 25:11; 24:31). As Govett has
well said, "Here were the types of the heavenly city and its
inhabitants with their dependence upon the great High Priest
above." Another has well remarked:

After playing many parts such as being a medium of decorative art, a standard of value, and a means of good and evil in society, along with higher usages in the coinage of empires and the representation of the Godhead, gold renders its last symbolic service in providing a pavement for the feet of the saints.[7]

All commentators and those who have written on this great passage have called attention, of course, to seven matters that are no longer present in the Holy City, five of them belonging to the bitter painful experiences of men and women since the beginning of history. We are told that here there will be neither tears nor crying (a fulfillment of Isa. 25:7-8; 35:10; Jer. 31:16). Our Lord wept. The apostles wept. There is no hint in the Scriptures that life here on earth, even of the holiest of men and women, will be free from tears. There are the tears, of course, of disappointment, of pain, of shame, of grief, and sorrow, of fear and of sympathy. There will not be cause of any kind in heaven for any tears to be shed, unless they would be those of joy, but even then our resurrection bodies will not be constituted for any form of weeping. In fulfilling Isaiah 35:10, we are told that there will be no more sorrow, not only that which is caused by the failures and disappointments of life and by death of loved ones, but sorrow for sin, for the barrenness of our lives, for the strange lukewarmness of our hearts, the absence of love for others. Not a shadow of all of this will ever appear to give one moment's cause for grief to the redeemed in glory. Closely identified with this, of course, is the fact that there will be no more pain. And pain seems to be multiplying in our modern civilizations, even though means for alleviating it are so easily available in countries of advanced culture. The words of the late C. J. Vaughan in a volume now too seldom read are worth remembering:

In the original language of this Holy Book there is but one word to express toil and pain. I scarcely know which of the two was intended, when the words now under notice were written down. Excessive toil, too severe for the strength, too trying to the brain, not allowed to break off, not allowed to pause, not allowed to rest, is at once pain too. Many of us have known it. In that respect we are all of us working men. . . . Whosoever among you is an ailing man or a feeble woman, never knowing what it is to enjoy a sense of vigor or robustness, never feeling equal to your day's work, and never refreshed by a sound night's repose, remember this will be all over forever in heaven.[8]

Of course, there will be no night there (22:5) because the city will be illuminated by a light infinitely greater than that which proceeds from the sun. This will be what we might call true illumination, not indirect, not dependent upon some heavenly body. "He who is even now the Light of the world shall be known as such in perfection by the saints of those high places: 'the lamp thereof is the Lamb.' It is to be much observed that, to all eternity, in heaven and on earth, the Lamb remains the lamp, the light-bearer, from whose face the light of the knowledge of the glory of God shines forth over the universe." That death will now be done away with forever is, of course, only the fulfillment of the hope of the redeemed and of the promises of God. The last enemy to be subdued by the Lord will be this universal foe of men—death (I Cor. 15:26). How comforting the promise that in glory "there shall be no curse any more" or as the margin reads, "no more anything accursed." I am sure this refers not only to mankind but to the whole universe which has suffered from the sin of men. Of course, hell itself is a demonstration of that which is accursed but we are here considering the great basic factors of the Holy City and, for that matter, a new and holy earth, and in that great universe there will be nothing which displeases God, nothing that will need to be punished, nothing that might ever serve as a temptation to the eternally redeemed. All that we have seen in this passage is made possible by the infinite glory and unchangeableness of our resurrection bodies, and it should be remembered that all of these items no longer present were endured by our Lord Himself—tears, sorrow, pain, death and darkness, and the reason why you and I will be in an eternity where all these will be absent is because He Himself first experienced them vicariously, and has thus delivered us from them all.

Finally, we are told that there will be no temple in this city. Of course not! Some have been confused and others have concluded that the book contradicts itself. They recall that in earlier chapters we are told of a temple that does exist in heaven, and now we are told that there is no temple. The apparent contradiction is certainly eliminated when we realize that the temple and its angelic messengers continue in action during the time of man's sin and the outpouring of the wrath of God, but after the old earth has disappeared, the temple has no longer any function. And as C. J. Vaughan reminds us, "The worship of heaven is now offered directly. It is as God Himself were the shrine in which man will then adore Him. The blessed will be so included in God that even when they worship He will be their temple—He the Lord God Almighty and the Lamb. . . . If we would hereafter worship in that temple which is God Himself, Christ Himself, we must know God now by faith, we must have life now in Christ; and then the words may be verified to us, 'I will see you myself and your hearts shall rejoice and your joy no man taketh from you'." In a former chapter, we have already discussed one truth in the conclusion of the description of this city, "His servants shall serve him," but the statement immediately following must be considered for a moment even though we are so conscious of our inadequacy to interpret its full meaning. "And they shall see his face, and his name shall be on their foreheads." In the New Testament we have the promise that the pure in heart shall see God (Matt. 5:8) and that though now we see through a glass darkly, that is, as in an enigma, then we shall see "face to face" (I Cor. 13:12). St. John himself echoes this truth in his precious words "Beloved, now are we children of God, and it is not yet made manifest what we shall be. We know that, if he shall be manifested, we shall be like him; for we shall see him even as he is" (I John 3:2). The reason that we carry pictures of our loved ones in our wallets or handbags is because when we are absent one from the other, we may be refreshed and renewed by looking upon their countenances, even if these are only photographs. How much greater the privilege and the inspiration to actually look into the face of a loved one, a privilege that is enhanced when we have been absent from each other for weeks and months or even years. We can tell almost instantly by looking upon the face of another to whom we are being introduced, either in person or by television, that he has a strong face or a weak face, whether that person seems to be trustworthy or deceitful, whether a person is accustomed to command or has a spirit of subserviency. How glorious it will be to look upon the face of Him who loved us and gave Himself for us, who has lived to make intercession for us, the One who fought many battles and won them all, in whose life there has never been one single moment of sin of any kind, in word or deed or thought, whose face will be radiant with unbroken victory, with unquenchable love and with perfect obedience to the holy will of God. Not only will we then look upon our Lord face to face, but we are told His name will be on our foreheads.

In the second part of the description of the Holy City in

which we find the details of natural beauty, we read that the angel showed John "a river of water of life, bright as crystal, proceeding out of the throne of God and of the Lamb, in the midst of the street thereof. And on this side of the river and on that was the tree of life, bearing twelve *manner of* fruits, yielding its fruit every month: and the leaves of the tree were for the healing of the nations" (22:1-2). This passage has given a great deal of trouble to students and justifies my quoting here the very excellent words of Lenski, who reminds us that both the Authorized and the Revised versions give the wrong idea by construing *potamou* with the adverbial phrases "on this side" and "on that." "According to their translations the river is in the middle of the avenue and the tree on the two sides of the river in the middle of the avenue." However, the text actually should read "between her avenue and the river on this side and on that wood of life bearing twelve fruits according to each month duly giving the fruit of it." Thus, the text really means the avenue was on one side and the river on the other side.

> If you are on the street and then look across to the river, you see the wood, and if you look at this middle area from the river to the street, you see the same wood and, of course, also you are at the river. In other words, there is a beautiful park running through the entire city which has the avenue on one side and the crystalline river on the other.[9]

Seiss considers this passage with a good deal of common sense when, after dispensing with the idea that this river stands for baptism, or knowledge flowing from God over the world, or the outpouring of the grace of God through preaching, or internal peace, or sanctifying influences, he asks:

> Why cannot men see and read that it does not belong to the earth at all, nor to any earthly people, or any earthly good. There is not a word said to show that these

waters in this particular form ever touch the earth, or any
dwellers on the earth. The river is a heavenly river, and
belongs to a heavenly city, and is for the use and joy of
a heavenly people. Its waters are literal waters, of a nature and quality answering to that of the golden city to
which they belong. Man on earth never knew such
waters, as men on earth never knew such a city; but the
city is a sublime reality,—the home and residence of the
Lamb and his glorious Bride,—and these waters are a
corresponding reality. Of old, the Psalmist sang, "There
is a river, the streams whereof shall make glad the city
of God, the holy place of the tabernacles of the Most
High" (Psalm 46:4), "the river of God's pleasures,"
where they that put their trust under the shadow of his
wings shall be abundantly satisfied with the fatness of
his dwelling-place, even at the headspring of life, amid
visions of light in the pavilion of his glory. (Psalm
36:7-9). Heaven is not a place of dust and drought. It
has its glad water-spring and everflowing river, issuing
direct from the eternal throne, whose crystal clearness
cannot be defiled. There flow the immortal waters, for
the joy of glorified natures, bright with the light of God,
and filling all with life-cheer as immortal as themselves.[10]

There is a glowing page in Horatius Bonar's volume on
Revelation, to which we have referred above, that I think
forms a perfect conclusion to our (incomplete) study of the
Holy City:

> Blessed City! City of peace, and love, and song! Fit
> accompaniment of the new heavens! Fit metropolis of
> the new earth, wherein dwelleth righteousness! How
> eagerly should we look for it! How worthy of it should
> we live! It has not yet arrived. Eye hath not seen it.
> But God points to it above, and assures us that it shall
> come. The right of citizenship is to be had now; and
> they who are to dwell in it are not angels, but men; not

the unfallen, but the fallen. It is as such that we apply for the "freedom of the city." He who is its Builder and Maker gives it freely. He who is its Prince, whose blood has bought and opened it, gives it freely. He waits to receive applications; nay, He entreats men to apply. He announces that whosoever will only take Him at His word, and trust Him for entrance into it, shall have it. He specially proclaims to us His own sacrifice, His infinite propitiation, His divine blood-shedding on the cross, and gives us to know that whosoever will receive the testimony to this great work of atonement shall enter in through the gates into the city. It is the blood that brings us to the mercy seat; it is the blood that brings us into the city. It will be a joy to enter that joyous city. By this joy we beseech you now to make sure of your citizenship, by making sure of your connection with the King. He who has the King has the city.[11]

PERIOD OF TIME WHEN THE HOLY CITY WILL APPEAR

This discussion of the Holy City, already quite extended, demands our facing a very important question: To what time period does this refer? There are five different views on this, each of which can only be referred to briefly. There is, first of all, the view, strange to say, that this refers to conditions now prevailing on earth though such a view might have seemed more possible in the lovely sunshine and false hopes of the first decade of our century than today. The late Professor William Milligan, who wrote four different volumes on the Apocalypse, himself believed that this New Jerusalem already existed on earth:

> The New Jerusalem has come; it has been in the midst of us for more than eighteen hundred years and is now in the midst of us and shall continue to be so wherever its King has those who love and serve Him and walk in His light and share His peace and joy. . . . We have essentially a picture not of the future but of the present.[12]

In one of his very few strange statements, no less an expositor than Dr. G. Campbell Morgan affirmed in three sermons
preached in Westminster Chapel in 1910 that cities on earth
ought to be true cities of God and that the church already is
such an institution.[13]

Some have insisted that the Holy City here shown to the
Apostle John is to be considered as nothing else but a
description of the earthly city of Jerusalem as it will be seen
during the millennium. But there is nothing here to make
us think of the earthly city of Jerusalem, either in its size or
in its character, nor in its location, for the text clearly indicates this is not a transformed earthly city but one that
originates in heaven and will be suspended over the earth.
This is the view, among others, of George Peters in his monumental work, *The Theocratic Kingdom of Our Lord, Jesus
Christ,* and also of F. W. Faber, John Brown and others.

Strange to say, a great group of conservative expositors
have held the view that two periods are referred to in this
description of the Holy City; that Revelation 21:1-8 refers
to the eternal state, while 21:9–22:5 is to be taken as a
recapitulation of the millennial age. This is the view of such
men as Joseph Seiss, William Kelly, Walter Scott, J. N.
Darby, A. C. Gaebelein and even G. R. Beasley-Murray in
the *New Bible Commentary.*

One of the best of recent commentators on the book of
Revelation, the late G. H. Lang, believes that the passage
speaks both of a millennial condition and of the eternal state,
and others have held the same view.

My own view of this passage, after studying it for years,
is that while there may be some millennial overtones here,
the entire passage from 21:1 to 22:5 refers to our eternal
state. One of the greatest students of prophecy of a century
ago, Bengel, strongly held this view in saying, "This new
city has no connection with the millennium, but belongs to

the state of perfect renovation and eternity, as is shown by the series of visions, the magnificence of the description, and the opposition to the second death." The late Professor Revere F. Weidner in one of the best commentaries on Revelation of the last two generations, to which, strange to say, one sees few references today, echoes Bengel's views emphatically. One can hardly deny this position:

> This holy city which John saw coming down out of heaven from God (21:10) is the same city which is referred to in 21:2 and belongs to the new heavens and the new earth of 21:1. The final consummation has taken place. . . . The occupants of the city are in their eternal state; there will be no change in their position or relation whatever.[14]

THE HOLY CITY AS THE CLIMAX OF REVELATION CONCERNING THE REDEEMED

The remarkable phenomenon of the Scriptures, which while written over a period of fifteen hundred years, yet continually sets forth its great themes with a remarkable unity, has been noted by all students of the Scriptures. There is not only a basic unity as the writers present the truths concerning God, Christ, the Holy Spirit, creation, redemption, sanctification, glorification, eternity, etc., but there is also equally remarkable evidence of what has been called progressive revelation.

Inasmuch as the canon of the Scriptures is closed, if God's revelation to men is complete as recorded in the Scriptures, then there must be a termination of truth concerning these great themes and if there is such a termination, and there is, these termini may well be expected to be both summarizing and climactic, with a tone of finality. This is preeminently true with the passage we are here discussing, unfolding for us this Holy City.

As we have already seen, this idea of a city of God in which redeemed men will dwell forever begins as far back as the times of Abraham. Here the promise of God to tabernacle with redeemed mankind finds its ultimate and permanent fulfillment. Both positively and negatively some of the greatest themes of Scripture are brought to their final conclusion. Life divinely bestowed, then lost through sin, replaced by death, restored to us in Jesus Christ, is here set forth in the concept of the water of life and the tree of life, with the total disappearance forever of any aspect of death. Here we have a condition characterized by light, a veritable synonym for God and also a synonym for new life in Christ, with the accompanying disappearance of night forever in the Holy City. Here the concept of holiness, which finds its roots far back in the sanctifying of the seventh day at the time of creation and which is, as we have previously said, the great objective of our redemption, becomes the prevailing characteristic of our eternal home. Here glory replaces everything that can be called shameful, fragmentary, disappointing or polluting. This time the new will remain permanent for eternity. At last God and man will be dwelling together, a communion never to be interrupted. Here at last we shall behold the face of Christ and shall be like Him when we see Him as He is.

Whatever may have been the vague dreams of the classical writers of Greece or non-Christian mystics regarding a paradise of the future, this is the one account which is not only more beautiful than anything ever penned by writers without divine inspiration, but it is made sure to us because it all relates to and derives from the purposes of God accomplished in Jesus Christ our eternal Redeemer.

NOTES

1. John Owen, *An Exposition of the Epistle to the Hebrews* (Edinburgh: 1855), VII, 70-72.
2. Moses Stuart, *A Commentary on the Apocalypse* (Andover, Mass.: 1845), II, 378.
3. C. Anderson Scott, *The Book of Revelation* (London: 1905), pp. 308-10.
4. This idea has been fully developed by George R. Berry in his *End of All Things* (London: 1912) (rev. ed., *The New Jerusalem* [Plymouth: 1917]).
5. F. W. Boreham, *Wisps of Wildfire* (London: 1924), pp. 202-3.
6. Joseph Seiss, *Lectures on the Apocalypse* (New York: 1901), III, 412-13. Also Horatius Bonar, *Light and Truth, The Revelation* (New York: 1872), pp. 370-78.
7. G. M. Mackie, "Gold," in Hastings, *Dictionary of Christ and the Gospels*, I, 683.
8. C. J. Vaughan, *Lectures on the Revelation of St. John* (4th ed.; London: 1875), II, 231.
9. R. C. H. Lenski, *The Interpretation of St. John's Revelation* (Columbus, Ohio: 1943), p. 650.
10. Seiss, *op. cit.*, pp. 424-25.
11. Horatius Bonar, *op. cit.*
12. William Milligan, *The Book of Revelation* (London: 1889), pp. 371, 373.
13. G. Campbell Morgan, *The Westminster Pulpit* (London: 1910), V, 209-32.
14. Revere F. Weidner, *Annotations on the Revelation of St. John the Divine* (New York: 1900), p. 308. On the significance of God *dwelling* in the Holy City, see some excellent remarks in G. B. Caird's recent volume, *A Commentary on the Revelation of St. John the Divine* (New York: 1966), pp. 263-64. A now long-forgotten discussion of some aspects of the Holy City by H. B. Swete is to be found in the *Interpreter* (Manchester: 1905), pp. 377-87, 468-78. As an example of preaching of the highest quality on subjects pertaining to the Holy City, refer to W. A. Criswell, *Expository Sermons on Revelation* (Grand Rapids: 1966), V, 103-33.

APPENDIXES

APPENDIX A

Some Great Hymns About Heaven

The advent of our Lord was accompanied by a great outburst of songs, on the part of the angels who announced His coming, and those who believingly received the message. And the Apostle Paul urges Christians to be faithful in instructing one another in psalms and hymns and spiritual songs. Many factors testify to the fact that the early church felt impelled to sing songs to their Redeemer out of the sheer gratitude of their hearts for His marvelous redemption. While there must have been scores and scores of hymns compiled by Christians during the first few centuries of our era, few of them have survived, and those that we do have naturally concentrate on themes relating to the Lord Jesus Christ, especially His birth, His death, His resurrection, and the greatness of His redemptive work. Hymns related to heaven were late in developing, and those of real importance did not appear until the Middle Ages.

The first great hymn writer was Peter Abelard (1079-1142), the distinguished philosopher, poet, musician and theologian, of whom it is said that "in dialectics and theology he was the master, without a rival." Abelard was so great a teacher that wherever he established a classroom, there huge crowds of students would gather. In addition to all of his theological labors, he produced an entire hymnbook of ninety-three hymns for use in the Abbey of the Paraclete at Nogent-sur-Seine. The only hymn found in this book that relates to our particular subject is the one beginning

> Oh, what the joy and the glory must be,
> Those endless Sabbaths the blessed ones see;
> Crown for the valiant, to weary ones rest;
> God shall be All and in all ever blest.

A contemporary of Abelard was Bernard of Morlaix, or as sometimes designated, of Cluny. Except that he flourished in the middle of the twelfth century, we have practically no details of his life. Bernard was the author of a poem of three thousand lines, *De Contemptu Mundi*. The theme of this huge composition is expressed in the opening lines of one of the stanzas:

> The world is very evil
> The times are waxing late
> Be sober and keep vigil
> The judge is at the gate.

Unexpectedly there occurs in the midst of this long poem the most famous hymn on heaven of all the Middle Ages, generally referred to by its Latin title, *Urbs beata Hierusalem*. In translation sometimes the title is given as "Jerusalem the Glorious" or "Jerusalem the Golden" or "Hail, Zion, City of Our God." It all depends upon which part of the poem is included in a given translation. The part of the poem that begins "Jerusalem the Golden" extends to five stanzas of eight lines each, while the section beginning "For thee, O dear, dear country" extends to five stanzas of the same length —a total of 104 lines.

The most familiar of the three hymns drawn from this composition of Bernard became famous throughout the Middle Ages and is the source for many, many hymns relating to heaven, emphasizing the golden city of the New Jerusalem. The hymn is so important that it deserves to be quoted here in its entirety:

Jerusalem the golden,
    With milk and honey blest,
Beneath thy contemplation
    Sink heart and voice oppressed:
I know not, O I know not,
    What social joys are there,
What radiancy of glory,
    What light beyond compare!

They stand, those halls of Zion,
    Conjubilant with song,
And bright with many an angel,
    And all the martyr-throng;
The Prince is ever in them,
    The daylight is serene,
The pastures of the blessed
    Are decked in glorious sheen.

Jerusalem the glorious,
    The joy of the elect,
O dear and future vision
    That eager hearts expect!
E'en now by faith I see thee,
    E'en here thy walls discern:
To Thee my thoughts are kindled,
    And strive and pant and yearn.

The cross is all thy splendour,
    The Crucified thy praise,
His laud and benediction
    Thy ransomed people raise:

Jesus, the crown of beauty,
  True God and Man, they sing;
Their never-failing portion,
  Their glorious Lord and King.

O mine, O golden Zion!
  O lovelier far than gold,
O sweet and blessed country,
  Shall I thy joys behold?
Jesu, in mercy bring us
  To that dear land of rest,
Where Thou art with the Father
  And Spirit ever blest.

A hymn that was discovered in manuscript form in the British Museum, and which may be dated at the end of the sixteenth century, is by an author of whom we have no information except the initials F.B.P. This was first published in 1601 and now and then has reappeared in part or in whole in various hymnals. It begins with the famous lines

Jerusalem, my happy home,
  When shall I come to thee?
When shall my sorrows have an end?
  Thy joys when shall I see?

The first stanza of Part II presents a theme that often reappears in these hymns on heaven:

Thy walls are made of precious stones,
  Thy bulwarks diamonds square;
Thy gates are of bright orient pearl;
  Exceeding rich and rare.

The hymn concludes with a longing of the author which has been echoed again and again down through the ages:

Jerusalem, my happy home,
  Would God I were in thee!
Would God my woes were at an end,
  Thy joys that I might see!

To the great mystic Thomas a Kempis (1380-1471) is ascribed a hymn that appears in a number of modern hymn-books, the first stanza of which reads as follows:

> Light's abode, celestial Salem,
>   Vision whence true peace doth spring,
> Brighter than the heart can fancy,
>   Mansion of the highest King;
> O how glorious are the praises
>   Which of thee the prophets sing!

Before we consider the hymns that were born at the time of the Reformation and immediately thereafter, we would do well to remind ourselves of the general nature of these medieval hymns on Heaven, so excellently set forth by Dr. Edward Dickinson in his invaluable *Music in the History of the Western Church.* Of Latin religious verse, from Hilary to Xavier, he says,

> The poetry is of the cloister, the work of men separated from the world, upon whom asceticism and scholastic philosophizing had worked to refine and subtilize their conceptions. It is the poetry not of laymen but of priests and monks, the special and peculiar utterance of a sacerdotal class, wrapt in intercessory functions, straining ever for glimpses of the Beatific Vision, whose one absorbing effort was to emancipate the soul from time and discipline it for eternity. It is poetry of and for the temple, the sacramental mysteries, the hours of prayer, for seasons of solitary meditation.

Luther was the great promoter of a new era of hymn-singing at the time of the Reformation, and it is commonly agreed that perhaps the hymns that were written, learned and sung, were as effective in teaching the great truths of the Reformed faith to the common people as were the actual prose writings of Luther and his co-workers. Luther himself wrote some thirty-six hymns, many of which were transla-

tions or adaptations of psalms; but of the five that were
completely original, none of them were directed to the subject of Heaven. As far as I know, the only hymn relating to
heaven that was produced in Germany during the Reformation that has been fairly extensively used in English and
American hymnals, especially Lutheran ones, is the one by
Johann M. Meyfart (1590-1642), the rector of the University
of Erfurt. This, like many other hymns, is based upon the
opening lines of Revelation 21, from which we might quote
the fourth stanza:

> O City beautiful! Thy light appears—
>   The gates by grace set wide—
> The Home for which through long, long exile years,
>   My weary spirit sighed—
> The false and empty shadows,
>   The life of sin, are past—
> God gives me mine inheritance,
>   The land of life at last.

The only other hymn on Heaven that we need to mention,
composed before the advent of Isaac Watts, is the brief
composition by Henry Vaughan (1621-95) which appears in
a great many of our hymnals. Richard Garnett once said that
apart from Milton, "there is now no poet of the Caroline
period except Herbert and Herrick who is more widely
known and one whose reputation is more solidly established."
The first stanza of Vaughan's hymn reads as follows:

> My soul, there is a country
>   Far beyond the stars,
> Where stands a winged sentry
>   All skilful in the wars.

We now come to the greatest hymn writer of modern
times, or perhaps of any time, Isaac Watts (1674-1748), who
gave to the Christian church 875 hymns and poetic render-

ings of the Psalms. Though there had been extensive singing of hymns throughout Central Europe as a result of the Reformation, and considerable singing in the Anglican church in Great Britain, the nonconformists, especially the Puritans, at first considered the singing of any hymns, except the Psalms, as worldly, due to the licentiousness of most of the songs that were sung by the common people at that time. Consequently Watts, who was a nonconformist himself, felt it necessary to write a long preface justifying the writing and singing of hymns among Christian people. He opens the famous preface to his lyric poems with these words:

> It has been a long complaint of the virtuous and refined world, that poesy, whose original is divine, should be enslaved to vice and profaneness; than an art inspired from heaven, should have so far lost the memory of its birthplace, as to be engaged in the interests of hell. How unhappily is it perverted from its most glorious design! How basely has it been driven away from its proper station in the temple of God, and abused to much dishonour! The iniquity of men has constrained it to serve their vilest purposes, while the sons of piety mourn the sacrileges and the shame.

Frederic Palmer has not exaggerated when he says that Watts "was the first Englishman who set the Gospel to music, and in his special field of song he has never been surpassed." His latest biographer echoes the same truth in saying that "Watts was the poet of that vast army of religious persons who read poetry not as a literary exercise but for spiritual food." When he was only thirty-three years of age, in 1707, Watts published his *Hymns and Spiritual Songs* in which 200 of his hymns were to be found. In the second edition, published two years later, he had 145 more. This is not the place for biographical details, but it may be interesting to note that possibly one of the three reasons why Watts

has given us so many beautiful hymns about heaven is because he took a great deal of interest in astronomy and in
1726 published a volume entitled *The Knowledge of the
Heavens and the Earth.*

It is practically impossible to decide which is the greatest
hymn on Heaven from the pen of this wonderfully gifted
hymnologist. Probably the best known is the one beginning
"There is a land of pure delight," which we will quote in
its entirety:

> There is a land of pure delight,
>   Where saints immortal reign;
> Infinite day excludes the night,
>   And pleasures banish pain.
>
> There everlasting spring abides,
>   And never-withering flowers;
> Death, like a narrow sea, divides
>   This heavenly land from ours.
>
> Sweet fields beyond the swelling flood
>   Stand dressed in living green;
> So to the Jews old Canaan stood,
>   While Jordan rolled between.
>
> But timorous mortals start and shrink
>   To cross this narrow sea,
> And linger shivering on the brink,
>   And fear to launch away.
>
> O could we make our doubts remove,
>   Those gloomy doubts that rise,
> And see the Canaan that we love
>   With unbeclouded eyes:
>
> Could we but climb where Moses stood,
>   And view the landscape o'er,
> Not Jordan's stream, nor death's cold flood,
>   Should fright us from the shore.

Among other hymns of Watts relating to Heaven is this:

> O! the delights, the heav'nly joys,
>   The glories of the place,
> Where Jesus sheds the brightest beams
>   Of his o'erflowing grace!

And two others begin

> Father, I long, I faint to see
> The place of thine abode

and

> How bright these glorious spirits shine

While there are more hymns by the Wesleys in most of the hymnals used in Great Britain and America than there are of any other writers of the seventeenth and eighteenth centuries, for some strange reason, nothing of what they wrote about heaven is today used in contemporary hymnals, with the single exception of the hymn beginning

> How happy is the pilgrim's lot,
> How free from every anxious thought,
>   From worldly hope and fear!
> Confined to neither court nor cell,
> His soul disdains on earth to dwell,
>   He only sojourns here.

Far more famous than this poem of Wesley's is the one by Samuel Stennett (1727-95), a dissenting Baptist minister of London, the author of some thirty-eight hymns of which the one we refer to is easily the most widely known. The first and last stanzas are as follows:

> On Jordan's stormy banks I stand,
>   And cast a wishful eye
> To Canaan's fair and happy land,
>   Where my possessions lie.

> Filled with delight, my raptured soul
>   Would here no longer stay:
> Though Jordan's waves around me roll,
>   Fearless I'd launch away.

A famous hymn of the early part of the eighteenth century and from Germany is by Heinrich Theobald Schenk (1656-1727), the only one of his which is found in almost all German hymnals:

> Who are these like stars appearing,
>   These before God's throne who stand?
> Each a golden crown is wearing;
>   Who are all this glorious band?
> Alleluia! hark, they sing,
> Praising loud their heav'nly King.

Probably the most famous hymn writer of the first half of the nineteenth century was James Montgomery (1771-1854), author of some four hundred different hymns of which seventy-one were thought important enough by John Julian to be listed in his famous *Dictionary of Hymnology*. Julian's tribute to Montgomery is worth quoting:

> His devotional spirit was of the holiest type. With the faith of a strong man, he united the beauty and simplicity of a child. Richly poetic, without exuberance, dogmatic without uncharitableness, tender without sentimentality, elaborate without effusiveness, richly musical without apparent effort. He has bequeathed to the church of Christ wealth which could only have come from a true genius and a sanctified heart.

Two stanzas of Montgomery's well-known hymn "Forever with the Lord" might well be included in our too severely condensed discussion of this subject:

> "For ever with the Lord!"
>   Amen; so let it be;

Life from the dead is in that word,
'Tis immortality.
Here in the body pent,
Absent from Him I roam,
Yet nightly pitch my moving tent
A day's march nearer home.

My Father's house on high,
Home of my soul, how near
At times to faith's foreseeing eye
Thy golden gates appear!
Ah! then my spirit faints
To reach the land I love,
The bright inheritance of saints,
Jerusalem above.

Probably no English hymn writer of the nineteenth century wrote as many beautiful hymns and poems regarding heaven as the Scottish divine and sainted pastor Horatius Bonar (1808-89). Note carefully in this hymn the personal element so often lacking in so many hymns on Heaven:

Upward where the stars are burning,
Silent, silent in their turning,
Round the never changing pole;
Upward where the sky is brightest,
Upward where the blue is lightest,
Lift I now my longing soul.

Far beyond that arch of gladness,
Far beyond these clouds of sadness,
Are the many mansions fair.
Far from pain and sin and folly,
In that palace of the holy,
I would find my mansions there.

The famous New Testament scholar, member of the Revision Committee of the New Testament, gifted preacher, Dean Henry Alford, wrote one hymn on Heaven that is found in

almost every hymnal of the last one hundred years, beginning
with these lines:

> Ten thousand times ten thousand,
>   In sparkling raiment bright,
> The armies of the ransomed saints
>   Throng up the steeps of light;
> 'Tis finished—all is finished—
>   Their fight with death and sin!
> Fling open wide the golden gates,
>   And let the victors in.

One hymn by a Roman Catholic mystic and scholar has
found its place in most of our hymnals, the one by Frederick
W. Faber (1814-63), each opening line of which emphasizes
the concept of paradise:

> O Paradise, O Paradise!
>   Who doth not crave for rest?
> Who would not seek the happy land
>   Where they that love are blest?
> Where loyal hearts are true
>   Stand ever in the light,
> All rapture through and through
>   In God's most holy sight.

One of the most exquisite writers of poetry of the last half
of the nineteenth century in Great Britain was Christina
Georgina Rossetti (1830-94). One of her best-known hymns
introduces again this idea of Jerusalem as the city of gold:

> Jerusalem is built of gold,
>   Of crystal, pearl and gem:
> O fair thy lustres manifold,
>   Thou fair Jerusalem!
> Thy citizens who walk in white
>   Have naught to do with day or night,
> And drink the river of delight,
>   The river of delight.

The other hymn by Miss Rossetti is built around something rarely found in hymns on Heaven, and that is an attempt to record a dream which she was supposed to have, which would make the hymn rather unsuitable for such a day as that in which we live. Her opening stanza is as follows:

> Once in a dream I saw the flowers
> That bud and bloom in Paradise;
> More fair they are than waking eyes
> Have seen in all this world of ours.
> And faint the perfume-bearing rose,
> And faint the lily on its stem,
> And faint the perfect violet
> Compared with them.

She does well to close with the following expression of her hope:

> I hope to see these things again,
> But not as once in dreams by night;
> To see them with my very sight.

A hymn well known to all of us is by one whose name will not be recognized in this generation, Mrs. Frank A. Breck (1895-1934):

> Face to face with Christ, my Saviour,
> Face to face—what will it be?
> When with rapture I behold Him,
> Jesus Christ who died for me.

Of course, the most gifted writer of hymns of our country was Fanny Crosby (1820-1915), who wrote over six thousand hymns during her lifetime, most of which was spent in total blindness. Of the many she wrote concerning Heaven, one is quite commonly used:

> When my life work is ended, and I cross the swelling tide,
> When the bright and glorious morning I shall see;

I shall know my Redeemer when I reach the other side,
And His smile will be the first to welcome me.

Finally, we might mention the hymn by the famous Boston pastor and Christian statesman A. J. Gordon, the first and last stanzas of which are as follows:

I shall see the King in His beauty,
In the land that is far away,
When the shadows at length have lifted,
And the darkness has turned to day.

I shall see Him, I shall be like Him,
By one glance of His face transformed;
And this body of sin and darkness
To the image of Christ conformed.

APPENDIX B

The Sign of the Son of Man in Heaven

The statement regarding the shaking of the powers of the heavens is found in all three accounts of the Olivet Discourse, but the statement regarding the sign of the Son of man in heaven is found exclusively in St. Matthew's narrative: "And then shall appear the sign of the Son of man in heaven: and then shall all the tribes of the earth mourn, and they shall see the Son of man coming on the clouds of heaven with power and great glory" (24:30).

Among the church Fathers, this prophecy was almost unanimously interpreted as referring to the cross of Christ, and this may be the meaning of the first reference we have to this passage in the earliest Christian literature appearing after the New Testament, in the *Didache,* generally called *The Teaching of the Twelve Apostles,* possibly the earliest Christian writing after the conclusion of the New Testament (*c.* 100 A.D.). In the strong eschatological conclusion, after speaking of the increase of lawlessness and persecution and the appearance of the "world deceiver as Son of God," the writer continues, "Then shall appear the Signs of the truth: first the Sign of expansion in heaven; then the Sign

279

of the voice of the trumpet; and the third the resurrection of the dead."[1] We are particularly concerned with this phrase "the Sign of expansion in heaven." The Greek word here translated as expansion, *ekpetasis,* does not occur in the New Testament nor even in the Septuagint, but in Plutarch, and means a spreading out. It became "the patristic term for the attitude of the crucified and (here) is probably the Sign of the Cross."[2]

Cyril of Jerusalem said, "A sign truly characteristic of Christ is the cross: a luminous sign of a cross goes before the king."[3] Hippolytus, quoting II Peter 3:12 and Revelation 6:14, amplifies this view as follows: "For the Sign of the cross shall arise from the East even unto the West in brightness exceeding that of the sun, and shall announce the Advent and manifestation of the Judge to give to everyone according to his works."[4] Origen introduced the idea that "as at the dispensation of the cross, the sun was eclipsed and darkness was spread over the earth, so when the Sign of the Son of Man appears in heaven, the light of the sun, moon, and stars shall fail, as though waning before the power of that Sign; this we understand to be the might of the cross."[5] Jerome followed Origen in this interpretation. Chrysostom held the very strange idea that our Lord actually took His cross into heaven with Him and that it was this actual cross on which He was crucified that is referred to by our Lord in referring to His second advent.[6]

Thomas a Kempis begins chapter 12 of his second book of *The Imitation of Christ* by echoing this ancient view: "This sign of the cross shall be in the heavens when the Lord shall come to judgment. Then all the servants of the cross who in their lifetime conformed themselves unto Christ crucified, shall draw near unto Christ the judge with great confidence." One who made a very careful study of this subject in the latter part of the nineteenth century reminds us: "This reference to the cross of Christ did not pass over to the exegetical tradition of Protestantism. The Protestant exegetes of the first two centuries leave it altogether undetermined what is to be understood by this sign." Calvin was inclined to believe, and most modern commentators follow him in this, that the sign of the Son of man was none other than the Son of man Himself. This was the view held by Bengel and Hengstenberg and others. The idea that this was a star of some miraculous nature has not won wide acceptance. Some have believed that our Lord is here simply referring to some great light that would appear in the sky, "something immediately connected with His personal appearance. Perhaps the dark clouds and tempest, the thunderings and lightnings in which the Redeemer is first shrouded." The great German exegete, H. A. W. Meyer, took such a view of the passage in stating that our Lord was simply referring to "a light-phenomena, the first radiance of the Messianic glory; perhaps becoming even more radiant and glorious until the Messiah comes forth from it in His glory." Lenski more or less combines these later views in his statement that "no sign, save a glowing, dazzling light shall hang over the earth for a shorter or longer period, after which sign the Son shall arrive. All will be one grand act: the Son's manifestation in glory will be what the tribes see."

I think all would agree that there is nothing in the text itself, or in any parallel statement to the phenomena of the second advent that would give us an indisputable interpretation of this passage. It does speak of something glorious at the time of our Lord's return. One cannot be dogmatic as to what this specifically might be.

NOTES

1. *Didache*, XVI.
2. Philip Schaff, *The Oldest Church Manual, called the Teaching of the Twelve Apostles* (Edinburgh: 1885).

3. Cyril, *Catechism*, XV, 22.
4. Hippolytus, in *Ante-Nicene Fathers* (New York: 1925), V, 251.
5. Origen, in Harold Smith, *Ante-Nicene Exegesis of the Gospels*, V, 149.
6. Chrysostom, *Homilies on Matthew*, LXXVI, 3.

See, for full treatment of various theories, Otto Zoeckler, *The Cross of Christ* (Eng. trans.; London: 1877), pp. 429-35; and Isaac Williams, *The Holy Week* (2d ed.; London: 1849), pp. 284-93.

APPENDIX C

"The Powers of the Heavens Shall Be Shaken"

In the Olivet Discourse there are two statements, one immediately following the other, in both of which the term "heaven" appears, and the exact meaning of these two statements is very difficult to determine. Both of them have given rise to a large number of different interpretations, yet in any book that attempts a comprehensive study of the meaning of Heaven in the Scriptures, these two verses require some consideration. We will begin with the first of these two utterances: "But immediately after the tribulation of those days the sun shall be darkened, and the moon shall not give her light, and the stars shall fall from heaven, and the powers of the heavens shall be shaken" (Matt. 24:29; see also Mark 13:25; Luke 21:26). We have already discussed in the chapter on the new heavens and the new earth the implications of the earlier part of this verse, so that here we shall but confine ourselves to the single clause "the powers of the heavens shall be shaken."

Three principal theories have been held. Some have insisted that this refers to what might be called astronomical powers, that is, the powers of gravity, the powers that hold the heavenly orbs in their orbits. Lenski has expressed this in a sweeping statement: "The whole siderial world shall collapse. All that holds the heavenly bodies in their orbits and enables sun and moon to light the earth will give way. . . . Let no man try to imagine this cataclysm! It is utterly beyond human conception. . . . God's omnipotent hand reaches down to wind up the affairs of earth and man." It seems to me that this is an extreme position to take. If what Lenski says is the meaning of this text, then the whole universe will collapse and this just seems contrary to reason. It has been here for billions of years, and it is hard to believe that all this enormous universe will be replaced by another. Also such an interpretation as this necessitates the utter dissolution of this earth, and that seems to invalidate many other prophecies concerning the future glory to rest upon this earth.

The view of the famous New Testament exegete of a century ago, Rudolf Stier, is somewhat indefinite but has been accepted by a number of writers: "It is chiefly the heaven of the church that is spoken of: the sun of revealed religion; the moon of intellectual culture and science, upon which the sun casts its rays; the stars of the heads of churches and ecclesiastical teachers—all these will be darkened in the great falling away, which takes place ever more and more at different periods." But Stier is closer to the truth, we believe, in saying that this passage is a figurative expression of "great tribulation and judgment upon nations." Many would agree with Stier in a more definite statement that these powers of the heavens are "the sustaining and working powers of the heavenly edifices with their influence upon the earth."[1]

The idea that the shaking of these powers embraces convulsive experiences prevailing among the nations of the earth at the end of this age is the view of A. B. Bruce who has said that "in true prophetic Oriental style, the colossal imagery of the physical universe is used to describe the political and social consequences of the great Jewish catastrophe: the physical stands for the social, the shaking of heaven for the shaking of earth (Haggai 2:6); or in the prophetic imagination the two are indissolubly blended: stars, thrones, city walls, temples, effete religions tumbling down into one vast mass of ruin."[2]

Somewhat similar to the view of Bruce is that of the late Professor Gould in his commentary on Mark's gospel: "This language is intended to portray the greatness of the doom of such nations as come under the judgment of God. . . . They are not events but only imaginative portrayal of what it means for God to interfere in the history of nations."

Finally, some have believed that this passage should be linked with the famous statement of the Apostle Paul where he speaks of those antagonistic principalities, powers, "the world rulers of this darkness, . . . spiritual hosts of wickedness in the heavenly places" (Eph. 6:12). Inasmuch as Satan is the prince of this world and is also called the prince of the power of the air, and inasmuch as the world as such "lieth in the evil one" (I John 5:19), it would seem to me that this phrase "the powers of the heavens" may refer to those powers which more or less control the corporate thinking and decision of nations which are opposed to the kingdom of God, such as we have seen in the blasphemous official legislative denial of the fact of God and the persecution of the church in such enormous areas as the Soviet Republic, Communistic China, and the whole of the Arab world. The day will come when these vast powers will be shaken by the omnipotence of God as the age draws to its end and righteous judgment approaches.

NOTES

1. R. Stier, *Words of the Lord Jesus* (rev. ed.; Edinburgh: 1873), III, 283.
2. A. B. Bruce, in *Expositor's Greek Testament*, I, 259.

BIBLIOGRAPHY

BIBLIOGRAPHY

As far as I know, this is the only comprehensive bibliography in English on the subject of Heaven that has been attempted. I have not felt it was necessary to list individual sermons on Heaven published in pamphlet form, nor pamphlets which discuss relevant subjects. No attempt has been made to include works on Immortality which, of course, is assumed in a discussion of Heaven, nor on Eschatology as such, nor the Second Advent, nor Hell. I have felt it necessary, however, to include books that are primarily devoted to a treatment of the doctrine of the Resurrection of believers. In the footnotes for some of the chapters of this book I have added brief bibliographies. I have examined all the books here listed that have been published since 1800, and most of those also published in the seventeenth and eighteenth centuries. Frequently, in pursuing this bibliographic study, I have discovered that titles were either quite misleading or the books to which they referred contained such ridiculous material, necessarily excluding them from any serious bibliography. For a long time I looked around for a volume by W. R. Hughes entitled *Little Journeys in the Heavenly Country*, but when I finally came upon the full title, I was aware at once that it would not appear in this list. The rest of the title reads *From Westham, Bossington, and Other Place Poems!* In 1897, a well-known Philadelphia publishing house issued a book with the comprehensive title *The Heaven and the Bible.* In these sixty pages are some strange subjects, as eight pages devoted to horses in heaven, and then industries in heaven, such as masons and stonecutters, papermakers, etc.

The first extended discussion of paradise in Christian literature is the treatise *de Paradiso,* by St. Ambrose of Milan, about A.D. 375. The Latin text is in Migne, xiv, 275-314; and a French translation in P. de Labriolle, *Saint Ambrose* (Paris: 1908). There is no English text.

An examination of the chronological data of this list reveals that fourteen of the books here listed were published in the seventeenth century (some of the greatest ever written on Heaven); seven were published in the eighteenth century; seventeen in the first half of the nineteenth century, and eighty-one in the second half of the nineteenth century; from 1900 to 1966, forty more volumes have appeared. Of the authors of these volumes, thirty-eight are in the *Dictionary of National Biography* or *The Dictionary of American Biography,* and eleven more in *Who Was Who,* or *Who Was Who in America,* which means that one-third of the authors of books on Heaven have been of sufficient importance to find a place in these basic biographical works.

Alford, Henry (1810-71). *The State of the Blessed Dead.* London: 1869. Pp. 96.

Amos, C. W. Hale. *Where Go the Dead?* London: 1929. Pp. xviii, 212.

Baillie, John. *And the Life Everlasting.* London: 1934. Pp. xii, 294.

Barrett, George S. *The Intermediate State.* London: 1896. Pp. vi, 275.

Bates, William (1625-99). *A Short Description of the Blessed Place and State of the Saints Above.* London: 1687. Pp. 102.

———. *The Everlasting Rest of the Saints in Heaven.* London: 1701. Pp. ix, 276.

Baxter, Richard (1615-91). *The Saints' Everlasting Rest, or a Treatise of the Blessed State of the Saints in their Enjoyment of God in Glory.* London: 1649, in *Works of Richard Baxter.* London: 1688, Vols. XXII and XXIII. Between 1649 and 1688 twelve editions were published.

The Cambridge History of English Literature (Vol. VII, p. 146), speaks of Baxter's work as "that book, which we all call immortal, though it is gradually sinking into the limbo whither much of seventeenth century prose, for all save scholars, has gone before us."

Baylee, Joseph. *The Intermediate State of the Blessed Dead* (1864). Pp. xvi, 176.

Bellarmine, Cardinal (1542-1621). *The Joys of the Blessed* (R.C.). Translated by Thomas Foxton. With an essay on the same subject written by Mr. Addison. London: 1772. Pp. ix, 136.

Bickersteth, Edward H. (1825-1906). *Hades or Heaven; or, What Does Scripture Reveal of the State and Employments of the Blessed Dead.* New York: n.d. Pp. 128.

Biederwolf, William E. *The Adventure of the Hereafter.* New York: 1934. Pp. xii, 173.

Bonar, Horatius (1808-89). *The Morning Glory.* London: 1850. Pp. 220.

———. *The Eternal Day.* London: 1853. Pp. 249.

Boudreaux, F. J. *The Happiness of Heaven* (R.C.) (3d ed.). London: 1881. Pp. 192.

Bounds, Edward M. *Heaven: A Place—A City—A Home.* New York: 1921. Pp. 151.

Branks, William. *Heaven Our Home* (3d ed.). Boston: 1864. Pp. 310.

———. *Life in Heaven.* Boston: 1865. Pp. 273.

———. *Meet for Heaven* (3d ed.). Boston: 1864. Pp. 306.

Brewster, Sir David (1781-1868). *More Worlds Than One: The Creed of the Philosopher and the Hope of the Christian* (1854). New ed., 1874. Pp. vii, 294.

Brown, John. *The Dead in Christ. Their State: Present and Future.* New York: 1855. Pp. 164.

Bryant, Alfred. *Attractions of the World to Come.* New York: 1853. Pp. 308.

Bunyan, John (1628-88). *The Holy City; or, the New Jerusalem* (1665) in his *Works.* London: 1784, IV, 2341-2414.

Burns, J. D. *The Heavenly Jerusalem.* London: 1856. Pp. 130.

Burns, James. *The Celestial City. Glimpses Within the Gates.* Boston: 1856. Pp. 130.

Bush, George. *Anastasis, or the Doctrine of the Resurrection of the Body Rationally and Scripturally Considered.* New York: 1845. Pp. 396.

Campbell, Archibald (1691-1756). *The Doctrines of a Middle State Between Death and the Resurrection.* London: 1721.

Campbell, James M. (1840-1926). *Heaven Opened. A Book of Comfort and Hope.* New York: 1924. Pp. 193.

Candlish, Robert S. *Life in a Risen Saviour.* London: 1848. New ed., 1863. Pp. 410.

Carlile, James. *The Station and Occupation of the Saints in Their Final Glory.* London: 1854. Pp. xl, 165.

Clarke, Rufus W. *Heaven and Its Scriptural Emblems.* Philadelphia: 1852. Pp. 269.

Cochrane, James. *The Resurrection of the Dead.* Edinburgh: 1869. Pp. 412.

Cooke, Richard J. *Outlines of the Doctrine of the Resurrection.* New York: 1884. Pp. 407.

Copland, Alexander. *Mortal Life; and the State of the Soul After Death.* London: 1832. Pp. 572. Published anonymously.

Courtenay, Reginald. *The Future States.* London: 1843. Pp. viii, 438.

Crampton, J. *The Three Heavens.* Dublin: 1871; London: 1876. Pp. xliv, 416.

Cremer, August Hermann. *Beyond the Grave.* Introduction by Dr. A. A. Hodge. New York: 1886. Pp. xxxviii, 153.

Cullmann, Oscar. *Immortality of the Soul or Resurrection of the Dead?* London: 1958. Pp. 60.

Dahl, Murdoch E. *The Resurrection of the Body*. Naperville, Ill.: 1962. Pp. 148.

Dahle, L. N. *Life After Death, and the Future of God's Kingdom*. Eng. trans., Edinburgh: 1897. Pp. xii, 455.

Dale, Robert W. (1829-95). *Christ and the Future Life*. London: 1895. Pp. 160.

Darragh, J. T. *The Resurrection of the Flesh*. London: 1921. Pp. xi, 324.

Davidson, Martin. *Stars and the Mind*. London: 1947. Pp. x, 210.
———. *The Heavens and Faith*. London: 1936. Pp. xv, 162.

Davies, Edwin. *Glimpses of Our Heavenly Home* (2d ed.). London: 1857. Pp. 260.
———. *The Hope of the Bereaved; or Recognition in Heaven* (2d ed.). Belfast: 1844.

Davis, Woodberry. *The Beautiful City, and the King of Glory*. Philadelphia: 1860. Pp. 255.

Dent, Arthur (d. 1607). *The Plaine-Man's Pathway to Heaven*. London: 1601; 18th impression, 1622. Pp. 430.

Dick, Thomas (1774-1857). *The Philosophy of a Future State*, Vol. I in *The Complete Works of Thomas Dick*. Cincinnati: 1853. Pp. iv, 99.

Dodsworth, J. *The Better Land, or, the Christian Emigrant's Guide to Heaven*. London: 1853.

Edmondson, Jonathan. *Scripture Views of the Heavenly World*. London: 1835; 3d ed., 1850; New York: 1856. Pp. 251.

Faber, George S. (1773-1854). *The Many Mansions in the House of the Father*. London: 1851. Pp. li, 423.

Fallows, Samuel (1835-1922). *The Home Beyond. Views of Heaven and Its Relation to Earth by over Four Hundred Prominent Thinkers and Writers*. Chicago: 1883. Pp. 410.

Fern, Robert. *A Treatise of the Celestial Work and Worship; or, the Sacred Employments and Services of the Blessed Spirits in Heaven*. London: 1721.

Figuier, Guillaume Louis. *Joys Beyond the Threshold* (R.C.). Eng. trans., Boston: 1893. Pp. iv, 321.

Fish, Henry C. *Heaven in Song.* New York: 1874. Pp. xxi, 742.

Foster, Randolf S. *Beyond the Grave.* New York: 1882. Pp. 269.

Freeman, Joseph. *Heaven Entered, or the Spirit in Glory Everlasting.* London: 1837. Pp. xi, 164.

Fyfe, James. *The Hereafter.* Edinburgh: 1890. Pp. 407. Very important on Sheol, Hades, etc.

Garbett, Edward. *The Soul's Life: Commencement, Progress, and Maturity.* London: 1869. Pp. 340.

Gasparin, Countess Valerie des. *The Near and Heavenly Horizons.* Edinburgh: 1861, pp. iv, 404; London: 1887, pp. vi, 311; London: 1908, with an introduction by Dr. G. Campbell Morgan, pp. viii, 183.

Gerhard, C. S. *Death and the Resurrection.* Philadelphia: 1895. Pp. 240.

Goodwin, Thomas (1600-1679). *Of the Blessed State of Glory Which the Saints Possess After Death,* in his *Works.* London, VII, 337-471.

Gordon, Samuel D. *Quiet Talks About the Life After Death.* New York: 1920. Pp. 197.

Grant, F. W. *Facts and Theories as to a Future State.* New York: 1879. Pp. 496.

Gray, George Z. *The Scriptural Doctrine of Recognition in the World to Come.* New York: 1875.

Gray, James M. (1851-1935). *Progress in the Life to Come.* New York: 1910. Pp. 60.

———. *A Picture of the Resurrection.* New York: 1917. Pp. 43.

Gregg, David (1845-1919). *The Heaven-Life.* New York: 1895. Pp. 168.

Gwynne, Walker (1845-1931). *Some Purposes of Paradise.* New York: 1893. Pp. 90.

Hall, John. *How Are the Dead Raised Up, and with What Body Do They Come?* Hartford: 1875. Pp. 216.

Hall, Joseph (1574-1656). *The Soul's Farewell to Earth and Approches to Heaven* in his *Works.* Oxford: 1837, VIII, 304-22.

———. *The Invisible World Discovered to Spiritual Eyes,* VIII, 323-423.

Hamilton, Thomas. *Beyond the Stars; or, Heaven, Its Inhabitants, Occupations, and Life.* First ed., 1888; 4th ed., Edinburgh. Pp. 270.

Hanna, William. *Resurrection of the Dead.* New York: 1872. Pp. 196.

Harbaugh, Henry. *The Heavenly Home; or, the Employments and Enjoyments of the Saints in Heaven* (9th ed.). Philadelphia: 1858. Pp. 365.

———. *Heaven; or, An Earnest and Scriptural Inquiry into the Abode of the Sainted Dead.* Seventeenth ed., 1848; rev. ed., Philadelphia: 1861. Pp. 290.

———. *The Heavenly Recognition* (1851); 9th ed., Philadelphia: 1856, pp. 288; 13th ed., 1859.

Hart, Burdett. *Aspects of Heaven.* New York: 1896. Pp. 256.

Heslop, William G. *Heaven. Our Father's House.* Grand Rapids: 1937. Pp. 104.

Hill, Henry F. *The Saints' Inheritance, or, the World to Come.* Boston: 1852; 5th ed., 1856. Pp. 264.

Hodge, J. Aspinwall. *Recognition After Death.* New York: 1889. Pp. 184.

Hoffman, H. S. *Life Beyond the Grave* (2d ed.). Philadelphia: 1899. Pp. 311.

Hough, Robert E. *The Christian After Death.* Chicago: 1947. Pp. 169.

Howe, John (1630-1705). *A Discourse Concerning the Redeemer's Dominion over the Invisible World, and the Entrance Thereunto by Death,* in his *Works.* London: 1821, I, 1-76.

———. *A Discourse Relating to the Expectation of Future Blessedness* in *Works* (1668), III, 347-95.

John Howe is an illustration of how some distinguished men of their own age are so soon forgotten. Howe was one of the most influential nonconformists of his generation; to him the *Dictionary of National Biography* devotes seven columns, but who today, except a few historical scholars, read his works?

Hudson, C. F. *Debt and Grace, as Related to the Doctrine of a Future Life* (2d ed.). Boston: 1858. Pp. viii, 472.

Hurlbut, Stephen A. (ed.). *The Picture of the Heavenly Jerusalem in the Writings of Johannes of Fecamp, De Contemplativa Vita, and in the Elizabethan Hymns.* Washington, D.C.: 1943. A very scholarly work on which the editor worked for a number of years.

Hutton, R. E. *The Soul in the Unseen World.* New York: 1902. Pp. 412.

Kellogg, Samuel H. *From Death to Resurrection.* New York: 1885. Pp. 63.

Killen, J. M. *Our Friends in Heaven, or the Mutual Recognition of the Redeemed in Glory Demonstrated* (1854). Pp. 225.

———. *Our Companions in Glory, or Society in Heaven Contemplated.* New York: 1862. Pp. 350.

Kimball, James William. *"My Father's House."* Boston: 1882. Pp. 248.

Kohler, Kaufmann (1843-1926). *Heaven and Hell in Comparative Religion* (1923). Pp. xix, 158.

Kuyper, Abraham. *Asleep in Jesus.* Eng. trans., Grand Rapids: 1929. Pp. x, 353.

Landis, Robert W. *The Doctrine of the Resurrection of the Body Asserted and Defended.* Philadelphia: 1846. Pp. 379.

Lowry, Edward P. *The Sayings of the Lord Jesus Concerning the Life to Come.* London: 1878. Pp. vii, 124.

McCarthy, J. P. *Heaven* (R.C.). New York: 1958. Pp. 143.

McClain, Joseph P. *The Doctrine of Heaven in the Writings of Saint Gregory the Great* (R.C.). Washington, D.C.: 1956. Pp. viii, 148.

McCullagh, Archibald. *Beyond the Stars; or, Human Life in Heaven.* New York: 1887. Pp. 106.

McCullough, J. W. *The Dead in Christ.* Baltimore: 1845. Pp. 202.

MacDonald, James M. *My Father's House.* New York: 1855. Pp. xiv, 376.

Macintyre, Ronald G. *The Other Side of Death. A Study in Christian Eschatology.* London: 1920. Pp. xiv, 359.

McNeile, Alan H. *The Problem of the Future Life.* Cambridge: 1925. Pp. viii, 155.

MacNeille, J. J. *Many Mansions. Sermons on the Future Life.* New York: 1926. Pp. 224.

Mant, Bishop Richard (1776-1848). *The Happiness of the Blessed Considered* (6th ed.). London, New York: 1853. Pp. 225. By 1871, seven editions had been printed in England.

Mather, Cotton (1663-1728). *Coelestinus. A Conversation in Heaven, Quickened and Assisted with Discoveries of Things in the Heavenly World.* Boston: 1723. Pp. 162. In the great bibliography of Cotton Mather by Thomas James Holmes is the following interesting comment: "*Coelestinus* consists of a series of seven Essays, which might be regarded as seven divisions of a lengthy sermon, in which is set forth this Doctrine: 'A *True and Right* Christian *is one of an* Heavenly Conversation: And, Christianity lies much in Conversing *with* and *like* the Heavenly World, which every Real Christian has a Lively Prospect of.' (P. 3.) The last six pages contain 'Accounts of the *Views* and *Joys*, which have been granted unto Souls *just Entring* into the *Paradise* of GOD.' He mentions the deathbed visions and testimonies of Mr. Wilkins of Salem Village; Mr. Tho. Parker, who had been a seafaring man; and a young man, Mr. J. Goodwin; a young woman, Mrs. Frothingam; a young gentlewoman, Mrs. Jerusha Oliver; a young gentlewoman, Mrs. Katharin Mather; a young gentlewoman, Mrs. Sarah Brown; a very gracious woman, Mrs. Rix" (Vol. I, p. 160).

Mather, Increase (1639-1723). *Meditations on the Glory of the Heavenly World.* Boston: 1711. Pp. 276. Inasmuch as this is the most comprehensive volume on Heaven to be published in America before the middle of the nineteenth century, the following paragraph from the definitive bibliography of the works of the author, by T. J. Holmes (Vol. I, p. 332), may be of interest:

"A year before the completing of his *Meditations on the Glory of the Heavenly World,* Increase Mather in the epistle To the Reader, in his *Earnest Exhortation to the Children of New-England,* dated November 9, 1710, wrote: 'Of making Many Books there is no End. Nor would I add to that *Vanity* which the Earth Groans under. Nevertheless, it has for several Years been in my Heart to Publish one Book more (and no more than one) being *Meditations on the Glory of the Heavenly World*: But I much Question whether I shall be able to Accomplish what I have had in my Heart to do.' Dying, though he thought himself to be, he nevertheless completed the work and lived thirteen years more to publish about twenty-two books after his *Meditations*."

In the author's *Several Sermons* (Boston: 1715) is a sermon entitled "That when Godly Men Dye, Angels carry their Souls . . . to a Better World."

Mattison, Hiram. *The Resurrection of the Dead, Considered in the Light of History, Philosophy, and Divine Revelation* (1866; 6th ed., 1874). Pp. 405.

Maxwell, Daniel. *The Glory of the Saints Between Death and the Resurrection Considered.* Belfast: 1856. Pp. 213.

Meek, Robert. *Heavenly Things; or, the Blessed Hope.* London: 1854. Pp. 246.

———. *The Mutual Recognition and Exalted Felicity of Glorified Saints.* London: 1830; 4th ed., 1844. Pp. iv, 126.

Milligan, William. *The Resurrection of the Dead.* Edinburgh: 1894. Pp. 246.

Molyneux, C. *The World to Come.* London: 1853.

Moody, Dwight L. *Heaven and How to Get There.* Chicago: 1880. Pp. 119. This appeared in many later editions, with varying titles. In twenty years it had sold 325,000 copies.

Moule, Handley C. G. *Christ's Witness to the Life to Come.* London: 1908. Pp. 256.

Muston, C. Ralph. *Recognition in the World to Come.* London: 1830; 4th ed., 1840. Pp. viii, 424.

Neale, John M. (1818-66). *The Unseen World.* London: 1847; 2d ed., 1853.

Nicoll, W. Robertson. *Reunion in Eternity.* New York: 1919. Pp. 295.

Pâche, René. *The Future Life.* Chicago: 1962. Pp. 376. Unusually good.

Patterson, Robert M. (1832-1912). *Paradise.* Philadelphia: 1874. Pp. 220.

Pickering, Henry (ed.). *Heaven, the Home of the Redeemed.* London: n.d. Pp. 127.

Pike, G. Holden (compiler). *The Heavenly World. Views of the Future Life by Eminent Writers.* London: 1880. Pp. vi, 328. This volume, which has practically been lost sight of by contemporary writers, is in some ways the best collection of sermonic material and testimonies regarding Heaven. It begins with fifty pages of material from Spurgeon, carrying the general title "The Glorious Inheritance," followed by material from Alexander Maclaren's writings under the heading "Ten Views of Heaven." There is considerable material by Robert Hall, Isaac Watts, Richard Baxter, Thomas Chalmers, John Bunyan, etc. The final seventy pages, with the general title "The Perfect World," contain testimonies relating to the hope of heaven on the part of some twenty-four clergy, poets, etc.

Pilcher, Charles Venn. *The Hereafter in Jewish and Christian Thought.* London: 1940. Pp. 206.

Porter, Jermain G. *Our Celestial Home. An Astronomer's View of Heaven.* New York: 1888. Pp. 116.

Reynolds, Joseph William. *The World to Come.* London: 1888. Pp. xxv, 310.

Ritchie, John. *Man's Future State.* Kilmarnock: 1912. Pp. 112.

Roberts, Joseph. *Heaven Physically and Morally Considered.* London: 1846. Pp. 106.

Robinson, John A. T. *The Body, A Study in Pauline Theology.* London: 1952. Pp. 95.

Salkeld, John (1576-1660). *A Treatise of Paradise.* London: 1617. Pp. 359.

Sasia, Joseph C. *The Future Life* (R.C.). New York: 1918. Pp. 562. A very comprehensive work.

Schoonhoven, Calvin R. *The Wrath of Heaven.* Grand Rapids: 1966. Pp. 187.

Scroggie, W. Graham. *What About Heaven?* London: 1940. Pp. 137.

Sewall, Samuel. *Phaenomena quaedam apocalyptica ad Aspectum Novi Orbis Configurata. Or, some few lines towards a description of the New Heaven as it makes to those who stand upon the New Earth.* Boston: 1697. Pp. 60.

Shimeall, Richard C. *The Unseen World.* New York: 1870. Pp. xxi, 446.

Simon, Ulrich. *Heaven in the Christian Tradition.* London: 1958. Pp. xviii, 310.

———. *The Ascent to Heaven.* London: 1961. Pp. 181.

Spear, Samuel T. *Meditations on the Bible Heaven.* New York: 1886. Pp. 403.

Spurgeon, Charles H. (1834-92). *Twelve Sermons on Heaven.* London: n.d. Pp. 60.

Stanton, Horace Coffin (1849-1925). *The Starry Universe* (5th ed.). New York: 1909. Pp. 362.

Steffe, John. *Five Letters. Scripture Proofs of a Separate Intermediate State of Existence After Death.* London: 1757.

Strong, Charles H. *In Paradise; or, the State of the Faithful Dead.* New York: 1893. Pp. 119.

Strong, James. *The Doctrine of the Future Life.* New York: 1891. Pp. 128.

Taylor, Isaac (1787-1865). *Physical Theory of Another Life.* London: 1836; new ed., London: 1866.

Tertullian. *On the Resurrection of the Flesh* in *Ante-Nicene Fathers,* III, 545-95. There are two excellent editions of this great work, by A. Souter (London: 1922); and by Ernest Evans (London: 1960), pp. xxxvi, 361; each containing both the Latin text and an English translation.

Thompson, Augustus C. *The Better Land; or, the Believer's Journey and Future Home.* Boston: 1854. Pp. 244.

Thompson, Edward. *Sermons upon the Future State of Happiness.* London: 1843. Pp. 264.

Townsend, Luther Tracy. *The Intermediate World.* New York: 1878. Pp. 250.

Vaughan, John S. *Life After Death.* London: 1895. Pp. xxiii, 219.

———. *Life Everlasting; or, the Delights Awaiting the Faithful Soul in Paradise.* London: 1922. Pp. xxix, 224.

Watts, Isaac (1674-1748). *Happiness of Separate Spirits* in his *Works*. London: 1812, II, 374-442.

———. *The World to Come; or, Discourses on the Joys and Sorrows of Departed Souls at Death*, VII, 1-315. This work was often reprinted, for example, Pittsburgh, 1846; pp. 563.

Watts-Ditchfield, J. E. *Here and Hereafter*. London: 1910. Pp. xii, 252.

Westcott, Brooke Foss. *The Gospel of the Resurrection*. London: 1865; 5th ed., 1874. Pp. xxxv, 276.

Whately, Richard (1787-1863). *A View of the Scripture Revelations Concerning a Future State* (3d ed.). Philadelphia: 1857. Pp. 308.

Whitley, J. T. *What Jesus Said About Heaven*. Nashville: 1925. Pp. 104.

Whiton, James Morris. *The Gospel of the Resurrection*. Boston: 1881. Pp. 271.

Whittley, John. *The Life Everlasting*. London: 1846. Pp. 588.

Wright, Theodore Francis. *The Realities of Heaven*. Philadelphia: n.d. Pp. 120.

Zartman, Rufus Calvin. *Heaven*. Reading, Pa.: 1893. Pp. 303.

INDEXES

Subject and Author Index

Inasmuch as the concluding Bibliography is alphabetically arranged, its authors have not been included in this index, unless they are referred to in the text itself.

Scripture Index